THE MOORE FAMILY

Early European Settlers In Wangaratta And Its Surrounds

THE MOORE FAMILY

Early European Settlers In Wangaratta And Its Surrounds

GARRY MOORE

Copyright © Garry Moore 2024
Cover design, Typesetting: Working Type Studio
(www.workingtype.com.au)

The right of Garry Moore to be identified as the Author of the Work has been asserted in accordance with the Copyright, Designs and Patents Act 1988.

All rights reserved. No part of this publication may be reproduced, stored in a retrieval system, or transmitted in any form or by any means without the prior written permission of the publisher, nor be otherwise circulated in any form of binding or cover other than that in which it is published and without a similar condition being imposed on the subsequent purchaser.

Garry Moore
The Moore Family: Early European Settlers
In Wangaratta And Its Surrounds
ISBN: 978-0-6486480-5-5

PREFACE

This book draws extensively on the wide and wise research effected over many years by a number of my relatives. I owe them all a great deal, and I would like to take this opportunity to express my sincere gratitude to them. Any errors appearing in this book are mine and not theirs.

I would like in particular to thank the late Rex Moore, Jenny Coates, Bill Willett and Professor David Lowe. Without the ability that I have had to access and draw upon their works, this book, and my earlier genealogical volumes, would not have been possible.

Garry Moore.
2 January 2024.

CONTENTS

Preface	v
Contents	vii
Introduction	1
John Moore's Background And Life Prior to His Marriage To Margaret Considine	3
Birth	3
John Moore's Antecedents	3
John Moore's Father	3
John Moore's Mother	5
John Moore's Parents' Marriage And Life Together	7
Phoebe Moore's Marriage To Thomas Buckman	12
John Moore's Life In England	14
The Lives Of John Moore's Sister, Half-Sisters And Half-Brother	18
Sarah Moore	18
Elizabeth Buckman	19
Mahala Buckman	20
George Buckman	22
Eliza Buckman	23
Sophia Buckman	24
John Moore's Life In Australia Prior To His Marriage	27
Margaret Considine's Background And Life Prior To Her Marriage To John Moore	31
Sixmilebridge	31
Margaret Considine's Antecedents	32

Voyaging To Australia ... 34
Margaret Considine's Life In Australia Prior To Her Marriage ... 39
The Lives of Margaret Considine's Siblings ... 40
    Bridget Considine ... 40
    Patrick Considine ... 42
    Ellen Considine ... 44

John And Margaret Moore's Life Together ... 47
Living At Springfield ... 47
The Faithfulls And North East Victoria. ... 48
The Moore Family At Ten Mile Hollow ... 50
The Move To Whorouly ... 54
Tenterfield ... 55
John Moore's Community Activities ... 56
The Death Of John Moore ... 58
John Moore's Will ... 60
Margaret Moore's Later Years And Death ... 61

John And Margaret Moore's Surviving Children ... 63
Henry Faithfull ... 63
Matilda Margaret Moore ... 71
John Moore Junior ... 77
William Moore ... 83
George Moore ... 94
Charles Moore ... 96
Harriet Jane Moore ... 99
Thomas Moore ... 103

Conclusion ... 109
Genealogical charts ... 110
Bibliography ... 117
Books ... 117
Articles ... 118
Genealogical Materials ... 121
Legislation ... 131
Government Gazette ... 131
Other Government Records ... 131
Newspapers ... 133
Miscellaneous Unpublished Documents ... 133

INTRODUCTION

John Moore and his wife, Margaret Moore (née Considine), were early European pioneers who settled in around 1843 in the North East of what was then known as the Port Phillip District of the Colony of New South Wales and is now the State of Victoria. Like the great majority of their fellow settlers, neither John nor Margaret was born in Australia.

John Moore was born in Woodchurch, Kent in 1816. He emigrated from England to New South Wales in 1838 when 22 years of age. In contrast, Margaret Considine was born at Sixmilebridge, County Clare in about 1818. She first arrived from Ireland in New South Wales in 1836 aged 18 years old.

Both John and Margaret came from poor rural stock. The prospect of a better life in Australia was no doubt the prime motivation for each to independently migrate across the world to New South Wales.

Soon after his arrival in Sydney, John found employment as a dairyman on a property known as *Springfield*, located a little to the south of Goulburn. This property was owned by the brothers William Pitt Faithfull and George Faithfull. It was while he was working on *Springfield* that John first met Margaret. At the time of this meeting, Margaret was also almost certainly employed on *Springfield*; in her case, as a domestic.

In 1839, John and Margaret were married in a Catholic wedding conducted in Goulburn. Prior to her marriage to John, Margaret had already borne a son to William Pitt Faithfull. At the time of the marriage, she was pregnant with her second child. The child, who proved to be a daughter, was also likely fathered by William Pitt Faithfull. After their marriage, John and Margaret went on to have a further eight children together; six of whom survived to adulthood.

In 1843, John was commissioned by William Pitt Faithfull to become overseer on Faithfull's *Ten Mile Hollow* squatting run on the King River in the Port Phillip District. Together with Margaret and their growing family, John lived and worked on that property until about 1949 or 1850. He then left Faithfull's employ and went to work as overseer on the *Whorouly* run of Dr George Mackay.

A little before 1856, John moved with his family from the King Valley to a property he had purchased straddling One Mile Creek to the west of the then new township of Wangaratta. He named the property *Tenterfield* and successfully farmed and grazed it and, in all likelihood, further land nearby, until his death in 1891. Margaret died some four years later in 1895.

John did not rise to any great height over the course of his life. Nevertheless, that life was one of changes and challenges; changes and challenges which he successfully negotiated. He was respected and well-regarded by those who came into contact with him. Similarly, Margaret successfully dealt with the substantial changes and challenges with which she was confronted during her life. Like her husband, she ended that life admired and liked by those who knew her.

In this book, I propose to trace the lives and circumstances of John and Margaret Moore in significantly greater detail than has been outlined in the brief thumbnail sketch to be found above.

In the first part of the book, I will deal with John's background and life prior to his marriage to Margaret. I will then turn to Margaret's background and life prior to her marriage to John. I'll next examine John and Margaret's life together after their marriage. I will conclude with a short biography of each of the children in John and Margaret's household.

JOHN MOORE'S BACKGROUND AND LIFE PRIOR TO HIS MARRIAGE TO MARGARET CONSIDINE

Birth

John Moore was born on 20 April 1816 in the Parish of Woodchurch, Kent. The second child and first son of Joseph Moore and his wife, Phoebe Moore (née Dunster), John was christened on 28 April 1816 in Woodchurch's All Saints Parish Church; very likely by the then-Curate of Woodchurch, the Reverend Michael Coysgarne.[1]

John Moore's Antecedents

John Moore's Father

There is some uncertainty surrounding both the year and the place of Joseph Moore's birth. However, it appears likely that he was born a little before 25 July 1791 in the Parish of High Halden in the West Ashford district of Kent; the son of Joseph Moore Snr and Anne (or Ann) Moore (née Johnson).[2] Although the backgrounds and circumstances of

---

1 See *WikiTree – John Moore (1816 – 1891)* (https://tinyurl.com/p7m48bsu) (at 11 September 2023); and *Woodchurch Local and Family History: Baptisms – John Moore (28 April 1816)* (https://tinyurl.com/yapeul4o) (at 11 September 2023). See also the Map of South Central Kent, England and photos 1, 2 and 3 below.

2 See *England, Births and Christenings, 1538 – 1975: Joseph Moore – 1791* (https://tinyurl.com/4exsd8xp) (at 11 September 2023). The *High Halden Register of Baptisms, 1558 – 1966* (P164/1/9) states that on 25 September 1792, "Joseph, son of Joseph and Anne Moore" was "received" into the Church after being privately baptised. Searches have not thus far identified any alternative year or place for Joseph's baptism. Importantly, he was buried in High Halden, as was his infant son, Richard Moore: see footnotes 46 and 48, together with their accompanying texts, below. As a poor man, he could well have been buried both in, and at the expense of, the parish of his birth. As to the location of High Halden, see the Map of South Central Kent, England below. See also photos 4 and 5 below.

his parents are also clouded by uncertainty, it seems likely that they were married on 4 April 1789 in the neighbouring Parish of Bethersden.[3] It is not presently known whether Joseph Moore Snr and Anne Moore had children together apart from Joseph Moore Jnr. Further, Anne (or Ann) Johnson may well have been born in Bethersden on 27 August 1769; the daughter of Samuel and Sarah Johnson.[4] In turn, it is possible that Joseph Moore Snr was born in Canterbury, Kent on 30 October 1763; the son of yet another Joseph Moore and the latter's wife, Sarah Moore.[5]

The Parishes of High Halden and Bethersden are located between the towns of Ashford and Tenterden to the south-east of London. Each Parish is centred on a village bearing the Parish's name.

It is unlikely that Joseph Moore Jnr. received much, if any, formal schooling as it appears that he was illiterate. At the time of his marriage in 1812 to Phoebe Dunster, he was unable to sign his name in the Woodchurch Parish Register. In consequence, he was required to "make his mark".[6]

Presumably, Joseph started working at an early age. In 1816, he was recorded in the Woodchurch Parish records as being a labourer.[7] In records relating to the immigration of Joseph's son, John Moore, to New South Wales in 1838, Joseph was described as having been an agriculturalist.[8] Most probably, Joseph's employment, like that of most of his male forebears, was that of a farm labourer.

It further appears likely that Joseph, firstly as a single man and later with his wife and children, was an itinerant worker who probably lived in accommodation provided by his employers. As Christine Bean has noted with respect to rural Kent:

> "By the last quarter of the 1700s the divide between land holders and their workers including husbandmen and other small land holders was increasing. This meant that farmers were living in their own grander houses. Farm workers were becoming itinerant and were less likely to have a permanent abode."[9]

---

[3] See *England, Select Marriages, 1538 – 1973: Joseph Moore and Anne Johnson - 1789* (https://tinyurl.com/bdeeawck) (at 11 September 2023). See also photo 6 below.

[4] See *England, Births and Christenings, 1538 – 1975: Anne Johnson – 1769* (https://tinyurl.com/jcca631) (as at 11 September 2023).

[5] See *England, Births and Christenings, 1538 – 1975: Joseph Moore – 1763* (https://tinyurl.com/gtjz3hd) (as at 11 September 2023).

[6] See *England, Selected Marriages, 1538 – 1973: Joseph Moore and Phoebe Dunster - 1812* (https://tinyurl.com/hknrauk) (at 12 September 2023);

[7] See *Woodchurch Local and Family History: Woodchurch Parish Chest, 1633 – 1842 - Joseph Moore* (Record Details, P400/13/5).

[8] See *Immigration Series: Entitlement Certificates of Persons on Bounty Ships, 1832 – 1842: John Moore* (AONSW 4/4830) (https://tinyurl.com/4334fnhc) (at 12 September 2023).

[9] See Christine Bean, *From Tradesman to the Poor House* (Gransden Family Website) (https://tinyurl.com/y7z2xkx4)

At an unknown time prior to his marriage in 1812, Joseph Moore moved to Woodchurch. Like High Halden and Bethersden, Woodchurch is both a parish and a village in the West Ashford district of Kent. The village of Woodchurch lies a little over 8 km to the south of Bethersden village and a little under 6 km to the south-east of High Halden.[10]

John Moore's Mother

Phoebe Dunster was likely born shortly prior to 17 March 1793 and baptised on the latter date in All Saints Church, Woodchurch.[11] Little is presently known of her early life and circumstances. There are Nineteenth Century Dunsters buried in the churchyards of All Saints Church, Woodchurch and of All Saints Church, Beckley in East Sussex.[12] The Dunster family may have been fairly widespread in southern England. The family probably took its name from the ancient village of Dunster in Somerset.[13]

Phoebe's father was Francis Dunster. He was born a little before 1 October 1758 and christened on that date in St Mildred's Church, Tenterden; Tenterden being a town some 5 km to the west of Woodchurch.[14] Like Joseph Moore, Francis Dunster probably worked most of his life as an agricultural labourer. However, life was clearly hard for him. He was described in Phoebe's christening records as being a pauper.[15]

Francis Dunster was the youngest of seven children born to James Dunster and Susanna Dunster (née Allard). In turn, James, who lived between about 20 July 1726 and about 18 December 1806, was a son of Jeremiah Dunster and Judith Dunster (née Reynolds). Jeremiah Dunster was born in about 1693 and died in about 1774. Judith Dunster lived between about 1695 and 1760. Francis' mother, Susanna, was born in about 1715 and died in about 1777.[16] Nothing is presently known of Susanna's antecedents.

Phoebe's mother, Sarah Dunster (née Barman), was born in about 1750, probably in

---

(at 12 September 2023).

10 See the Map of South Central Kent, England below.

11 See *Woodchurch Local and Family History, Baptism Details* (17 March 1793, Phoebe Dunster) (https://tinyurl.com/ybwpvctk) (at 12 September 2023); and *FreeREG Baptism Entry – Phoebe Dunster* (https://tinyurl.com/yd6bzk40) (at 12 September 2023).

12 See photo 7 below.

13 With respect to the village of Dunster, see *Wikipedia – Dunster* (https://tinyurl.com/y8jfnalw) (at 12 September 2023). It is of interest to note that a Thomas Dunster was serving as a marine on Captain James Cook's *Endeavour* when Cook explored the east coast of the Australian mainland in 1770: see Historical Records of New Zealand, *Crew of Lieutenant Cook's Ship Endeavour, 1770* (https://tinyurl.com/5n7rurts) (at 12 September 2023); and James Cook, *A Journal of the Proceedings of His Majesty's Bark Endeavour,* 1770, p. 31 (https://tinyurl.com/m89enu5d) (at 12 September 2023). Phoebe had an uncle named Thomas Dunster, who would have been about the right age to have been the Thomas Dunster on the *Endeavour*: see *WikiTree – Thomas Dunster (1754)* (https://tinyurl.com/ybznj33j) (at 12 September 2023). However, it has not as yet been established that the two Thomas Dunsters were in fact one and the same.

14 See *WikiTree – Phoebe (Dunster) Buckman (1793 – 1866)* (https://tinyurl.com/ycba75yz) (at 12 September 2023).

15 See *FreeREG Baptism Entry – Phoebe Dunster* (https://tinyurl.com/yd6bzk40) (at 12 September 2023).

16 See *WikiTree – Phoebe (Dunster) Buckman (1793 – 1866)* (https://tinyurl.com/ycba75yz) (at 12 September 2023).

Woodchurch, the second of at least seven children born to William Barman and Sarah Barman Snr.[17]

On 29 August 1775, the younger Sarah Barman (as she then was) married her first husband, John Burt, in All Saints Church, Woodchurch.[18] Sarah and John had two children together. John Burt Jnr was born in 1775 and baptised in All Saints Church in that village on 21 September 1775.[19] James Burt was born in 1777 and christened in the same church on 16 November 1777.[20]

John Burt Snr died shortly prior to 8 April 1778. He was buried in the All Saints churchyard in Woodchurch on the latter date.[21] Following John's death, his widow married her second husband, Francis Dunster, in All Saints Church, Woodchurch on 26 March 1780.[22] Although Francis was probably born in Tenterden, it would appear that he lived all his married life with Sarah in nor around Woodchurch.

Francis and Sarah Dunster went on to have not less than seven children together. Phoebe Dunster was their second last child. Their remaining children were:

- Elizabeth Dunster, baptised on 23 July 1780.[23]

- Mary Dunster, baptised on 12 March 1784.[24]

- Francis Dunster, baptised on 29 October 1786.[25]

- William Dunster, baptised on 5 October 1788.[26]

---

17 See *WikiTree – Sarah (Barman) Dunster (abt. 1750 – 1828)* (https://tinyurl.com/3etdx3cb) (at 12 September 2023).

18 *Ibid.*

19 See *Woodchurch Local and Family History, Baptism Details* (21 September 1775, John Burt) (https://tinyurl.com/y9q2dcr7) (at 13 September 2023).

20 See *Woodchurch Local and Family History, Baptism Details* (16 November 1777, James Burt) (https://tinyurl.com/hyt293u) (at 13 September 2023).

21 See *Woodchurch Local and Family History, Burial Details* (8 April 1778, John Burt) (https://tinyurl.com/yxgyu2r4) (at 13 September 2023)..

22 See *WikiTree – Sarah (Barman) Dunster (abt. 1750 – 1828)* (https://tinyurl.com/3etdx3cb) (at 13 September 2023); *Woodchurch Local and Family History, Marriage Details* (26 March 1780, Francis Dunster and Sarah Burt) (https://tinyurl.com/ya72ts4g) (at 13 September 3023); and *FreeREG Marriage Entry – Francis Dunster and Sarah Burt* (https://tinyurl.com/yxf2u6k7) (at 13 September 2023).

23 See *Woodchurch Local and Family History, Baptism Details* (23 July 1780, Elizabeth Dunster) (https://tinyurl.com/yd4wn9ye) (at 13 September 2023).

24 See *Woodchurch Local and Family History, Baptism Details* (12 March 1784, Mary Dunster) (https://tinyurl.com/y848pwb8) (at 13 September 2023).

25 See *Woodchurch Local and Family History, Baptism Details* (29 October 1786, Francis Dunster) (https://tinyurl.com/y7zt7osf) (at 13 September 2023).

26 See *Woodchurch Local and Family History, Baptism Details* (5 October 1788, William Dunster) (https://tinyurl.com/y9dh4vly) (at 13 September 2023).

- George Dunster, baptised on 9 January 1791.[27]

- James Dunster. Baptised on 13 April 1794.[28]

Each of the above, like Phoebe, was christened in All Saints Church, Woodchurch. Francis Dunster died shortly prior to 27 January 1828. He was buried on that date in the churchyard of All Saints Church, Woodchurch.[29] Sarah Dunster died less than 12 months later. On 14 December 1828, she, like her second husband, was buried in the All Saints churchyard in Woodchurch.[30]

Phoebe Dunster almost certainly had the benefit of little, if any, formal schooling. Like both of her husbands, she appears to have been illiterate; being of necessity needing to "make her mark" when required to sign her name.[31] It seems highly likely that Phoebe was fully occupied with domestic and family duties from an early age.

John Moore's Parents' Marriage And Life Together

On 19 April 1812, Joseph Moore and Phoebe Dunster were married by the Reverend Coysgarne in All Saints Church, Woodchurch.[32] The marriage produced three children:

- Sarah Moore was probably born a little before 14 February 1813. She was christened by the Reverend Coysgarne in All Saints Church, Woodchurch on that date.[33]

- A mentioned above, John Moore was born on 20 April 1816. On 28 April 1816, he, like his sister, was baptised in All Saints Church, Woodchurch.[34]

---

27 See *Woodchurch Local and Family History, Baptism Details* (9 January 1791, George Dunster) (https://tinyurl.com/ycvkyzvf) (at 13 September 2023).

28 See *WikiTree – James Dunster (1794)* (https://tinyurl.com/2zkcdj2r) (at 14 September 2023).

29 See *FreeREG Burial Entry – Francis Dunster* (https://tinyurl.com/3rmm6rmv) (at 14 September 2023).

30 See *FreeREG Burial Entry – Sarah Dunster* (https://tinyurl.com/y55raanw) (at 14 September 2023).

31 See *Woodchurch Local and Family History, Marriage Details* (19 April 1812, Phoebe Dunster and Joseph Moore) (https://tinyurl.com/ydycnspq) (at 14 September 2023); and *FreeREG Marriage Entry – Phoebe Moore and Thomas Buckman* (https://tinyurl.com/yc6znkuj) (at 14 September 2023).

32 See *Woodchurch Local and Family History, Marriage Details* (19 April 1812, Joseph Moore and Phoebe Dunster) (https://tinyurl.com/ydycnspq) (at 14 September 2023); and *England, Select Marriages, 1538 – 1973 Joseph Moore and Phoebe Dunster* (https://tinyurl.com/hknrauk) (at 14 September 2023).

33 See *Woodchurch Local and Family History, Baptism Details* (14 February 1813, Sarah Moore) (https://tinyurl.com/y8n7448a) (at 14 September 2023); and *FreeREG Baptism Entry – Sarah Moore* (https://tinyurl.com/y974x83y) (at 14 September 2023).

34 See *WikiTree – John Moore (1816-1891)* (https://tinyurl.com/p7m48bsu) (at 14 September 2023); *Woodchurch Local and Family History, Baptism Details* (28 April 1816, John Moore) (https://tinyurl.com/yapeul40) (at 14 September 2023); and *FreeREG Baptism Entry – John Moore* (https://tinyurl.com/ycwajrq2) (at 14 September 2023).

- Richard Moore was born in Bethersden, and christened on 27 September 1818 in Bethersden's St Margaret's Church.[35] Richard died less than a year later in Bethersden, and was buried in the churchyard of St Mary the Virgin's Church, High Halden.[36]

Within months of the birth of their son, John, Joseph and Phoebe Moore found themselves on hard times. Towards the middle of 1816, and undoubtedly then unemployed, Joseph applied to the Woodchurch Parish for poor relief.

The precise reason for Joseph's unemployment in 1816 is not known. Christine Bean has observed that during the late 1700s and early 1800s, farming in Kent went through some radical changes:

"New crops were being introduced and some of the older crops no longer had a market."

Bean went on to note that the population of Kent was increasing during this period.[37] The rural labour market in Kent may also have been adversely affected in 1816 by two compounding factors. In the first place, there was probably an influx around that time of discharged soldiers and sailors following the end of the Napoleonic Wars.[38]

In the second place, Joseph Moore and his family might well have been victims of the so-called "Year Without a Summer". In April 1815, the Mt Tambora volcano on the Dutch East Indian island of Sumbawa erupted. The eruption was the largest in recorded history.

---

35 See *FreeREG Baptism Entry – Richard Moore* (https://tinyurl.com/ycmdzzlo) (at 14 September 2023).

36 See *FreeREG Burial Entry – Richard Moore* (https://tinyurl.com/yagekwpb) (at 14 September 2023).

37 See Bean, *op. cit.* The population of Woodchurch rose from 698 in 1801 to 1,187 in 1831, a rise of 489 (or 70%) in just 39 years: see Josie Mackie, "Social Conditions and Agriculture" ("*Social Conditions*") in Woodchurch Ancestry Group (eds.), *Leaving Woodchurch: Emigration from Woodchurch since the Seventeenth Century* (2011), p. 13. Rural unemployment in the Parish during this period was probably exacerbated by the introduction of threshing machines: Mackie, *Social Conditions, op. cit.* p. 14. See also Carl J. Griffin, "Parish farms and the poor law: a response to unemployment in rural southern England, c. 1812 – 1835" in (2011) 59 *Agricultural History Review* 176 at p. 177.

38 See Marjorie Bloy, "Causes of Discontent and Distress, 1812 – 22" in *A Web of English History: The Age of George III* (https://tinyurl.com/4aw7vfyy) (at 14 September 2023). It is interesting to note that in "Social Conditions and Agriculture", Josie Mackie observed:

"The end of the Napoleonic Wars in 18115 saw soldiers returning home looking for agricultural work coupled with a series of bad harvests. And, of course, Woodchurch was overwhelmingly an agricultural parish."

See Mackie, *Social Conditions, op. cit.*, p. 13. It might also be noted that the Reverend George Gleig, of Waltham near Canterbury, referred to the impact of the returning soldiers and sailors thus:

"multitudes of disbanded soldiers and sailors...[were] sent back to their parishes."

This led to "a competition among men to find masters". An initial resistance to reduced wages inevitably led to farmers:

"strik[ing] off a certain number from their employ leading to numbers of young, healthy, and willing persons [who] no longer knew where to apply for a day's work."

According to Gleig, parish vestries:

"could neither understand nor manage it. They would not listen to the applications of the young and healthy, but refused them peremptorily both relief and employment."

See George Gleig, *The Chronicles of Waltham* (1835), pp. 80-81. See also Griffin, *op. cit.*, p. 180.

It threw some 175 cubic km of ash and other volcanic debris into the atmosphere. The ash ultimately encircled the earth, producing profound climate changes over the ensuing three years. In Europe, it caused a pronounced drop in temperatures, crop failures and famine. The year 1816 saw food riots and other civil disturbances in England.[39] It follows that Joseph and his family could well have been, in part, victims of climate change; albeit temporary climate change.

Joseph's application for poor law relief to the Woodchurch Parish was refused. His entitlement to such relief in Woodchurch was examined by two local Justices of the Peace. On 4 July 1816, these Justices ruled as follows:

> "Whereas Complaint has been made unto us,...being two of his Majesty's Justice of the Peace, in and for the...County of Kent,...by the Churchwardens and Overseers of the Poor of the...Parish of Woodchurch, that Joseph Moore, Labourer, with Phobe [sic] his wife and Sarah aged three years and a half and John aged nine [sic] months his children, did lately come to inhabit in the said Parish of Woodchurch not having gained a legal Settlement there; nor produced any Certificate owning them to be settled elsewhere, and that the said Joseph Moore and his said wife and children are actually chargeable to the said Parish of Woodchurch. We the said Justices, upon due proof made thereof, as well as upon the Examination of the said Joseph Moore upon Oath as otherwise, and likewise upon due Consideration had of the Premises, do adjudge the same to be true, and we do also adjudge that the lawful Settlement of the said Joseph Moore and his said wife and children is in the... Parish of Bethersden in the said County of Kent. We do therefore require you the said Churchwardens and Overseers of the Poor of the said Parish of Woodchurch... to remove and convey the said Joseph Moore and his said wife and children from and out of your said Parish of Woodchurch to the said Parish of Bethersden and them to deliver to the Churchwardens and Overseers of the Poor there,...together with this our Order...;and we do also hereby require you the said Churchwardens

---

39 See Clive Oppenheimer, "Climatic, environmental and human consequences of the largest known historic eruption: Tambora volcano (Indonesia) 1815" in (2003) 27(2) *Progress in Physical Geography* 230—259; and Gillen D'Arcy Wood, *Tambora: The Eruption That Changed The World* (2014), pp. 60-62. Peter Frankopan has further observed:

"In the three years before Tambora erupted, global temperatures had already become distinctly cooler, partly because of the eruptions of Mount Soufrière in the Caribbean and Mount Mayon in what is now the Philippines in 1812 and 1814 respectively. If these magnified the effects of Tambora, it did not help that 1816 corresponded to an unusually weak maximum in the sunspot cycle, a phenomenon that is known to affect sea surface temperatures. The impacts around the world were so great that 1816 has become popularly known as 'the year without a summer'. The consequences were dramatic. In July 1816, *The Times* of London warned that dangers lay ahead: 'Should the present wet weather continue', the paper noted, harvests were likely to fail 'and the effects of such a calamity at such a time cannot be otherwise than ruinous to the farmers and even to the people at large'."

See Peter Frankopan, *The Earth Transformed: An Untold History* (2023), p. 456.

and Overseers of the Poor of the said Parish of Bethersden to receive and provide for them according to Law."[40]

The Churchwardens and Overseers of the Poor referred to in the Justices' Removal Order were officers appointed by the Parish Vestry in each parish charged by law to feed, clothe, house and find work for the poor inhabitants of their parishes where necessary. They, like the Justices of the Peace, were required to discharge their duties with respect to the poor in accordance with the *Poor Law Relief Act 1662* (UK) (also known as the *Settlement Act*)[41], as amended by the *Poor Relief Act 1691* (UK).[42]

As parishes were required to fund the poor relief administered by them from their own resources (i.e. from parish taxes and donations), the legal entitlements of applicants to local poor law relief were examined closely. Under the provisions of the *Poor Relief Act 1612* (UK), only those legally "settled" in a parish could be entitled to relief in and from that Parish. Those not so "settled" were liable to be removed to their parishes of legal settlement – by force if needs be – in each case on the order of two Justices of the Peace.[43]

The *Poor Relief Act 1662* (UK) provided that a person born in a parish had a settlement entitlement in that parish. A person born outside the parish could gain a settlement entitlement within it if he or she met one or more of the following conditions:

- having married into the parish;

- having been hired for at least a year and a day within the parish;

- having held an office within the parish;

- paying £10 per year or more in rent for a property located in the parish;

- paying not less than £10 per year in taxes in the parish;

---

40 See *Woodchurch Local and Family History; Woodchurch Parish Chest, 1633 – 1842: Joseph and Phoebe Moore* (Record Details, P400/13/5). See also the copy of the Removal Order below. The two Justices of the Peace appear from their signatures on the Removal Order to have been Thomas Law Hodges and Robert Monypenny. Thomas Law Hodges, of Hemsted House, Benenden in Kent, lived from 1776 until 1857. A Deputy Lieutenant of Kent and a Major in the West Kent Militia, he served as a Whig Member of Parliament for Kent (and later for West Kent) between 1832 and 1852: see *Wikipedia – Thomas Law Hodges* (https://tinyurl.com/bd2kpnke) (at 14 September 2023). Robert Monypenny, of Merrington Place, Rolvenden in Kent, lived from 1771 until 1834: see Robert Sewell, *Monypenny of Pitmilly* (https://tinyurl.com/ycky8kdx) (at 14 September 2023).

41 14 Car. 2, c. 12.

42 3 Will. & Mary, c. 11. See Mackie, *Social Conditions, op. cit.*, p. 14. See also Jennie Light, "Overseers of the Poor and the Vestry Meeting (1757 – 1850)" in Woodchurch Ancestry Group (eds.), *A Social History of Woodchurch: The People* (2014), pp. 69-70.

43 See James Paterson, "Protection of the Body against Want and Destitution" in *Commentaries on the Liberty of the Subject and the Laws of England Relating to the Security of the Person* (1877); and Marc Linder, "The Joint Employment Doctrine: Clarifying Joint Legislative-Judicial Confusion" in (1989) 10(2) *Hamline Journal of Law and Public Policy* 321.

- having previously gained poor relief in and from the parish;

- having entered into a seven year apprenticeship with a settled parish resident; and

- having lived in the parish for at least 40 days without complaint.

With respect to the last of these conditions, the amending *Poor Relief Act 1691* (UK) obliged parish officers to publicly publish arrival registrations in writing in their local churches' Sunday circulars, and also to read them to the congregation. The 40 day period would only commence thereafter.

Given this statutory framework, the refusal of Joseph Moore's application for poor relief, and the Justices' order for his and his family's removal from Woodchurch to Bethersden, are puzzling to say the least. Although it is likely that Joseph's mother had been born in Bethersden, it is also likely that Joseph was himself born in High Halden rather than Bethersden.[44]

It is possible that Joseph, although born in High Halden, could have become "settled" in Bethersden prior to moving to Woodchurch and marrying Phoebe Dunster. This could have occurred in either of two ways. Firstly, his parents might have moved with him from High Halden to Bethersden at some stage after his birth. Secondly, Joseph might have been raised by his parents in High Halden but have himself settled in Bethersden after leaving his parent's High Halden home.

What is even more puzzling about the removal is that Joseph would seem to have qualified for settlement in Woodchurch on at least two of the grounds recognised under the *poor Relief Act 1662* (UK). In the first place, his wife, Phoebe Dunster, had been unambiguously born and baptised in Woodchurch, and he had married her in Woodchurch's All Saints Church. In the second place, not only had he married a Woodchurch girl in Woodchurch, but his two older children had been born and baptised in that Parish. During the period covering his marriage, the birth of his two older children and the making of his application for poor relief, it appears most likely that he would have lived in Woodchurch Parish for at least 40 consecutive days without complaint.

It is, of course, conceivable that both Joseph and Phoebe Moore could have somehow acquired settlement in Bethersden after their marriage. However, given the subsequent births and christenings of their first two children in Woodchurch, this seems highly unlikely.

The precise circumstances surrounding the Moore family's removal from Woodchurch to Bethersden in 1816 are likely to remain clothed in a measure of mystery. However,

---

44 See footnote 2 above. Fairly thorough searches of the relevant Bethesden Parish records have not provided any indication that Joseph was born or baptised in that Parish.

there would appear to be strong grounds for concluding that the removal was unlawful, and that the family were the subjects of unjust treatment.

The fate met by Joseph Moore and his family after their removal from Woodchurch to Bethersden is presently unknown, They may well have spent a period of time in the Bethersden workhouse.[45] In 1777, the latter apparently accommodated 20 inmates. Clearly, life there would have been difficult. Alternatively, they may have found lodgings and sustenance with relatives in Bethersden.

Whether Joseph Moore ever again found employment after his removal to Bethersden is also unknown. In the event, he died early in 1819. His cause of death is not known. He was buried in the churchyard of St Mary the Virgin's Church in High Halden on 14 February 1819.[46]

Joseph was probably about 28 years old when he died. Life expectancy for males in early Nineteenth Century England was around 40 years. However, a man who survived the dangers of childhood and adolescence could ordinarily expect to live into his 60s.[47]

A mere four months after Joseph Moore's death and burial, he was followed to the grave by his infant younger son, Richard Moore. Richard was buried in his father's grave at St Mary the Virgin's Church, High Halden on 20 June 1819.[48]

Phoebe Moore's Marriage To Thomas Buckman

How Phoebe Moore supported herself and her two small children following Joseph's death is not presently known. However, it seems that she did not return to Woodchurch; remaining instead in Bethersden. Some two and a half years after Joseph death, on 11 August 1821, Phoebe Moore married her second husband, Thomas Buckman, in St Margaret's Church, Bethersden. The marriage was officiated by the Vicar of St Margaret's Church, the Reverend Patrick Keith.[49]

Thomas Buckman appears to have been born in Hothfield, Kent in 1798.[50] Like Phoebe and Joseph Moore, Thomas was illiterate – "making his mark", rather than signing, the Bethersden Parish Register.[51] When and where he first met Phoebe is now lost in time.

---

45 See Historic England, *4-8 Batemans Corner* (https://tinyurl.com/39k8df9h) (at 15 September 2023).

46 See *WikiTree – Joseph Moore (1791 – 1819)* (https://tinyurl.com/3yz2bjd9) (at 15 September 2023).

47 See Tim Lambert, *A History of Life Expectancy in Britain* (https://tinyurl.com/h2mzho7) (at 15 September 2023).

48 See *FreeREG Burial Entry – Richard Moore* (https://tinyurl.com/yagekwpb) (at 15 September 2023).

49 See *FreeREG Marriage Entry – Phoebe Moore and Thomas Buckman* (https://tinyurl.com/yc6znkuj) (at 16 September 2023); and *WikiTree – Phoebe (Dunster) Buckman (1793 – 1865)* (https://tinyurl.com/ycba75yz) (at 16 September 2023).

50 See *WikiTree – Thomas Buckman (1798 – 1865)* (https://tinyurl.com/y8bv66p9) (at 16 September 2023); and the *1861 England Census* (https://tinyurl.com/39ffzbm5) (at 16 September 2023).

51 See *FreeREG Marriage Entry – Thomas Buckman and Phoebe Moore* (https://tinyurl.com/yc6znkuj) (at 16 September 2023).

It is likely that Thomas spent his entire working life as an agricultural labourer and timber sawyer.[52]

It would appear that Phoebe and Thomas Buckman had the five following children together:

- Elizabeth Buckman, born in Bethersden in 1823.[53]

- Mahala Buckman, born in Bethersden on 14 July 1828 and baptised on 29 June 1849.[54]

- George Buckman, born in Bethersden in about 1831 and baptised on 24 April 1853.[55]

- Eliza Buckman, born in Bethersden in about 1833.[56]

- Sophia Buckman, born in Bethersden in about 1835.[57]

Both Mahala and George Buckman were christened in St Margaret's Church, Bethersden.

Following her marriage to Thomas Buckman, Phoebe almost certainly lived the balance of her life in Bethersden. She is recorded as living at Maylan Corner, Bethersden in the *1841 England Census*[58], the *1851 England Census*[59] and the *1861 England Census*.[60] Shortly prior to 7 June 1865, Thomas Buckman died. On the latter date, he was buried in the churchyard of St Margaret's Church, Bethersden.[61] Phoebe also died in Bethersden in 1865. On 20 August 1865, she, too, was buried in St Margaret's churchyard.[62]

---

52 See the *1861 England Census* (https://tinyurl.com/yku2575u) (at 16 September 2023).

53 See the *1861 England Census* (https://tinyurl.com/4973svuj) (at 16 September 2023). No contemporaneous record of Elizabeth Buckman's birth has currently come to light. Nor does there appear to be any record of her having been christened.

54 See *FreeREG Baptism Entry – Mahala Buckman* (https://tinyurl.com/y8wbuw3c) (at 16 September 2023); and *WikiTree – Mahala Buckman (1828)* (https://tinyurl.com/y8gq4nns) (at 16 September 2023).

55 See *FreeREG Baptism Entry – George Buckman* (https://tinyurl.com/y62ldgnv) (at 16 September 2023); and *WikiTree – George Buckman (abt. 1831)* (https://tinyurl.com/y72hedud) (at 16 September 2023).

56 See *WikiTree – Eliza Buckman (abt. 1833)* (https://tinyurl.com/y8bx7vw7) (at 16 September 2023).

57 See *WikiTree – Sophia Buckman (1835)* (https://tinyurl.com/y9cwwlsq) (at 16 September 2023).

58 See the *1841 England Census* (https://tinyurl.com/3tyxvzbw) (at 16 September 2023).

59 See the *1851 England Census* (https://tinyurl.com/yyg9xqbh) (at 16 September 2023).

60 See the *1861 England Census* (https://tinyurl.com/5bas5xk4) (at 16 September 2023).

61 See *FreeREG Burial Entry – Thomas Buckman* (https://tinyurl.com/ybnkalcv) (at 16 September 2023); and *WikiTree – Thomas Buckman (1798 – 1865)* (https://tinyurl.com/y8bv66p9) (at 16 September 2023).

62 See *FreeREG Burial Entry – Phoebe Buckman* (https://tinyurl.com/y9swkvsc) (at 16 September 2023); and *WikiTree – Phoebe (Dunster) Buckman (1793 – 1865)* (https://tinyurl.com/ycba75yz) (at 16 September 2023).

John Moore's Life In England

Little is known of John Moore's early years Unlike his parents, he was literate.[63] This suggests that he must have had at least a modicum of formal schooling. A now missing photograph of John as a youngish man has been said to show him to be of a stocky build, probably not tall, with a beard and with his hair parted to the right.[64] He probably spoke with a local Kentish accent all of his life.[65]

Undoubtedly the most significant events impacting on John's early life would have been his family's removal from Woodchurch to Bethersden, the death of his father and his mother's remarriage to Thomas Buckman. Given that John was not yet three years of age when Joseph Moore died, it is unlikely that he would have had any memory of his father. Like his sister and his half-sisters and half-brother, John grew up in the Bethersden home of his mother and stepfather.

It would seem that John, like both his father and stepfather, worked as a farm labourer in England. He was recorded in December 1837, when he was 21 years of age, as being an "agriculturist".[66] There would seem to be no surviving record of John's English employer or employers.

In 1838, John left England and his family for good; emigrating to Australia. He was 22 years old at the time of his departure.

What caused John to immigrate to Australia is not now known. It is possible, although perhaps unlikely, that friction with his stepfather, and a desire to remove himself from the latter's environs, played a part. It is worth noting that his sister, Sarah Moore, continued living in the home of her mother and stepfather in Bethersden until at least 1841. This might suggest that Thomas Buckman was not an unkindly or difficult man with whom to live. Moreover, had John wished to escape his stepfather, he could simply have moved further afield in England. More likely, John was motivated by a desire to better himself and his economic prospects in Australia.

As mentioned above, economic hardship and dislocation were almost certainly the reasons for Joseph Moore's unsuccessful application to the Woodchurch Parish for poor

---

63   See *Immigration Series: Entitlement Certificates of Persons on Bounty Ships, 1832 – 1842: John Moore* (AONSW 4/4830) (https://tinyurl.com/2eexvfb6) (at 16 September 2023).

64   The photograph is referred to in an anonymous document dated September 1994. I am currently unaware of both the identity of the author and the provenance of the document.

65   The oldest child raised in the household of John Moore and his wife, Margaret, was variously known as "Henry Moore" and "Henry Faithfull". In a hand-written list of the members of John and Margaret's family inscribed at the front of a Bible (which is currently in the possession of Judy Field of Wangaratta), Henry's name is spelled "Henery". This spelling may well reflect the way in which John, with his Kentish accent, pronounced Henry's name. See the photocopied Bible page below.

66   See *Immigration Series: Entitlement Certificates for Persons on Bounty Ships, 1832 – 1842: John Moore* (AONSW 4/4830) (https://tinyurl.com/2eexvfb6) (at 17 September 2023).

relief in 1816.⁶⁷ It would seem that economic circumstances for Kent farm workers had not improved by the late 1830s to any appreciable extent, if at all. A decline in demand for English Southdown wool, which was being ousted from markets during this period by wool from German sheep crossed with Spanish Merinos, contributed to a reduced demand for rural labour in Kent.⁶⁸ The widening use of newly-introduced threshing machines further undermined local employment.⁶⁹

Economic conditions in southern England were such that the Reverend Thomas Sockett, the Rector of the West Sussex Parish of Petworth, wrote in 1833:

> "Here, however industrious and frugal a labouring man may be, there is no longer a demand for his labour sufficient to enable him to bring up a family, without assistance from a parish; much less to lay by any provision for old age: and especially, if he marry, and have several children, he has no prospect before him but hard labour, and hard fare, during his youth and middle age, and the work-house in the close of his days."⁷⁰

Life in this period became so distressing for agricultural labourers that parish officials began to encourage them to emigrate.⁷¹ By way of example, the *Introduction to the Woodchurch Parish Church* states that many people emigrated from that Parish to the United States and to Australia in the 1830s to escape the high levels of unemployment. It would see that 80 Woodchurch parishioners immigrated to Australia alone between 1820 and 1859.⁷²

Although John Moore emigrated from Bethersden rather than Woodchurch, it seems close to certain that he did so in the context of very similar circumstances as confronted the Woodchurch emigrees.

It should be pointed out that rural unemployment and associated distress led to riots and other forms of civil unrest in England, particularly in the south-east, in the 1830s. Rioting commenced with the so-called *Swing Riots* in the early part of that decade.⁷³ In

---

67   See footnotes 37, 38 and 39, together with their accompanying texts, above.

68   See *Australia's Early Immigration Schemes: The Bounty Scheme* (https://tinyurl.com/yd2gegpa) (at 17 September 2023).

69   See Mackie, *Social Conditions, op. cit.*, p. 14.

70   See Thomas Sockett, *Emigration: A Letter to a Member of Parliament* (1834, 2ⁿᵈ ed.), p. 13. By 1830, over 200 Woodchurch parishioners were either unemployed or residing in the nearby Tenterden workhouse: see Light, *op. cit.*, p.70.

71   See John Chaplin and Pauline Gardiner, "Introduction" in Woodchurch Ancestry Group (eds.), *Leaving Woodchurch: Emigration from Woodchurch since the Seventeenth Century* (2011), p. 7.

72   See Robert A Chown, "The Population of Woodchurch and Emigration" in Woodchurch Ancestry Group (eds.), *Leaving Woodchurch: Emigration from Woodchurch since the Seventeenth Century* (2011), p. 12.

73   See *Wikipedia – Swing Riots* (https://tinyurl.com/n9gry8t) (at 17 September 2023); and Eric Hobsbawm and George Rudé, *Captain Swing* (1969), p. 73.

1838, there was a riot in Woodchurch. On 9 July 1838, an angry assembly of over 100 Woodchurch villagers confronted William Sidders, one of the officers of the Sheriff of Kent, together with several of Sidders' assistants. Sidders' intention was to serve a Writ of Possession on one of the villagers, Aaron Daw.[74]

Daw was one of a number of poor inhabitants of Woodchurch who were individually occupying two large blocks of land which had formerly been village common land used for cattle grazing. These blocks were locally known as *Townland Green* and *Lower Green*. The occupiers, without authority, had divided both blocks into broadly rectangular garden plots on which to grow vegetables. Some, including a William Dunster, had built their residences on the land they were cultivating.[75] In all, a total of six Dunsters have been identified as individually occupying garden plots on the two blocks.[76] All would undoubtedly have been related to Phoebe Buckman and John Moore; with William Dunster very likely being one of Phoebe's older brothers and an uncle of John's.[77]

By 1838, both *Townland Green* and *Lower Green* were owned by a William Deedes of Sandling Park.[78] Deedes elicited the support of Sidders to remove the squatters. The villagers refused to voluntarily yield up possession of the lands they occupied. On 9 July 1838, and as they attempted to serve the Writ of Possession on Daw, Sidders and his men were driven off by the villagers; who apparently made violent threats against them and pelted them with stones and other objects.[79]

In the event, William Dunster and five other villagers, who were all taken to be the ringleaders of the rioting villagers, were charged with riot and with obstructing a Sheriff's officer. All six were committed to stand trial at the Kent County Assizes in Maidstone on 6 August 1838. As matters turned out, the trial of the men did not proceed. In the words of Josie Mackie:

> "At the Assizes they each pleaded guilty but, as reported in the *South Eastern Gazette* on 21 August, Deedes decided not to proceed against the men, so they were all discharged. It would be interesting to know why he decided this. The

---

[74] See Josie Mackie, "Riot in Woodchurch: A Summer of Discontent" ("*Riot in Woodchurch*") in (2019) 1 *Scuppets & Scutchell* 60, at pp. 65 – 66. See also Woodchurch Ancestry Group, *Facebook Posts Page*, Entry for 9 July 2018 (https://tinyurl.com/ybnlg4q6) (at 17 September 2023).

[75] William Dunster built his home on *Townland Green*: see Mackie, *Riot in Woodchurch, op. cit.*, p. 62.

[76] See Mackie, *Riot in Woodchurch, op. cit.*, pp. 62 and 64.

[77] See footnote 26 and its accompanying text above.

[78] William Deedes lived from 1796 until 1862. He held office as Member of Parliament for East Kent from 1845 until his death in 1862: see *The Peerage: Person Page 31884 – William Deedes* (https://tinyurl.com/yxapd3gd) (at 17 September 2023).

[79] See Mackie, *Riot in Woodchurch, op. cit.*, p. 66.

newspaper report merely says that the men had seen the error of their course of action. Lord Denman, then Lord Chief Justice, said that they should be 'grateful to the prosecutor for his kindness'."[80]

Following the abandonment of the charges brought against them, the six men returned to Woodchurch; with William Dunster reoccupying his *Townland Green* home. It may be that he, like the other occupants of the plots of land, agreed to pay rent to Deedes. In any event, in 1859, the latter sold all of the plots to their then occupants.[81]

It is not now known whether John Moore was aware of the 1838 Woodchurch riot, or of the charges levied against his uncle, William Dunster, and the ultimate disposition of those charges. However, it seems that both geographic and family proximity would have rendered it likely that he would at least have been aware of the riot and of his uncle's involvement in it. In any event, it is clear that those events would have played no appreciable part in John's decision to emigrate from England to Australia. Although he did not leave his home shores until after the charges against William Dunster had been abandoned, the processes leading to his departure were already in train no later than December 1837.[82]

John travelled from England to Australia as a bounty immigrant. The bounty immigration scheme was a program, initiated by the New South Wales Colonial Government, which ran from 1835 until 1841. Colonists in New South Wales paid bounties to agents in Britain, who then recruited suitable tradesmen and labourers, and paid for their passages to Australia. On arrival, the sponsoring colonists would employ the immigrants; with the colonists being reimbursed by the Colonial Government for the immigrants' costs of passage and the agents' fees. Prospective immigrants had to show themselves to be suitable candidates for assisted passage. They had to be young, healthy and "useful" in their work experiences.[83]

The most significant of the English bounty immigration agents was a John Marshall. It was the latter who arranged John Moore's passage to Australia. Like other bounty immigrants, John was the subject of an Entitlement Certificate which was presented to the Colonial authorities in Sydney on his arrival in that city. Among other particulars recorded

---

80   *Ibid.*

81   See Mackie, *Riot in Woodchurch, op. cit.*, p. 67. The land on which William Dunster's house once stood is now the location of a convenience store and post office known as *Townland Stores and Post Office*. The property is situated at 74 Front Road, Woodchurch: see Mackie, *Riot in Woodchurch, op. cit.*, p. 65.

82   See *Immigration Series: Entitlement Certificates of Persons on Bounty Ships, 1832 – 1842: John Moore* (AONSW 4/4830) (https://tinyurl.com/2eexvfb6) (at 17 September 2023); and footnote 66 and its accompanying text above.

83   See *Heritage Genealogy: Immigration Indexes* (https://tinyurl.com/y9m7tqfk) (at 18 September 2023). See also Chaplin and Gardiner, *op. cit.*, p. 8.

on his Certificate were the facts that he was a Protestant and in good bodily health. The Certificate also revealed that John had been certified as being of good character by the Reverend Richard Bennett, the Vicar of Bethersden, and by a John Lade. The latter was a Bethersden landowner who may well have at one time employed John.[84]

John Moore sailed for Australia from Plymouth on 28 August 1838. He was 22 years old at the time of his departure. John travelled as a steerage passenger on the *James Pattison*; a vessel of 573 tons captained by a James Cromarty. John was one of around 300 immigrant passengers on Board. During the voyage, there were 5 births and 11 deaths of children. At one point, the *James Pattison* became becalmed and it was necessary for her to sail round Van Diemen's Land rather than through Bass Strait. The ship docked at Sydney on 11 December 1838 after a voyage of 106 days.[85]

Before turning to John Moore's life in Australia, and to Margaret Considine, I first propose to shortly examine the lives of John's sister and his half-sisters and half-brother. On leaving England, John was not to see any of them again, as none followed in his tracks to Australia. If he had any subsequent contact of any sort with any of them, that contact is lost in the mists of time.

The Lives Of John Moore's Sister, Half-Sisters And Half-Brother

Sarah Moore

Little is presently known of Sarah Moore's life. In the *1841 England Census*, she was recorded as being a female servant then living with her mother, stepfather and half-siblings in Thomas Buckman's house at Maylan Corner, Bethersden.[86] Who her employer was at this time is not now known, and details of her life after 1841 are somewhat opaque.

Sarah was not living with her mother and stepfather in Bethersden at the time of the *1851 England Census*. Indeed, her name does not seem to appear in that Census. However, it does appear from the *1861 England Census* that she was living in 1861 at Rye, Sussex in the home of a Stephen Norley, and was working as Norley's servant.[87]

Sarah Moore seems never to have married or to have produced any children outside

---

84 See *Immigration Series: Entitlement Certificates of Persons on Bounty Ships, 1832 – 1842: John Moore* (AONSW 4/4830) (https://tinyurl.com/2eexvfb6) (at 18 September 2023).

85 See *Wikipedia – James Pattison (1828 ship)* (https://tinyurl.com/2jwtuyzu) (at 18 September 2023); The Ratbag Encyclopedia, *Researching a Convict Ship* (https://tinyurl.com/4sbpn37x) (at 18 September 2023); and *Ozships: Australian Shipping 1788 – 1968: Arrivals: James Pattison – 11 December 1838* (https://tinyurl.com/y83da271) (at 18 September 2023); and the *Sydney Herald*, Wednesday, 12 December 2023, p. 3. See also photo 8, a copy of an 1837 painting of the *James Pattison*, below.

86 See the 1841 England Census (https://tinyurl.com/374964a7) (at 18 September 2023).

87 See the *1861 England Census* (https://tinyurl.com/3v8w4j3u) (at 18 September 2023).

marriage. It is likely that she died at the age of 55 years a little prior to 27 October 1868, and was buried on that date in the churchyard of St Margaret's Church, Bethersden.[88]

Elizabeth Buckman

There is also significant uncertainty surrounding the life of the oldest of Phoebe and Thomas Buckman's children, Elizabeth Buckman. Elizabeth does not seem to appear in the *1841 England Census*. She would then have been about 18 years of age. Presumably, she was living and working away from the home of her mother and stepfather at the time of the Census, and for some now unknown reason went unrecorded in it.

Elizabeth was, however, recorded in the *1851 England Census*. She was there said to be living as a lodger in the home of a George Hixson, a master blacksmith, and his family. Her occupation was given as that of a nurse.[89]

The *1851 England Census* further recorded that three of Phoebe and Thomas Buckman's grandchildren were then living with Phoebe and Thomas in their Bethersden home. The three grandchildren were named in the Census as John Buckman, aged 9 years old, and the twins Elizabeth Buckman Jnr and Margaret Buckman, who were both said to be 7 years old. John was recorded as having been born in Bethersden and the twins in Woodchurch. All three were said in the Census to be "scholars".[90]

The two young girls were the illegitimate daughters of Elizabeth Buckman Snr and a William Willis. Both Elizabeth Jnr and Margaret were baptised under the recorded surname of "Willis" on 23 May 1844 in All Saints Church, Woodchurch.[91] Although he does not appear to have been baptised, John Buckman was almost certainly an earlier child of Elizabeth Buckman Snr. Each of the latter's three younger sisters was clearly too young to have given birth to him. It is possible, but perhaps a little unlikely, that William Willis was also the boy's father.[92]

In the *1861 England Census*, Elizabeth Buckman was said to be a housekeeper living and working in the household of a farmer, Thomas Pitcher, on Park Gate Road, Eltham,

---

88 See *England, Select Deaths and Burials, 1538 – 1991: Sarah Moore – 1868* (https://tinyurl.com/4mkabkyx) (at 18 September 2023).

89 See the *1851 England Census* (https://tinyurl.com/2pb5vcck) (at 18 September 2023).

90 See the *1851 England Census* (https://tinyurl.com/584dtme6) (at 18 September 2023).

91 See *Woodchurch Local and Family History, Baptism Details* (23 May 1844, Elizabeth and Margaret Willis) (https://tinyurl.com/y56pecuk) and (https://tinyurl.com/y4cc4dnc) (both at 18 September 2023). William Willis was likely a son of a Thomas Willis, a tinker from Woodchurch, and the latter's wife, Rebecca Willis. William was christened in All Saints Church, Woodchurch on 10 July 1825: see *Woodchurch Local and Family History, Baptism Details* (10 July 1825, William Willis) (https://tinyurl.com/y3tvkah2) (at 18 September 2023). The *1841 England Census* reveals that he was 15 years old, unmarried and living with his parents and five siblings in Woodchurch in that year: see the *1841 England Census* (https://tinyurl.com/yxqe9ha4) (at 18 September 2023).

92 William Willis would have been about 16 years of age when John Buckman was born.

Kent. She was then 38 years of age and unmarried.⁹³ The *1871 England Census* recorded Elizabeth as still being unmarried and working as a nurse. However, rather than living and working in Thomas Pitcher's household in Eltham, as she had been in 1861, she was listed in the *1871 England Census* as living and working back in Bethersden in the home of another farmer, Horace Brown, and his family.⁹⁴

Elizabeth Buckman was 48 years old in 1871. Thereafter, she appears to almost completely disappear from the record. It is not known whether Elizabeth had any continuing contact with any of her three children. However, it seems quite likely that she died in the first quarter of 1884 on the Isle of Thanet in Kent.⁹⁵

Mahala Buckman

Phoebe and Thomas Buckman's second daughter, Mahala Buckman, was baptised in St Margaret's Church, Bethersden on 29 June 1849; some 21 years after her birth on 14 July 1828.⁹⁶ The *1851 England Census* noted that Mahala was then living with her parents in Phoebe and Thomas Buckman's Bethersden home and was employed as a seamstress.⁹⁷ Later in 1851, she left that home upon her marriage. On 5 October 1851, Mahala married Alfred Law in St Nicholas' Church, Sevenoaks in Kent. Although they married in Sevenoaks, Alfred Law, like Mahala, was apparently born in Bethersden.⁹⁸

The record appears to be largely silent with respect to the movements and doings of Mahala and Alfred Law for some 20 years following their marriage in 1851. It would seem that they were not listed in the *1861 England Census*. However, in the *1871 England Census*, Mahala and Alfred were said to be living in Woodchurch; with Alfred working as a farm bailiff.⁹⁹

---

93 See the *1861 England Census* (https://tinyurl.com/4973svuj) (at 18 September 2023). The same Census recorded that Margaret Buckman, Elizabeth Buckman's daughter, was still living with her grandparents, Phoebe and Thomas Buckman in their Bethersden home. However, Elizabeth Buckman's two other children, John Buckman and Elizabeth Buckman Jnr, were apparently living and working and working elsewhere at locations which are currently unknown: see the *1861 England Census* (https://tinyurl.com/5bas5xk4) (at 19 September 2023). It would seem that John Buckman married a Sarah Hephziba Reeves on 25 December 1863 in St Margaret's Without Rochester Church in Kent: see *England, Select Marriages, 1538 – 1973: John Buckman and Sarah Reeves – 1863* (https://tinyurl.com/2szsy4jn) (at 19 September 2023). Nothing further is currently known concerning Elizabeth Buckman Jnr.

94 See the *1871 England Census* (https://tinyurl.com/yku2575u) (at 19 September 2023).

95 See *England and Wales, Civil Registration Death Index, 1837 – 1915: Elizabeth Buckman* (https://tinyurl.com/y4p3ntgc) (at 19 September 2023). It should, however, be noted that in this *Death Index* record, Elizabeth Buckman is said to have been 61 years old at the time of her death. This would see her as having been born in about 1823, and not 1824.

96 See *FreeREG Baptism Entry – Mahala Buckman* (https://tinyurl.com/y8wbuw3c) (at 20 September 2023).

97 See the *1851 England Census* (https://tinyurl.com/yyg9xqbh) (at 20 September 2023).

98 See *Kent, England, Church of England Baptisms, Marriages and Burials, 1538 – 1914: Mahala Buckman* (https://tinyurl.com/3wdhefwv) (at 20 September 2023). It is possible that Mahala Buckman's christening as an adult in 1849 was undertaken by her in accordance with the precepts of the Church of England in preparation for her marriage to Alfred Law: see footnotes 54 and 96, together with their accompanying texts, above.

99 See the *1871 England Census* (https://tinyurl.com/bdcubjfe) (at 20 September 2023).

The *1871 England Census* further records that Mahala and Alfred Law had five children at that time living with them in Woodchurch; being:

- Thomas Law, born in about 1855.

- Louisa Law, born in about 1861.

- Emily Law, born in about 1863.

- Julia Law, born in about 1864.

- Harriet Law, born in about 1866.

All were born in Bethersden save for Harriet, who was born in Faversham, Kent.[100]

However, it would seem that Mahala and Alfred had a sixth child, Mahala Law Jnr, who, for some currently unknown reason, was not living with her parents at the time of the *1871 England Census*. Mahala Law Jnr was born on 20 September 1857. She was baptised in St Margaret's Church, Bethersden on 23 May 1858.[101]

The *1881 England Census* lists Mahala and Alfred Law as living in St Nicholas-at-Wade on the Isle of Thanet. Alfred was said to be still employed as a farm bailiff. Mahala and Alfred's youngest daughter, Harriet Law, was residing with them; as was a baby girl, Alice Law, who was stated to be one year of age. The identity of Alice Law is a mystery. She was initially recorded in the Census as being a "Visitor". The word "Visitor" was then crossed out and replaced with the words "Nurse Child".[102]

What became of Mahala and Alfred Law after 1881 is presently unclear. Neither appeared in the *1891 England Census*. However, there is a record of a Mahala Law dying in the third quarter of 1884 on the Isle of Thanet.[103] Given that Mahala and Alfred Law were said in the *1881 England Census* to be living on the Isle of Thanet, the Mahala Law who died on the Isle in 1884 could well have been Alfred Law's wife or widow.[104]

---

100 *Ibid.*

101 See *FreeREG Baptism Entry – Mahala Law* (https://tinyurl.com/yxo7y7sd) (at 20 September 2023). It is, perhaps, interesting to note that Mahala Law Jnr and her younger sister, Harriet Law, were both listed in the *1901 England Census* as then residing in Tottenham, London, and both working as "lodging house keepers (seaside)": see the *1901 England Census* (https://tinyurl.com/y4zf67jb) (at 20 September 2023).

102 See the *1881 England Census* (https://tinyurl.com/3bmky5tn) (at 20 September 2023). St Nicholas-at-Wade is a small village lying about 11 km to the west-south-west of the Kent seaside town of Margate on the Isle of Thanet.

103 See *England and Wales, Civil Registration Death Index, 1837 – 1915: Mahala Law* (https://tinyurl.com/y5n40gnh) (at 20 September 2023).

104 However, it is worth noting that Mahala Law (née Buckman) should have been about 56 years old in 1884. The Mahala Law who is recorded as having died on the Isle of Thanet in 1884 was said to have been only 51 years of age at her death: see *England and Wales, Civil Registration Death Index, 1837 – 1915: Mahala Law* (https://tinyurl.com/y5n40gnh) 9at 20 September 2023). This may have simply been an error in the *Death Index* entry.

George Buckman

Like his older sister, Mahala, Phoebe and Thomas's only son, George Buckman, was baptised as an adult. He was christened on 24 April 1853 in St Margaret's Church, Bethersden. At the time of his baptism, he was 22 years old, and it was noted that he was employed as a labourer.[105] A little over six months later, on 3 November 1853, George married a Rebecca Reeves in the same church.[106]

In all, George and Rebecca Buckman had a total of nine children; those being:

- Thomas Buckman, born in 1854.

- Rebecca Buckman, born in 1856.

- Harriet Buckman, born in 1858.

- Franklin ("Frank") Buckman, born in 1860.

- Albert Buckman, born in 1863.

- Henry Buckman, born in 1865.

- Jane ("Jennie") Buckman, born in 1867.

- William ("Willie") Buckman, born in 1871.

- Beatrice Buckman, born in 1875.[107]

In 1867, George and Rebecca Buckman emigrated with their then existing children from England to the United States.[108] They made their way to upstate New York, where they established their home at or near to the small town of Stockbridge.[109] In the *1870 United*

It is also worth noting that Mahala Law's older sister, Elizabeth Buckman, likewise apparently died on the Isle of Thanet in 1884: see footnote 95 and its accompanying text above. Perhaps the two sisters moved into a house together on the seafront at, say, Margate after Alfred Law's death. Perhaps that house was then inherited by Mahala Law Jnr and Harriet Law after the deaths of Elizabeth Buckman and Mahala Law Snr in 1884. Perhaps Mahala Law Jnr and Harriet Law jointly operated the property as a lodging house thereafter: see footnote 101 and its accompanying text above. This is, of course, all pure speculation.

105 See *FreeREG Baptism Entry – George Buckman* (https://tinyurl.com/y62ldgnv) (at 20 September 2023). See also *England, Births and Christenings, 1538 – 1975: George Buckman – 1853* (https://tinyurl.com/4w9htr7t) (at 20 September 2023).

106 See *FreeREG Marriage Entry – George Buckman and Rebecca Reeves* (https://tinyurl.com/y5a8hk6e) (at 20 September 2023. See also footnote 98 above.

107 See the *1861 England Census* (https://tinyurl.com/m6vbey34) (at 20 September 2023); and the *1880 United States Federal Census* (https://tinyurl.com/52t4ns7k) (at 20 September 2023).

108 The *1905 New York State Census* recorded that George Buckman had lived in the United States for 38 years: see the *1905 New York State Census* (https://tinyurl.com/4ud43sb4) (at 20 September 2023).

109 Stockbridge lies about 45 km to the east-south-east of the City of Syracuse in New York State. Rather than travelling directly from England to New York City, and then moving overland northwards to Stockbridge, the Buckman family journeyed across the Atlantic in the *Nova Scotian* to Canada; landing in Quebec City in May 1867: see the *All Canadian*

States Federal Census, George was recorded as working as a farm labourer.[110] By 1875, George had purchased his own farm in the Stockbridge area. He continued to farm that propert until his death in 1909. He lies buried in the Stockbridge Cemetery at Munnsville, New York.[111]

Eliza Buckman

On 27 June 1858, Phoebe and Thomas Buckman's penultimate child, Eliza Buckman, married Walter Heathfield in St Nicholas' Church, Sevenoaks in Kent. Walter was 22 years old at the time of the marriage and working as an agricultural labourer. At 25 years of age, Eliza was three years older than her new husband.[112]

It is not presently known why Eliza and Walter chose to marry in Sevenoaks. At least prior to 1851, Eliza had been living with her parents in their Bethersden home.[113] For his part, Walter was born and raised in Smarden, Kent.[114] Sevenoaks is some 37 km to the north-west of Smarden and about 42 km to the north-west of Bethersden.[115]

In 1861, it would seem that in addition to their daughter, Sophia Buckman, and their grand-daughter, Margaret Buckman, a grandson, James Buckman, was also living with Thomas and Phoebe Backman in their Bethersden home. James was 5 years old at the time of the *1861 England Census*.[116] Whereas Margaret Buckman was Elizabeth Backman's daughter, it is clear that James Buckman was the son of Eliza Buckman. Walter Heathfield was very likely James' biological father. The *1871 England Census* records a James Heathfield as living in Smarden with Eliza and Walter Heathfield. James was said to be Walter and Eliza's son and to be 15 years old.[117] This would place his birth in 1856 – two years prior to Walter and Eliza's marriage and five years prior to the *1861 England Census*.

Passenger Lists, 1865 – 1935 : George Buckman (https://tinyurl.com/y5077zzy) (at 20 September 2023). Presumably, they then sailed up the St Lawrence River to the south shore of Lake Ontario and travelled overland southwards to Stockbridge.

110 See the *1870 United States Federal Census* (https://tinyurl.com/y75wdhsq) (at 20 September 2023).

111 See the *1875 New York State Census* (https://tinyurl.com/mpd7smhd) (at 20 September 2023); the *1880 United States Federal Census* (https://tinyurl.com/52t4ns7k) (at 20 September 2023); the *1905 New York State Census* (https://tinyurl.com/4ud43sb4) (at 20 September 2023); and *Find a Grave Memorial – George Buckman* (https://tinyurl.com/yxfacgqy) (at 20 September 2023).

112 See *Kent, England, Church of England Baptisms, Marriages and Burials, 1538 – 1914* (https://tinyurl.com/22bvmrze) (at 21 September 2023).

113 See the *1851 England Census* (https://tinyurl.com/yyg9xqbh) (at 21 September 2023).

114 See the *1861 England Census* (https://tinyurl.com/4pa85xxa) (at 21 September 2023).

115 Perhaps either Eliza or Walter was working in or near to Sevenoaks at the time of their marriage. It is worth noting that Eliza's older sister, Mahala Buckman, was also married in Sevenoaks. Mahala married Alfred Law in St Nicholas' Church, Sevenoaks on 5 October 1851: see footnote 98 and its accompanying text above. It is likewise now unknown why Mahala married so far from her Bethersden home. It's possible that the connection with Sevenoaks for both sisters was an unidentified Buckman relative.

116 See the *1861 England Census*: (https://tinyurl.com/5bas5xk4) (at 21 September 2023).

117 See the *1871 England Census:* (https://tinyurl.com/4c6jxe7v) (at 21 September 2023).

If James Buckman was indeed Walter Heathfield's child, then Eliza and Walter were to have five children in all:

- James Heathfield (in his early days known as James Buckman), born in 1856.

- Eliza Heathfield Jnr, born in 1859.

- Rose Florence Heathfield, born in 1862.

- Sophia Heathfield, born in 1866.

- Cordelia Heathfield, born in 1868.[118]

By the time of the *1861 England Census*, Walter and Eliza Heathfield were living in Walter's home village of Smarden, where Walter continued to work as an agricultural labourer.[119] Smarden continued to be the couples' home for the balance of their respective lives.[120] Eliza Heathfield died in Smarden in the second quarter of 1894. She was 61 years old when she died.[121]

Sophia Buckman

Thomas and Phoebe Buckman's youngest child, Sophia Buckman, was also the last of their children to leave the Buckmans' Bethersden home.[122] On 6 April 1868, Sophia married John Clinch in St Clement's Church, Hastings, Sussex. At the time of her marriage, she was 32 years old. John Clinch, at 27 years of age, was five years younger than his bride and born in Chilham, Kent.[123]

Sophia and John Clinch had five children together; being:

- Charles Clinch, born in 1869.

- Alice Clinch, born in 1870.

---

118   *Ibid.*

119   See the *1861 England Census*: (https://tinyurl.com/yc7fapdr) (at 21 September 2023).

120   See the *1871 England Census*: (https://tinyurl.com/4c6jxe7v) (at 21 September 2021); the *1881 England Census*: (https://tinyurl.com/4jbj5mpr) (at 21 September 2023); and the *1891 England Census* (https://tinyurl.com/bddj88k5) (at 21 September 2023).

121   See *England and Wales, Civil Registration Death Index, 1837 – 1915: Eliza Heathfield* (https://tinyurl.com/2f586pxm) (at 21 September 2023).

122   See the *1861 England Census* (https://tinyurl.com/5bas5xk4) (at 22 September 2023). In that Census, Sophia was described as a "needle woman". See also photo 9 below.

123   See *England, Select Marriages, 1538 – 1973: Sophia Buckman and John Clinch – 1868* (https://tinyurl.com/y4y20656) (at 22 September 2023).

- Isabella Flora Clinch, born in 1873.

- Evangeline Clink, born in 1875.

- Jessie Clinch, born in 1878.

Of these five children, only the oldest, Charles Clinch, was born in England.[124]

In 1869, John, Sophia and Charles Clinch immigrated to the United States.[125] Upon their arrival, they initially settled in Stockbridge, New York. It will be recalled that Sophia's brother, George Buckman, had emigrated from England to Stockbridge two years earlier in 1867.[126] There seems to be little doubt that a letter or letters from George to Sophia would have encouraged the latter and her husband to make the move to the United States with their small son. However, it is interesting to note that in the *1870 United States Federal Census*, John, Sophia and Charles Clinch were recorded as living in the same Stockbridge home as George and Ann Clinch and their two young children; Rowe Clinch and Ruth Clinch.[127] It seems clear that George Clinch must have been a close relative of John Clinch – perhaps a cousin.

At some point in time between 1875 and 1880, John and Sophia Clinch moved with their children from Stockbridge to Hastings, New York; where it would seem that John acquired a farm.[128] By 1900, the couple had moved even further from Stockbridge to a new farming property at Hounsfield, New York.[129]

John and Sophia Clinch continued to live on their farm at Hounsfield until John's death in 1912.[130] Following her husband's death, Sophia returned to Stockbridge to live with her married daughter, Isabella Day (née Clinch), and the latter's husband, Elmer Day, on the latter's farm.[131] She continued to live with the Days until her own death in 1922. Sophia was buried in John Clinch's grave in the Dexter Cemetery at Dexter near Hounsfield.[132]

---

124 See the *1880 United States Federal Census* (https://tinyurl.com/2s3utnfu) (at 22 September 2023).

125 See the *1890 United States Federal Census* (https://tinyurl.com/y4lfqoyl) (at 22 September 2023).

126 See footnote 108 and its accompanying text above.

127 See the *1870 United States Federal Census* (https://tinyurl.com/2s42vks8) (at 22 September 2023). George and Ann Clinch and their children may well have accompanied John , Sophia and Charles Clinch from England to the United States. Both John and George were stated in the Census to be employed in Stockbridge as "day labourers". See also the *1875 New York State Census* (https://tinyurl.com/2wsjshj4) (at 22 September 2023).

128 See the *1880 United States Federal Census* (https://tinyurl.com/2s3utnfu) (at 22 September 2023). Hastings is located about 60 km to the north-west of Stockbridge.

129 See the *1900 United States Federal Census* (https://tinyurl.com/yeympdj7) (at 22 September 2023). See also photo 10 below. Hounsfield lies some 65 km to the north of Hastings and about 110 km to the north-west of Stockbridge.

130 See the *1905 New York State Census* (https://tinyurl.com/3xxj9rds) (at 22 September 2023); the *1910 United States Federal Census* (https://tinyurl.com/yj6zay8z) (at 22 September 2023); and *Find a Grave Memorial – John Clinch* (https://tinyurl.com/2ep6f3z8) (at 22 September 2023).

131 See the *1915 New York State Census* (https://tinyurl.com/y8xrqwu5) (at 22 September 2023).

132 See *Find a Grave Memorial – Sophia Buckman Clinch* (https://tinyurl.com/32r8peh8) (at 22 September 2023).

Of John and Sophia Clinch's five children, the one who is, perhaps, of most interest is Alice Clinch. Alice was the first of the Clinch children to be born in the United States.[133] On 19 October 1898, she married a native-born New Yorker, LaVerne Judson LaBarr.[134] Like Alice, LaVerne was born in 1870.[135]

At around the time of his marriage to Alice, LaVerne became an officer in the Salvation Army. Alice joined the Salvation Army but apparently did not become an officer in it like her husband.[136] The *1910 United States Federal Census* recorded that Alice and LaVerne were then living with two of their children in Rutland, New York, and that LaVerne was employed as a clergyman in the Salvation Army.[137]

At some point in time between 1910 and 1928, LaVerne, Alice and their children moved from Rutland to Greensboro in North Carolina. After arriving in Greensboro, LaVerne apparently joined the Ku Klux Klan. According to a local newspaper article published on 21 February 1928, he rose (if that be the right word) to become the Secretary of the Klan's Greensboro Klavern. It seems that by about this stage he, and presumably Alice, had left the Salvation Army. The *1930 United States Federal Census* noted that the family were living in Greensboro; with LaVerne working as a building contractor.[138] Ten years later, in 1940, LaVerne and Alice were still living in Greensboro. However, by then, LaVerne had seemingly retired.[139]

Alice LaBarr died on 26 January 1950 in Greensboro of pellagra. She had been frail for some time prior to her death, and had suffered a heart attack on 24 December 1949.[140] Following a funeral service held in the First Evangelical and Reformed Church, Alice was buried in the Montlawn Cemetery in Raleigh, North Carolina.[141]

Following Alice's death, LaVerne LaBarr moved from his home in Greensboro to Raleigh to live with two of his unmarried daughters: Myrtle and Mabel LaBarr. He died of a likely heart attack on 7 April 1958. His funeral service was conducted in the First

---

133 See the *1875 New York State Census* (https://tinyurl.com/2wsjshj4) (at 22 September 2023).

134 See the *New York State Marriage Index, 1881 – 1967* (https://tinyurl.com/ck62ru5z) (at 22 September 2023).

135 See *North Carolina Death Certificates, 1909 – 1976: LaVerne Judson LaBarr* (https://tinyurl.com/yaothuhy) (at 22 September 2023).

136 See photo 11 below.

137 See the *1910 United States Federal Census* (https://tinyurl.com/yhhvctah) (at 22 September 2023). Rutland is a small town lying around 20 km to the east of Hounsfield.

138 See the *1930 United States Federal Census* (https://tinyurl.com/3fjmzwb5) (at 22 September 2023).

139 See the *1940 United States Federal Census* (https://tinyurl.com/46navp9s) (at 22 September 2023).

140 See *North Carolina Board of Health: Certificate of Death – Alice Ellen Clinch LaBarr (1870 – 1950)* (https://tinyurl.com/3f5n5erx) (at 23 September 2023).

141 See *Find a Grave Memorial – Alice Ellen Clinch LaBarr (1870 – 1950)* (https://tinyurl.com/ydk99h2r) (at 23 September 2023). Raleigh is the Capital of North Carolina and is situated some 100 km to the south-east of Greensboro.

Presbyterian Church in Raleigh, and he was then buried in the Montlawn Cemetery near his wife, Alice.[142]

John Moore's Life In Australia Prior To His Marriage

After landing in Sydney from the *James Pattison* on 11 December 1838, John Moore appears to have been engaged to work as a dairyman on William Pitt Faithfull's squatting run, *Springfield*, located some 15 km to the south of Goulburn in New South Wales. At that time, *Springfield* was being managed by William Pitt Faithfull in conjunction with his younger brother, George Faithfull. John probably started work on *Springfield* in late December 1838 or in early January 1839.[143]

William Pitt Faithfull was born on 11 October 1806 at Richmond in New South Wales. His brother George was born at Canterbury in the Colony on 5 January 1814. Their father, William Faithfull Snr, arrived in Sydney in February 1792 as a Private in the New South Wales Corps.[144] Their mother, Susanna Faithfull (née Matcham) was a distant relative of Admiral Horatio Nelson. William and Susanna were married in Sydney in 1804.[145]

Little is known of John Moore's early days on *Springfield*. However, in an obituary marking his death, he was described as "an exceptionally good and reliable young man" during his first years on the property.[146] Intriguingly, the same obituary went on to assert with respect to John that:

> "he was entrusted with the charge of a mob of cattle to be driven overland to Colac, then known as Western Port, which new country was then [being] taken up. The undertaking was a trying and hazardous one in those days (1839) – no roads, bridges, punts, or even known fords, and the native blacks to be encounted all along the dreary journey. The fatigues and vicissitudes of the little party led by

---

142 See *North Carolina State Board of Health: Certificate of Death – LaVerne Judson LaBarr (1870 – 1958)* (https://tinyurl.com/7yku97dh) (at 23 September 2023); and *Find a Grave Memorial – LaVerne Judson LaBarr (1870 – 1958)* (https://tinyurl.com/bdf67y6t) (at 23 September 2023).

143 See "John Moore Senior and Family" in John Faithfull and Jim Lewis, *From 16000 to 5* (2003, 2nd ed.), Appendix N, p. 147.

144 William Faithfull Snr. gained some notoriety in Sydney in 1795 when he and another soldier were successfully sued for assault. This led to William appealing the verdict to Governor Hunter – the first such appeal in the Colony – but to no avail: see *Historical Records of Australia* ("*HRA*"), Series 1, Volume 1, p. 608; Victor Windeyer, "A Birthright and Inheritance" in (1961) 1 *Tasmania University Law Review* 635, at pp. 664 – 665; and Malcolm Henry Ellis, *John Macarthur* (1963), pp. 82 – 83.

145 See Fred and Diana Bienvenu, *Faithfulls of Omeo* (1983), p. 3. See also photo 12 below.

146 See the *Wangaratta Despatch*, Wednesday, 5 August 1891. A transcribed copy of this obituary was in the possession of the late Charles Bertram ("Bert") Moore, one of John Moore's great-grandsons.

> Mr Moore were very considerable, but the work was successfully accomplished, and he returned to Goulburn..."[147]

This account of John's droving expedition from *Springfield* to Colac in 1839 was replicated almost word for word in a subsequent obituary published in 1895 following the death of John's widow, Margaret Moore (née Considine).[148]

There are reasons to question the accuracy of these droving expedition accounts. In the first place, a different obituary for Margaret Moore published in *The Age* on Saturday, 13 July 1898 stated that the destination of expedition was Port Fairy and not Colac.[149]

In the second place, it would seems strange that William Pitt Faithfull would entrust the leadership of the expedition as described to a young man from England who had been in his employ for a year or less. The distance from Goulburn to Colac "as the crow flies" is around 680 km. It would surely be a longer trek moving cattle along the way. And, as the obituaries both indicated, the cattle would need to be moved through trackless, difficult country to a destination entirely foreign to John Moore and the men he allegedly led.

In the third place, the Colac region had only recently been occupied by Europeans when the expedition was said to have taken place.[150] That raises the issue of how William Pitt Faithfull could have concluded that it would have been worthwhile to send cattle to that locality. The cost of the exercise would have been large and the reward speculative at best.

Finally, there does not appear to be any historical record relating to either Goulburn or Colac which would in any way support the expedition account contained in the two obituaries. One would have thought that an expedition of the sort described in the obituaries would have also been documented elsewhere.

One intriguing possibility is that rather than taking the herd of cattle from *Springfield* to Colac, John might have taken them to Colac Colac. The latter is a district on the Courang Creek, some 8 km to the south-west of Corryong and currently given over to grazing. It is located some 240 km to the south-west of Goulburn.[151] This area was first taken up by overlanders from New South Wales north of the Murray River in 1839.[152]

---

147 *Ibid.*

148 See the *Ovens and Murray Advertiser*, Saturday, 20 May 1895, p. 5.

149 See *The Age*, Saturday, 13 July 1895, p. 8.

150 Hugh Murray was the first European to occupy land in the vicinity of Lake Colac. He arrived with a flock of sheep in Geelong from Van Diemen's Land on board *The Gem* in September 1837. Murray went on to occupy some 34,000 acres of land around Colac centred on three squatting properties. He was soon joined by other sheep graziers from Van Diemen's Land: see *Wikipedia – Colac, Victoria* (https://tinyurl.com/pf3vjfsb) (at 24 September 2023).

151 See *Wikipedia – Colac Colac, Victoria* (https://tinyurl.com/7v9b74w6) (at 24 September 2023).

152 J. J. Howell and the Hassell brothers were the first Europeans to occupy land in the Colac Colac area: see Arthur

However, again, there would appear to be no historical record extant which might substantiate this conjecture.

What can be said with certainty regarding John Moore and 1839, is that on 3 September of that year, John, an Anglican from England, married Margaret Considine, a Catholic from Ireland, in a Catholic ceremony in Goulburn.[153]

Andrews, *First Settlement on the Upper Murray, 1835 – 1845* (1920), p. 106; Kelly Gang and Friends, *Adjie* (https://tinyurl.com/2u8h7yzt) (at 24 September 2023) and *The Corryong Courier*, Thursday, 27 October 1932, p. 6.

153 See Marriage Entry No. 7 for John Moore and Margaret Considine in the records of Sts. Peter and Paul's Catholic Old Cathedral, Goulburn.

Map of South Central Kent, England, showing the locations of the villages of Bethersden, High Halden and Woodchurch and the town of Tenterden.

KENT to wit. To the Churchwardens and Overseers of the Poor of the Parish of *Woodchurch* in the County of Kent; and to the Churchwardens and Overseers of the Poor of the Parish of *Bethersden* in the said County

WHEREAS Complaint has been made unto us, whose names are hereunto set and seals afixed, being two of his Majesty's Justices of the Peace, in and for the said County of Kent, and one of us of the Quorum, by the Churchwardens and Overseers of the Poor of the said Parish of *Woodchurch* that *Joseph Moore Labourer with Phebe his wife and Sarah aged three years and a half and John aged nine months his Children*

did lately come to inhabit in the said Parish of *Woodchurch* not having gained a legal Settlement there; nor produced any Certificate owning *him* to be settled elsewhere, and that the said *Joseph Moore and his said wife and children are* actually chargeable to the said Parish of *Woodchurch*.

We the said Justices, upon due proof made thereof, as well upon the Examination of the said *Joseph Moore* upon Oath as otherwise, and likewise upon due Consideration had of the Premises, do adjudge the same to be true, and we do also adjudge that the lawful Settlement of the said *Joseph Moore and his said wife and children*

is in the said Parish of *Bethersden* in the said County of *Kent*. WE do therefore require you the said Churchwardens and Overseers of the Poor of the said Parish of *Woodchurch* or some, or one of you to remove and convey the said *Joseph Moore and his said wife and children*

from and out of your said Parish of *Woodchurch* to the said Parish of *Bethersden* and there to deliver to the Churchwardens and Overseers of the Poor there, or to some or one of them, together with this our Order or a true copy thereof, at the same time shewing them the original: and we do also hereby require you the said Churchwardens and Overseers of the Poor of the said Parish of *Bethersden* to receive and provide for *them* according to Law. GIVEN under our Hands and Seals, the *fourth* Day of *July* in the Year of our Lord One Thousand, Eight Hundred and *sixteen*.

1816 Order for the removal of Joseph and Phoebe Moore from Woodchurch to Bethersden.

Photo 1: The village of Woodchurch, Kent, England.

Photo 2: All Saints Church, Woodchurch, Kent, England.

Photo 3: The ancient font in All Saints Church, Woodchurch, Kent, England.

Photo 4: The village of High Halden, Kent, England.

Photo 5: St. Mary the Virgin's Church, High Halden, Kent, England.

Photo 6: St. Margaret's Church, Bethersden, Kent, England.

Photo 7: A Dunster Gravestone, All Saints Church, Woodchurch, Kent, England.

Photo 8: The James Pattison (painting by Petrus Cornelis Weytes, c. 1837)

Photo 9: Sophia Buckman, c. 1865.

Photo 10: Sophia Clinch (née Buckman) (on the left), Jessie Clinch (in the centre) and John Clinch (on the right), Hounsfield, New York, United States of America.

Photo 11: Alice and LaVerne LaBarr in Salvation Army uniform.

Photo 12: William Pitt Faithfull (portrait by Joseph Backler, 1845).

MARGARET CONSIDINE'S BACKGROUND AND LIFE PRIOR TO HER MARRIAGE TO JOHN MOORE

Sixmilebridge

Margaret Considine was born on or about 7 July 1818 in the small village of Sixmilebridge, County Clare, Ireland.[154]

Sixmilebridge is situated about halfway between the town of Ennis and the city of Limerick, and in part functions now as a dormitory for both and for the nearby town of Shannon. In 1681, Thomas Dineley explained the origin of its unusual name thus:

> "From Bunratty, the seat of the Earl of Thurmond, into the town of Sixmilebridge, belonging also to that noble family, is 3 miles; from whence to the city of Limerick, to which are two ways, namely by the oil mills and the seat of the McNamaras beyond it, or over the high mountain, famous for its admirable prospect, hanging as it were over Sixmilebridge town and commonly known as Gallows Hill; this is the upper, and the other the lower, way to Limerick; and from town to city six miles either way, whence the town has its name."[155]

The Irish name for the village was and remains Droichead Abhann Ó gCearnaigh,

---

154 See *Geni – Margaret Moore (Considine)(1818 – 1895)* (https://tinyurl.com/4erxud4w) (at 24 September 2023); *WikiTree – Margaret Considine (1818 – 1895)* (https://tinyurl.com/4zu7wu66) (at 24 September 2023); and the *Moore Considine Family Website – Margaret Considine* (https://tinyurl.com/j33nctz: access code - seemoore) (at 24 September 2023).

155 See *Sixmilebridge Historical Background* (https://tinyurl.com/y8kfkp8x) (at 24 September 2023). See also the Map of County Clare, Ireland, showing Sixmilebridge and the Map of Sixmilebridge c. 1850, both below.

which translates in English as "Bridge of the River O'Kearney".[156] According to Patrick Comerford:

> "The original village grew up around a crossing place on the O'Garney River, which flows through the village. Donough O'Brien, the 4th Earl of Thurmond, built the bridge in 1610 – and from then until 1804, when the bridge at Bunratty was built, traffic between Limerick and Ennis passed through Sixmilebridge.
>
> The village has wide streets and large squares that were laid out by the O'Brien family from the 17th century. By the end of the 17th century, development here was linked to the industrialisation of the area as people of Dutch origin found the river very suitable for milling. The east of the village was once its commercial part, with water powered mills, a brewery, a market house and a fair green.
>
> Sixmilebridge became a river port where goods including rape seed oil and soap were exported by boat from the mills just south of the village. Boats from Amsterdam sailed up the river almost as far as the village in the 17th and 18th centuries. But by the early 18th century the village had gone into decline and the river trade came to an end in 1784 when Henry d'Esterre built a toll bridge at Rosmanagher....
>
> The remains of the quay walls, warehouses, soap factory and stone mill wheels can still be seen. Many of the old buildings in the village have been preserved and have found new uses."[157]

There were said to be 229 houses in Sixmilebridge in 1831.[158]

Margaret Considine's Antecedents

Very little appear to be known about Margaret Considine's antecedents, or about her circumstances whilst she was living in Ireland. It is known that she was a daughter of Michael Considine and his wife, Bridget Considine (née McMahon).[159] Michael Considine is stated in some family websites to have been born in Sixmilebridge in about

---

156 See photo 13 below.

157 See Patrick Comerford, *The Old Bridges, Mills and Ducks on the River at Sixmilebridge* (https://tinyurl.com/yckz2372) (at 24 September 2023). See also photos 14, 15 and 16 below.

158 See Samuel Lewis, *A Topographical Dictionary of Ireland* (1837), Vol. 2, p. 556.

159 See *Geni – Margaret Moore (Considine) (1818 – 1895)* (https://tinyurl.com/4erxud4w) (at 24 September 2023); *WikiTree – Margaret Considine (1818 – 1895)* (https://tinyurl.com/4zu7wu66) (at 24 September 2023); and the *Moore Considine Family Website – Margaret Considine* (https://tinyurl.com/j33nctz) (at 24 September 2023).

1786.¹⁶⁰ His occupation was said to be that of a general labourer.¹⁶¹ Although her place of birth in Ireland is presently unascertained, it has been asserted that Bridget McMahon was born in 1790.¹⁶²

David Lowe, however, has argued convincingly that these birth dates ascribed to Michael Considine and Bridget McMahon are probably incorrect. Noting that no relevant records for Sixmilebridge existed prior to 1828, Lowe has observed that all that can presently be said is that given the likely dates of the births of their children, Michael and Bridget were probably both born at some time shortly before 1795.¹⁶³

The date and place of Michael and Bridget's marriage is similarly unascertained at present. However, it might reasonably be supposed that they were married in Sixmilebridge. One might further reasonably suppose that following the marriage, Bridget was primarily engaged in domestic and family duties.

Nothing concrete is currently known regarding the ancestors of either Bridget McMahon or Michael Considine.

The Considine surname is the anglicised version of the original Gaelic Mac Consaidin, meaning "son of Consaidin". The name is relatively new among Irish surnames. It does not appear to have had a Greek or a Roman origin. Rather, it seems that the Mac Consaidins were originally O'Briens who, for some now lost reason, were inspired to rename themselves after the first Christian Emperor of Rome. The progenitor of the Mac Consaidins is said to have been Consaidin Ua Brianin, a Bishop of Killaloe in the Twelfth Century. The O'Briens were a sept of the Uí Thairdelbaig. In turn, the latter were a junior branch of the Dál gCais (or Dalcassian in English) tribe, which was centred in Clare. The Uí Thairdelbaig furnished a number of High Kings of Ireland. These included Brian Boru (941 – 1014), who founded the O'Brien dynasty.¹⁶⁴ It might also be noted that the McMahons were also a sept of the Uí Thairdelbaig.¹⁶⁵

In addition to Margaret Considine, Michael and Bridget Considine had at least three other children: Patrick, Bridget Jnr and Ellen Considine. All appear to have been born

---

160 See *Lamb – McInnis Family Tree: Michael Considine* (https://tinyurl.com/y83sb3gr) (at 24 September 2023); and *Geni – Michael Considine* (https://tinyurl.com/yabvj7g2) (at 24 September 2023).

161 See *Death Registered in New South Wales – Bridget Humphries* (https://tinyurl.com/2da79mmw) (at 24 September 2023).

162 See *Lamb – McInnis Family Tree: Bridget McMahon* (https://tinyurl.com/2p8r6hf2) (at 24 September 2023); and *Geni – Bridget McMahon* (https://tinyurl.com/4yw3kxut) (at 24 September 2023).

163 See *WikiTree – Michael Considine (bef. 1795 – aft. 1820)* (https://tinyurl.com/43wp8n39) (at 24 September 2023).

164 See photo 17 below.

165 See generally here *Greek Origins of Mac Considine from Constantine* (https://tinyurl.com/yd3bawut) (at 24 September 2023); *Wikipedia – Delcassians* (https://tinyurl.com/yamgmb4b) (at 24 September 2023); and Catherine Swift, "Hunting for the genetic legacy of Brian Boru in Irish historical sources" in Seán Duffy (ed.) *Medieval Dublin XVI – Proceedings of Clontarf 1014 – 2014* (2017), pp. 7 – 8 and 12 – 13. Many Considines and Considine businesses are still to be found in and around County Clare: see photo 18 below.

in Sixmilebridge. Unfortunately, Irish birth records for all four Considine children have not as yet been located. In the absence of such records, it is not possible to be sure of their respective birth dates. The *Moore Considine Family Website* records Patrick Considine as having been born in 1811, Bridget Considine Jnr in 1817, Margaret Considine in 1818 and Ellen Considine in 1820. These years broadly accord with those to be found in other genealogical websites.[166]

A number of family websites record that Michael Considine and his wife, Bridget Considine Jnr, both died in 1820.[167] No causes of death have been suggested. If they did indeed both die in 1820, they would have left their children as very young orphans; with Ellen Considine being only an infant. What became of Margaret Considine and her siblings in the years immediately following their parents' death is presently unknown. There were no orphanages in the 1820s in Sixmilebridge or in nearby Limerick. Presumably, the orphans went to live with relatives or with another local family or families.

It seems likely that Margaret received little, if anything, in the way of formal education. In addition to English, she may have spoken at least some Irish.[168] She was probably put to some paid employment as a menial at an early age. No photo of her as a young woman is known to exist.[169] It would appear that she was known to her immediate family as "Maggie".

Voyaging To Australia

In 1836, Margaret Considine and her sister, Bridget Considine Jnr, took ship and emigrated from Ireland to Australia. They clearly did so in order to better their lives As Elizabeth Rushen has put it:

---

166 See the *Moore Considine Family Website* (https://tinyurl.com/j33nctz: access code: seemoore) (at 24 September 2023). The *Moore Considine Family Website* does not provide a source or sources for these birth years. It might be noted that in a table drawn from British emigration records, Elizabeth Rushen has Bridget Considine Jnr's age in 1836 at the time of the latter's emigration from Ireland to Australia as being 21 years. Margaret Considine is stated in the same table to have been 20 – 22 years old when she emigrated at the same time with Bridget: see Elizabeth Rushen, *Colonial Duchesses: The Migration of Irish Women to New South Wales Before the Great Famine* (2014), p. 209. These ages would see Bridget having been born in 1815 and Margaret between 1814 and 1816. Interestingly, the Death Certificates for both Bridget and Margaret appear to indicate that each was born in 1818: see footnote 161 above; and *Death Certificate – Margaret Moore* (https://tinyurl.com/yfwkew4u) (at 2 October 2023). A number of other family websites go further and suggest that both women were born on 7 July 1818: see, for example, *Ancestry – Bridget McMahon* (https://tinyurl.com/ya9jhc6n) (at 2 October 2023). None of these other websites provide a source for these dates. Nor would there appear to be any family "folk memory" suggesting that Margaret and Bridget had been twins.

167 See footnote 160 above and *Lamb – McInnes Family Tree – Bridget McMahon* (https://tinyurl.com/2p8r6hf2) (at 2 October 2023). However, David Lowe has again noted that there does not appear to be any valid source for this date: see *WikiTree – Michael Considine (bef. 1795 – aft. 1820)* (https://tinyurl.com/43wp8n39) (at 2 October 2023).

168 In Ireland, Irish went from being the predominant language in 1700 to being the primary language of only a quarter of the population by 1850: see J. P. Mallory, *The Origins of the Irish* (2015), p. 271. However, the Irish language was still strong in Counties Clare and Galway during the Nineteenth Century, and it has been estimated that at least half of the 150,000 Irish immigrants to Victoria in that century spoke Irish: see Val Noone, *Hidden Ireland in Victoria* (2012), p. 12.

169 See photo 19 below for an image of Margaret's younger sister, Ellen Cook (née Considine). The two sisters may well have resembled one another.

"The women who departed Ireland in the mid-1830s chose to escape the entrenched poverty and afflictions of their homeland for a life of opportunity."[170]

Rushen went on to state that the Irish population grew rapidly from around 5,200,000 in 1800 to 8,200,000 in 1841. She also noted that the British Government's 1833 *Inquiry into the Condition of the Poorer Classes in Ireland* established that in County Clare, female servants earned at most £7 per year. Such women suffered from "grinding poverty and backbreaking drudgery".[171]

The British Government's response to the plight of the poor and destitute in Britain and Ireland in the 1830s was to encourage emigration to the colonies. In 1832, the Government appointed a committee of philanthropists from a London charitable body, the *Refuge for the Destitute*, to constitute the *Committee for Promoting the Emigration of Single Women*. This ultimately became known as the *London Emigration Committee*. Between 1833 and 1836, this Committee chartered 14 ships to convey female emigrants to the colonies. Four sailings took emigrants from Cork to Sydney.[172] To select suitable women emigrants in Ireland, local Emigration Committees were established in Dublin and Cork.[173]

Applicants for a berth on one of the *London Emigration Committee's* ships were required to be single or widowed, of "unexceptional" character, aged between 15 and 30 years and desirous of emigrating. Preference was given to "strong and healthy country servants".[174] An application form had to be completed by, or on behalf of, each applicant. The application form was required to be certified by the applicant's parish clergyman, and to be accompanied by two references from magistrates or other "respectable" persons.[175]

Having made successful applications to the Cork Emigration Committee, Margaret Considine and her sister Bridget joined some 234 other single or widowed women and a number of paying families on board the *Duchess of Northumberland* in Cork harbour on or shortly prior to 25 May 1836 for the voyage to Sydney.[176]

---

170 See Rushen, *op. cit.*, p. 3.

171 *Ibid.*

172 See Rushen, *op. cit.*, pp. 8 – 9.

173 See Rushen, *op. cit.*, pp. 10 – 11.

174 See Rushen, *op. cit.*, p. 21.

175 See Rushen, *op. cit.*, p. 30.

176 See Rushen, *op. cit.*, p. 17. On 25 May 1836, the *Cork Evening Herald* reported that the *Duchess of Northumberland* was:"now lying off Cove, and ready to sail with an overflow cargo of respectable, well conducted, but alas! impoverished of the fair sex."
See Rushen, *op. cit.*, p. 63. Weighing 541 tons, and built in 1834, the *Duchess of Northumberland* was captained on this voyage by a David Roxburgh: *Ibid*. See also photos 20 and 21 below.

The *Duchess of Northumberland*'s voyage from Cork to Sydney took 130 days. It was by no mean all smooth sailing. On 29 June 1836, two possible pirate ships were sighted. One of the passengers on board the *Duchess of Northumberland*, a Thomas Trotter, kept a diary of the voyage. Of the two suspect vessels, he wrote that they:

> "came in sight...and caused consternation as to their being Pirates; our cannon, four in number were got ready for defence, and the muskets, boarding pikes and small arms all got ready with ammunition, but about midnight they parted and although ...seen in the morning, they left us; all the passengers were determined to fight as they...were in their mercy if we submitted."[177]

Moreover, in a private log he kept of the voyage, the ship's Third Officer, Henry Wren, recorded a particularly strong gale on 5 August 1836. Wren noted:

> "Blowing strong gale from the West...heavy sea...women very fright'd...cutter mast... carried away...shipped a great deal of water and nearly drowned a dozen of the poor women. It was a great mercy they were not washed overboard. Gave them a great fright below."[178]

In fine weather, the women emigrants spent their time knitting and making garments from fabric supplied to them by the Emigration Committees and other donors.[179]

The *Duchess of Northumberland* dropped anchor in Sydney Harbour on 3 October 1836. However, it was not until the morning of 6 October that the emigrants disembarked. The *Sydney Gazette and New South Wales Advertiser* described their disembarkation in the following terms:

> "The landing of the girls by the ship *Duchess of Northumberland*, took place on Thursday morning, at 9 o'clock, at the Government Jetty. A great many persons assembled to witness the interesting exhibition of youth, health and beauty; and, notwithstanding many of the lower orders were present, the arrangements made on the occasion prevented the slightest indecorum. The Government Launch was

---

177 See Thomas Trotter, *Diary, 25 May 1836 – 6 August 1836* (29 June 1836) (State Library of New South Wales, ML, MSS 774).

178 See Henry Wren, *Private Journal, Ship Duchess of Northumberland 5 May – 8 November 1836* (5 August 1836) (State Library of New South Wales, ML, MSS 763). See also Rushen, *op. cit.*, p. 77.

179 See Rushen, *op. cit.*, p. 78. See also photo 22 below.

used for the purpose, and as each succeeding cargo was landed on the wharf, a hearty cheer, from the crew and passengers that conveyed them to our shore, was heard to welcome their arrival. They are, generally, an interesting looking class of females; and many, on first putting their feet on *terra firma*, were heard to thank God for his mercies, in guarding them from the dangers with which they were lately encompassed. Poor girls, we trust they will find New South Wales a happy asylum, and that they may never have cause to look back with regret to the day that they joined the *Duchess of Northumberland*, and were wafted by the favouring gale, far, far from their native soil."[180]

More prosaically, the *Sydney Monitor* recorded the emigrants arrival thus:

"The Female Emigrants [off] the "Duchess of Northumberland" disembarked on Thursday morning and were lodged in the temporary building near Government House appropriated to their reception. The majority of them are strong. healthy looking women."[181]

The landing of the Irish emigrant women from the *Duchess of Northumberland* in 1836 was attended by a measure of sectarian controversy in Sydney. The *Sydney Herald*, in particular, was scathing in its critique:

"Another batch of Free Females has arrived by the *Duchess of Northumberland*, drawn from that focus of agitation, the county of Cork, and adjacent districts. The public object to this exclusive importation of Irish orphans and tenants of poorhouses, and receive them with apprehensions of evil. The force of the undercurrent of Irish feeling both in England and in the Colony, is too obvious in this instance, to admit for one moment of any doubt.

Why, it is asked, do the Government in most of their recent importations to New South Wales, make selections only from the south of Ireland? Why do they import Roman Catholic females only, or chiefly? Why do they relieve the Irish

---

180 See the *Sydney Gazette and New South Wales Advertiser*, Saturday, 8 October 1836, p. 2. The report continued: "The future welfare of these young women depends entirely upon their own conduct – that they will obtain good situations, if they are found deserving, we are quite satisfied, and if double the number had arrived they would find no lack of employment now; but as there are many temptations and allurements held out by the vicious, to decoy and corrupt the innocent female, on her landing here, so it will require a double degree of circumspection and prudence on their part to steer clear of the rocks and shoals with which they will find themselves encircled."
Ibid.

181 See the *Sydney Monitor*, Monday, 10 October 1836, p. 2.

landowners, who pay no poor rates, of a surplus population which should be drawn from enlightened England, where landholders tax themselves for the maintenance of their parochial poor?"[182]

Subsequently, the *Sydney Herald* saw fit to mount a more personal attack on at least some of the *Duchess of Northumberland*'s women. The Cork Immigration Committee had dispatched a letter on that vessel to Governor Bourke in Sydney in which the Committee had warranted with respect to the women that:

> "The utmost care and judgment has been exercised in their selection, and we hesitate not to recommend them as industrious and virtuous, and also desirous to earn and procure in a foreign land that subsistence denied them at home."[183]

Yet, on 3 November 1836, the *Sydney Herald* gave voice to a rumour that the women had not been selected with proper care, and that many had been "swept up" from the streets without reference to their character. The newspaper observed, *inter alia*, that:

> "Among the women by this ship *Duchess of Northumberland*, it is a matter of notoriety, that several made no secret that their object in coming out here was to establish brothels, and were endeavouring, during the voyage, to induce others of the females to enter their service as prostitutes."[184]

This rumour has since been largely discredited by historians. To this end, it is worth pointing out that in a report to the Colonial Office in London, Governor Bourke noted that:

> "I am inclined to think that the generality of the women received from Ireland have turned out better in point of morals than those from England; arising perhaps from a more careful selection of the former."[185]

---

182 See the *Sydney Herald*, Thursday, 13 October 1836, p. 2.
183 See *The Australian*, Tuesday, 4 October 1836, p. 3; and *The Colonist*, Thursday, 6 October 1836, p. 3.
184 See the *Sydney Herald*, Thursday, 3 November 1836, p. 2. See also the *Sydney Gazette and New South Wales Advertiser*, Tuesday, 11 October 1836, p. 2.
185 See Bourke to the Secretary of State, 11 October 1836, TNA, CO 714/114, p. 96. See also Rushen, *op cit.*, pp. 46 and 113.

Margaret Considine's Life In Australia Prior To Her Marriage

Once safely ashore, the female emigrants from the *Duchess of Northumberland* were interviewed by prospective local employers.[186] There seems little doubt but that Margaret Considine was soon engaged to work as a domestic servant by a member of the Manning family. In an obituary published in the *Ovens and Murray Advertiser* following her death in 1895, it was observed that:

"For about two years, she resided in the family of Sir Robert Manning."[187]

However, it is clear that there was no Sir Robert Manning living in New South Wales in or about 1836. It accordingly seems likely that Margaret was in fact engaged by John Edye Manning.

John Edye Manning was born in 1783 in Exeter, England. In 1804, he married Matilda Cooke and began practising law in England. Manning was appointed Registrar of the Supreme Court of New South Wales in August 1828. In May 1829, he arrived in Sydney with his wife and five of his children to take up his appointment. In addition to his legal duties, Manning quickly acquired significant land holdings in New South Wales. Among his acquired properties was land in the vicinity of Goulburn. Manning became insolvent in 1841, returned to England in 1849 and died there in 1870.[188]

Margaret Considine may well have initially worked for John Edye Manning in premises owned by him in Sydney. However, by the middle of 1837 at the latest, it is likely that she was living and working in the Goulburn district. The circumstances in which she arrived in that district are uncertain. She may have been sent there by Manning to work on his Goulburn property. According to her obituary in the *Ovens and Murray Advertiser*, she remained in the employ of the Mannings for about two years.[189] In its obituary, the *Wangaratta Chronicle* asserted that she continued in Manning employment

---

186 See the *Sydney Gazette and New South Wales Advertiser*, Saturday, 8 October 1836, p. 4.

187 See the *Ovens and Murray Advertiser*, Saturday, 20 July 1895, p. 6. Interestingly, the *Wangaratta Chronicle*, in its obituary, noted that Margaret:
"came to New South Wales with the well-known Manning family as far back as 1837."
See the *Wangaratta Chronicle*, Saturday, 13 July 1895, p. 2. However, as may be seen above, Margaret arrived in New South Wales in 1836, rather than in 1837. Moreover, it is clear from shipping records that there were no Mannings who sailed on the *Duchess of Northumberland* with her.

188 See R. J. M. Newton, "Manning, John Edye (1783 – 1870)" in *Australian Dictionary of Biography* (https://tinyurl.com/y6v2q57j) (at 6 October 2023). It is interesting to note that Margaret's first daughter was christened "Matilda". She shared that name with John Edye Manning's wife.

189 See the *Ovens and Murray Advertiser*, Saturday, 20 July 1895, p. 6

until her marriage to John Moore in 1839.[190] However, it could be that she left Manning's employ in Sydney to join her sister, Bridget, who had moved to Goulburn in 1836. And, after arriving in Goulburn, she may well have found new employment on William Pitt Faithfull's *Springfield* property.

Whatever be the case, it is clear that by the middle of 1837, Margaret Considine was in an intimate relationship with William Pitt Faithfull.

On 5 March 1838, Margaret gave birth to a son. Notwithstanding his mother's Catholic faith, the infant boy was baptised into the Church of England; being christened in Goulburn by the Reverend William Sowerby.[191] Margaret's firstborn was at varying times known as Henry Moore and Henry Faithfull.[192] There can be almost no doubt that he was the son of William Pitt Faithfull.[193]

As mentioned above, on 3 September 1839, Margaret Considine married John Moore, who was then working for the Faithfulls on *Springfield*.[194] Although John was a life-long Anglican, the marriage was solemnised in Goulburn in accordance with the rites of the Catholic Church. Margaret's sister and brother-in-law, Ellen and Christopher Cook, served as witnesses to the marriage.[195]

The Lives of Margaret Considine's Siblings

Bridget Considine

Following her disembarkation from the *Duchess of Northumberland* on 6 October 1836, Margaret's sister, Bridget Considine, does not seem to have tarried long in Sydney. On 14 December 1836, she married Robert Humphries in Goulburn.[196]

Robert Humphries was born at Westminster, London in England in 1810.[197] A bricklayer and plasterer by occupation, he was convicted in London's Old Bailey on 21 January

---

190   See the *Wangaratta Chronicle*, Saturday, 13 July 1895, p. 2.

191   See *Ancestry – Australia, Births and Baptisms, 1792 – 1821: Henry Concidine* [sic] (FHL Film No. 993952) (https://tinyurl.com/5f7vrp37) (at 7 October 2023).

192   See footnote 65 above.

193   See Bienvenue, *op. cit.*, pp. 6 and 16. See also Jenny Coates, "Margaret Considine (c.1818 – 1895)" in *Conversations with Grandma* (https://tinyurl.com/52apm3p3) (at 7 October 2023). Given the disparity in their positions in colonial society, William Pitt Faithfull would clearly have given little thought to marrying Margaret Considine before or after Henry's birth.

194   See footnote 153 and its accompanying text above.

195   See Marriage Entry No. 7 for John Moore and Margaret Considine in the records of Sts. Peter and Paul's Catholic Old Cathedral. See also Coates, *op. cit.*

196   See *New South Wales; Births, Deaths and Marriages – Marriages: Robert Humphries and Bridget Considine* (https://tinyurl.com/4hfkj6xt) (at 7 October 2023).

197   See *New South Wales; Certificate of Freedom (1835): Robert Humphries* (https://tinyurl.com/3uu24t2n) (at 7 October 2023).

1828 for stealing a handkerchief valued at 3s. from the person of a William Gaven and sentenced to be transported to New South Wales for seven years.[198] He gained his Certificate of Freedom in Goulburn on 23 April 1835.[199]

Robert and Bridget Humphries had the following five children together:

- Michael Humphries, born in Goulburn on or shortly before 14 December 1837.

- Robert Charles Humphries, born in Goulburn in 1839.

- Elizabeth Humphries, born in Goulburn on or a little before 12 September 1841.

- Ernest Humphries, born at Millbank near Collector on or shortly before 19 April 1846.

- James Humphries, born at Millbank near Collector on or shortly prior to 19 April 1846.[200]

In or about 1847, Bridget separated from Robert Humphries and entered into a de facto relationship with George James Reynolds.[201] A labourer born in 1813 at Chelsea, London in England, Reynolds was convicted of highway robbery at the Old Bailey on 25 October 1828 and sentenced to death. This sentence was commuted to transportation to New South Wales for life.[202] Whilst living near Goulburn, Reynolds received a Conditional Pardon from New South Wales Governor FitzRoy on 20 December 1848.[203]

Bridget had five further children with Robert Humphries; they being:

- Henry Reynolds, born near Collector on or a little before 12 March 1848.

- Emily Reynolds, born at Goulburn on or shortly prior to 10 April 1849.

---

198 See *Old Bailey Records – Robert Humphries* (https://tinyurl.com/af8n358b) (at 7 October 2023); and *Australian Convict Transportation Registers: Other Fleets and Ships, 1791 – 1868: Robert Humphries* (https://tinyurl.com/zhvu8j3k) (at 7 October 2023).

199 See *New South Wales; Certificate of Freedom (1835): Robert Humphries* (https://tinyurl.com/3uu24t2n) (at 7 October 2023).

200 As to each of these children, see the *Manwaring Family History Website – Bridget Considine* (https://tinyurl.com/9mpba2np) (at 7 October 2023).

201 *Ibid.*

202 See *Old Bailey Records – George Reynolds* (https://tinyurl.com/kzsxjr8v) (at 7 October 2023); and *New South Wales, Australia, Convict Indents, 1788 – 1842: George Reynolds* (https://tinyurl.com/vysxb54y) (at 7 October 2023)

203 See *New South Wales, Australia, Convict Registers of Conditional and Absolute Pardons, 1788 – 1870: George Reynolds* (https://tinyurl.com/kvfkpmex) (at 7 October 2023).

- Mary Ann Reynolds, born at Jewerra near Collector on or shortly before 15 March 1852.

- Susan Margaret Reynolds, born at Bungonia near Goulburn on or a little before 11 January 1854.

- William Henry Reynolds, born at Millbank near Collector on or shortly prior to 12 August 1856.[204]

Bridget died on 13 October 1898 whilst living on or close to the *Millbank* run of John Macauley near Collector in New South Wales. She was buried in the Anglican Cemetery at Collector.[205] George Reynolds died in Goulburn on 5 December 1904 and was buried in the Anglican Cemetery at Goulburn.[206]

Patrick Considine

It would appear that Margaret's brother, Patrick Considine, worked as a "farm servant" (likely, as a farm labourer) in the vicinity of Sixmilebridge while still living in Ireland.[207] In or about 1829, he married Honora Downs in Sixmilebridge.[208] The couple produced two children in Ireland – Michael Considine, born shortly prior to 25 March 1831 and baptised in Sixmilebridge on that date[209]; and John Considine, born a little before 18 October and christened in Sixmilebridge on that date.[210]

On 19 September 1837, Patrick and Honora Considine departed Limerick, Ireland as bounty emigrants on board the *Strathfieldsaye*. They were accompanied on the voyage by their son, Michael Considine, and by Patrick's youngest sister, Ellen Considine.[211]

---

204 See with respect to each of these children the *Manwaring Family History Website – Bridget Considine* (https://tinyurl.com/9mpba2np) (at 7 October 2023)

205 See *Deaths Registered in New South Wales – Bridget Humphries* (https://tinyurl.com/2da79mmw) (at 8 October 2023).

206 See *New South Wales Death Certificate – George Reynolds* (https://tinyurl.com/2d7cpz6s) (at 8 October 2023). Robert Humphries had earlier died at Gunning on 20 January 1898 and been buried in the Gunning Cemetery: see *New South Wales Death Certificate – Robert Humphries* (https://tinyurl.com/akb4e8wk) (at 8 October 2023).

207 See *New South Wales, Australia, Assisted Passenger Lists, 1828 – 1896: Patrick Considine* (https://tinyurl.com/365wcyv3) (at 8 October 2023); and *Immigration Record – Patrick Considine* (https://tinyurl.com/4kx2cf6u) (at 8 October 2023).

208 See *Ireland, Catholic Parish Registers, 1655 – 1915 for Patritius* Consden (Patrick Considine) (https://tinyurl.com/2kx2yb2c) (at 9 October 2023). See also the *Keir Fisher -Montgomery Moore Family Tree: Patrick Considine* (https://tinyurl.com/4j7erfz6) (at 8 October 2023).

209 See *Ireland, Catholic Parish Registers, 1655 – 1915 for Michael Considine* (https://tinyurl.com/4ej9ahp7) (at 9 October 2023).

210 See *Ireland, Catholic Parish Registers, 1655 – 1915 for Joannes* (John) *Considine* (https://tinyurl.com/3579p72s) (at 9 October 2023).

211 See *New South Wales, Australia, Assisted Passenger Lists, 1828 – 1896: Patrick Considine* (https://tinyurl.com/365wcyv3) (9 October 2023); and *New South Wales, Australia, Assisted Passenger Lists, 1828 – 1896: Ellen Considine* (https://tinyurl.com/y4y6z7x8) (at 9 October 2023).

Patrick and Honora were not accompanied by their younger son, John Considine. Although John's fate is currently unknown, it seems almost certain that he died as an infant at some time prior to his parents leaving Ireland.

The *Strathfieldsaye* anchored in Port Jackson on 26 January 1838.[212] Following his arrival in New South Wales, Patrick Considine secured employment as a farm labourer on Major Archibald Innes' *Lake Innes* pastoral property near Port Macquarie.[213] Although he was to work as a farm labourer for the balance of his life, Patrick did not remain in the Port Macquarie area for long. Soon after his and his family's arrival in Australia, his wife, Honora Considine, died; and by 1841 at the latest, Patrick and his young son, Michael Considine, had moved to the Goulburn, area where Patrick's sisters, Margaret Considine and Bridget Humphries (née Considine), were residing. On 10 April 1841, Patrick married his second wife, Flora McInnes, in a Catholic ceremony conducted in Goulburn.[214]

Patrick Considine spent the balance of his life in the Goulburn district. He and Flora Considine had the following four children together:

- Mary Considine, born at Taralga near Goulburn on or a little before 16 February 1842.

- Margaret Considine, born at Richlands near Goulburn on or shortly prior to 16 March 1843.

- James Considine, born at Richlands near Goulburn on or shortly before 6 November 1844.

- Patrick Peter Considine, born at Richlands near Goulburn on or a little before 15 April 1847.[215]

Flora Considine died at Richlands near Goulburn on 29 December 1852. Patrick Considine died on 17 November 1853 at Tarlo near Goulburn after being kicked in the chest by a horse.[216]

---

212 See *WikiTree – Bounty Immigrant Voyages to Australia, Arrivals in New South Wales – Strathfieldsaye 26 January 1838* (https://tinyurl.com/2xytysb3) (at 9 October 2023).

213 See the *Moore Considine Family Website – Patrick Considine* (https://tinyurl.com/j33nctz: access code - seemoore) (at 9 October 2023).

214 *Ibid.*

215 *Ibid.*

216 *Ibid.* See also the *Goulburn Herald and County of Argyle Advertiser*, Saturday, 19 November 1853, p. 2.

Ellen Considine

It would seem that after disembarking from the *Strathfieldsaye* in Sydney on or shortly after 26 January 1838, Ellen Considine made directly for Goulburn, where her older sisters, Margaret Considine and Bridget Humphries (née Considine), resided. In her immigration documentation, her occupation was listed as that of a housekeeper.[217] Presumably, she found employment in that, or some similar capacity, after reaching Goulburn. On 17 June 1839, she was married in Goulburn to Christopher Cook in an Anglican ceremony conducted by the Reverend William Sowerby.[218]

Christopher Cook's background is clouded with uncertainty. It appears that he was born on or about 8 December 1804 in Goole, Yorkshire; that he may have been convicted of the theft of a coat in 1825 after a trial in the Old Bailey; and that may have been transported to Australia for a term of seven years.[219] He almost certainly worked in manual capacities over his entire working life.

At some presently unknow point in time between 1851 and 1854, Christopher and Ellen Cook moved south from Goulburn across the Murray River and down to the Wangaratta district in Victoria. After moving to that district, they appear to have lived in close proximity to Ellen's older sister, Margaret Moore (née Considine), for most of the balance of their respective lives.

Ellen and Christopher raised a total of 11 children together; being:

- Mary Ann Cook, born in Goulburn on or shortly before 17 May 1840.

- Daniel Grear Cook, born in Goulburn on or a little before 17 January 1842.

- Jane Cook, born in Goulburn on or shortly prior to 25 August 1843.

- Elizabeth Cook, born in Goulburn on or shortly before 19 April 1845.

- Ellen Nellie Cook, born in Goulburn on or shortly prior to 21 July 1847.

- William Cook, born in Goulburn on or shortly before 5 May 1849.

---

217   See *New South Wales, Australia, Assisted Passenger Lists, 1828 – 1896: Ellen Considine* (https://tinyurl.com/y4y6z7x8) (at 9 October 2023). See also photo 19 below.

218   See *Certificate of Marriage – Christopher Cook and Ellen Considine* (https://tinyurl.com/5eddp5k2) (at 9 October 2023).

219   See the *Moore Considine Family Website – Christopher Grear Cook* (https://tinyurl.com/j33nctz: access code - seemoore) (at 9 October 2023).

- Queenie Eliza Cook, born in Goulburn on or a little before 8 November 1851.

- Emily Susan Cook, born in Whorouly on or shortly before 3 May 1854.

- John Edward Grear Cook, born in Wangaratta on or shortly prior to 4 April 1855.

- Margaret Matilda Cook, born at Three Mile Creek, Wangaratta on or a little before 24 March 1859.

- James Robert Cook, born at Three Mile Creek, Wangaratta on or shortly before 5 April 1862.[220]

Christopher Cook died in Wangaratta at the advanced age of 97 years on 8 March 1902.[221] Ellen Cook died shortly after her husband on 12 August 1902.[222] Both lie buried in the same grave at the Wangaratta Cemetery, together with one of their sons, William Cook.[223]

In 1865, Christopher and Ellen Cook's fifth child, Ellen Nellie Cook, married the Derbyshire-born Silas Porter in Wangaratta. Silas, who lived between 1836 and 1888, and worked as painter in Beechworth before moving to Wangaratta and plying the same trade.[224] Silas and Ellen Porter had a total of six children together. Following her husband's death in 1888, Ellen Porter ran a boarding house in Wangaratta until her own death in 1925.[225]

Silas and Ellen Porter's fourth child, Amy Ellen Porter, lived from 1876 until 1902. In 1898, Amy married David McEwan in Wangaratta. David was born in around 1881 At the time of the marriage, he was a widower with two young children and worked as a pharmacist at Dows Pharmacy in Chiltern. David and Amy McEwan had two children together – John McEwan was born in Chiltern on or shortly before 29 March 1900. His sister, Amy Ellen McEwan Jnr, was born in the same town in February 1902. Shortly

---

220

221 See the *Moore Considine Family Website – Christopher Cook* (https://tinyurl.com/j33nctz: access code - seemoore) (at 9 October 2023).

222 See the *Moore Considine Family Website – Ellen Considine* (https://tinyurl.com/j33nctz: access code - seemoore) 9at 9 October 2023).

223 See *Billion Graves – Christopher, Ellen and William Cook* (https://tinyurl.com/266axe25) (at 9 October 2023).

224 See the *Moore Considine Family Website – Silas Porter* (https://tinyurl.com/j33nctz: access code - seemoore) (at 10 October 2023).

225 See the *Moore Considine Family Website – Ellen Nellie Cook* (https://tinyurl.com/j33nctz: access code - seemoore) (at 10 October 2023).

after the birth of her daughter, Amy McEwan Snr died in Chiltern in March 1902.[226] David McEwan died in Chiltern in 1907.[227]

Following the early death of their parents, John McEwan and Amy Ellen McEwan were largely raised in frugal circumstances by their maternal grandmother, Ellen Nellie Porter, in her Wangaratta boarding house.[228]

John McEwan left school at the age of 13 years to support his family. Studying at night, he joined the Commonwealth Crown Solicitor's Office in Melbourne in 1916. He enlisted in the AIF in 1918, but the First World War ended before he could see overseas service. However, his enlistment enabled him to participate in the soldier-settlement scheme. This led to him acquiring farming land near Stanhope.

A successful farmer, John McEwan joined both the Victorian Farmers' Union and the Country Party. In 1934, he won the seat of Echuca for that party in the House of Representatives. In 1937, he was appointed Minister for the Interior in the Lyons Government. In 1940, he was appointed Minister for External Affairs in the first Menzies Government. He became Minister for Commerce and Agriculture in 1949 in the second Menzies Government and then Minister for Trade in 1956.

In 1958, John McEwan succeeded Sir Arthur Fadden as Leader of the Country Party and Deputy Prime Minister of Australia. Over the course of a long and distinguished ministerial career, he was influential in orientating the Australian economy towards protectionism as against free trade. Following Prime Minister Harold Holt's death, John McEwan was appointed caretaker Prime Minister on 19 December 1967. He served in that capacity until being succeeded by John Gorton on 10 January 1968. He was knighted in 1971 following his retirement in that year.

Sir John McEwan died at Toorak on 20 November 1980 at the age of 80 years.[229] His body was cremated and his ashes interred at the Springvale Botanical Cemetery.[230]

---

226 See the *Moore Considine Family Website – Amy Ellen Porter* (https://tinyurl.com/j33nctz: access code - seemoore) (at 10 October 2023).

227 See the *Moore Considine Family Website – David James McEwan* (https://tinyurl.com/j33nctz: access code - seemoore) (at 10 October 2023).

228 See the *Moore Considine Family Website – Ellen Nellie Cook* (https://tinyurl.com/j33nctz: access code - seemoore) (at 10 October 2023).

229 See the *Moore Considine Family Website – John McEwan* (https://tinyurl.com/j33nctz: access code - seemoore) (at 10 October 2023); and C. J. Lloyd, "McEwan, Sir John (1900 – 1980)" in *Australian Dictionary of Biography* (https://tinyurl.com/2avhu9hp) (at 10 October 2023).

230 See *Billion Graves – John McEwan* (https://tinyurl.com/ntffsn8j) (at 10 October 2023).

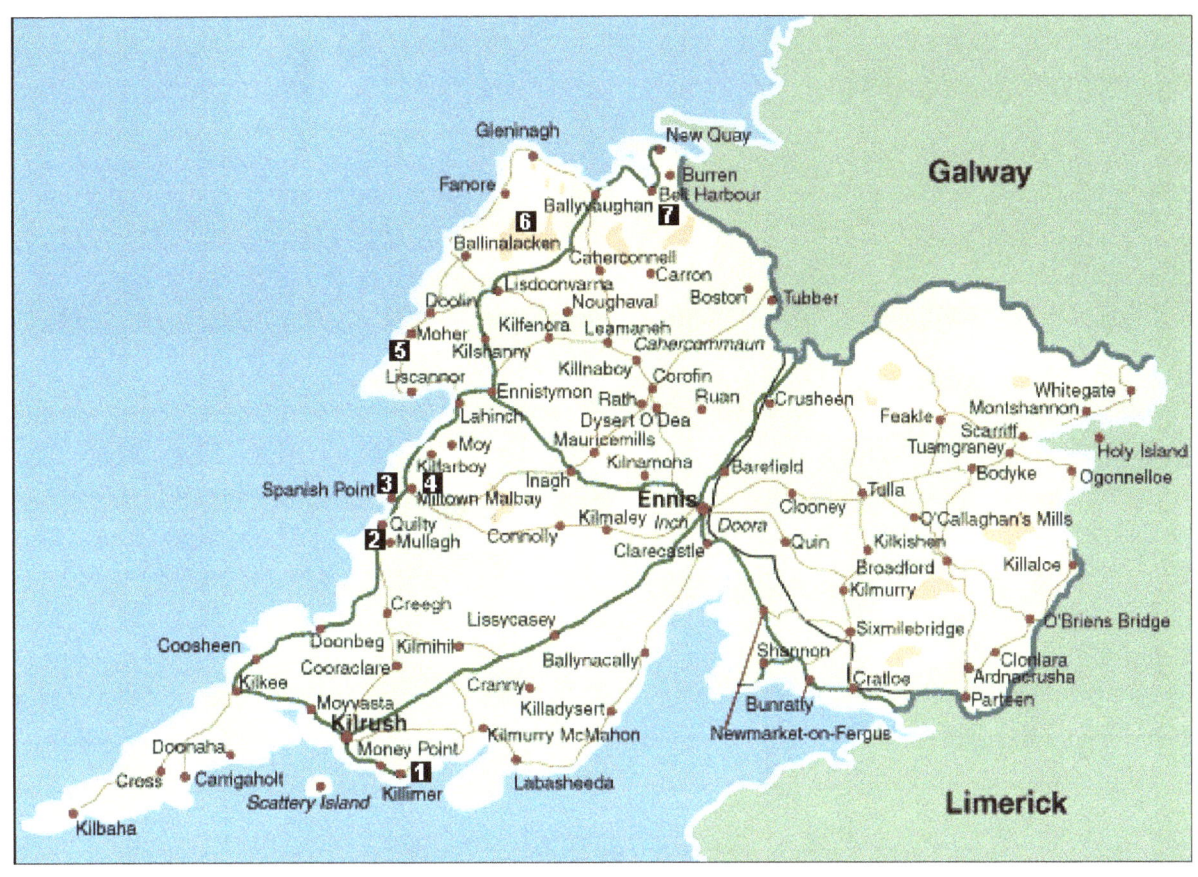

Map of County Clare, Ireland, showing Sixmilebridge.

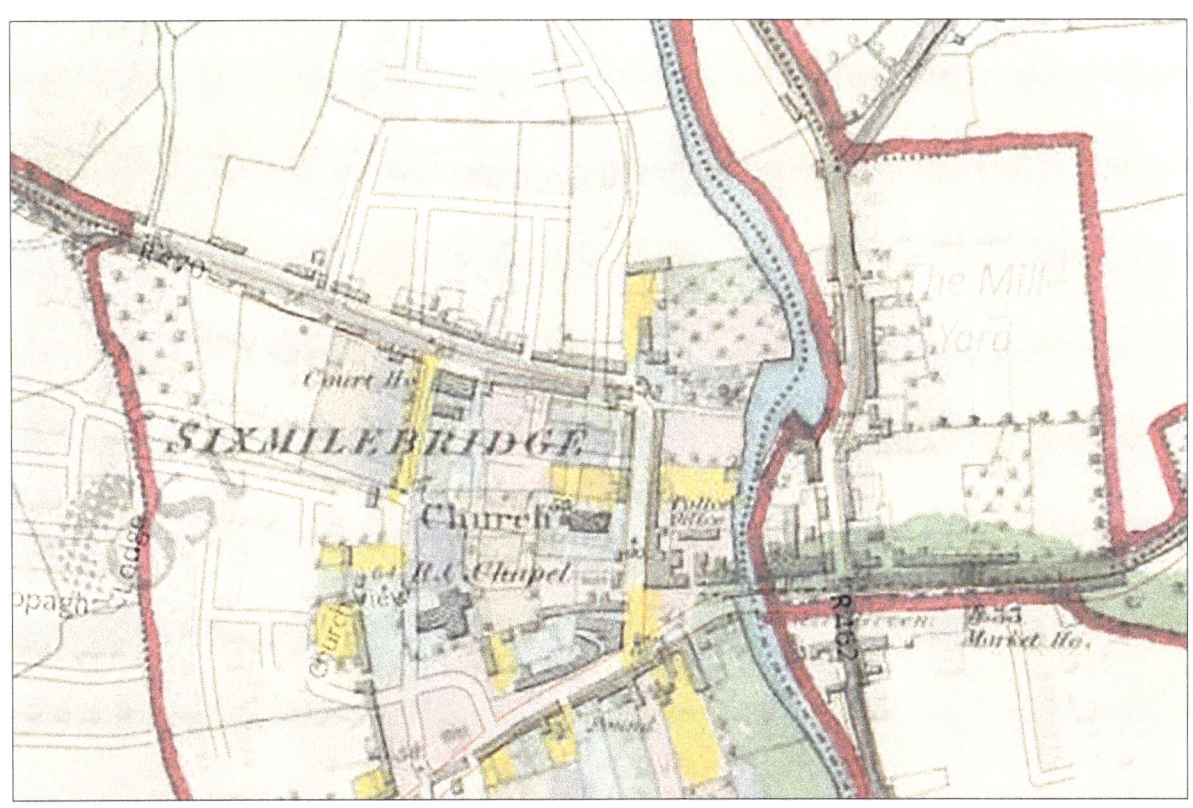

Map of Sixmilebridge, c. 1850.

Photo 13: Road signs at the outskirts of Sixmilebridge, County Clare, Ireland.

Photo 14: An early photo of central Sixmilebridge, County Clare, Ireland.

Photo 15: Central Sixmilebridge, County Clare, Ireland, in 2019.

Photo 16: The O'Garney River at Sixmilebridge, County Clare, Ireland.

Photo 17: The reputed Grave of Brian Boru outside the wall of St. Patrick's Church of Ireland Cathedral, Armagh, County Armagh, Ireland.

Photo 18: Considine's Bar, St. Brigid's Well, Liscannor, County Clare, Ireland.

Photo 19: Ellen Cook (née Considine).

Photo 20: A drawing of the Duchess of Northumberland.

Photo 21: A scrimshaw engraving of the Duchess of Northumberland.

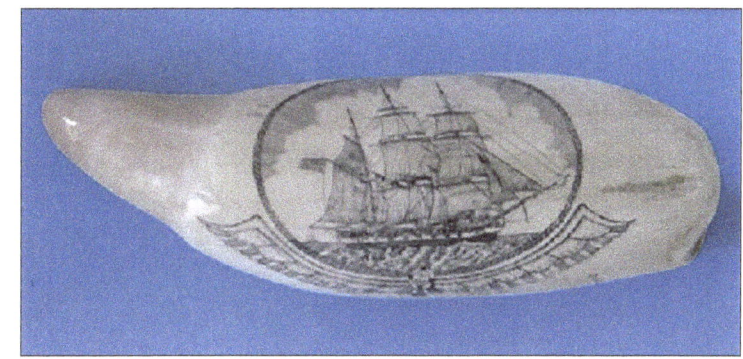

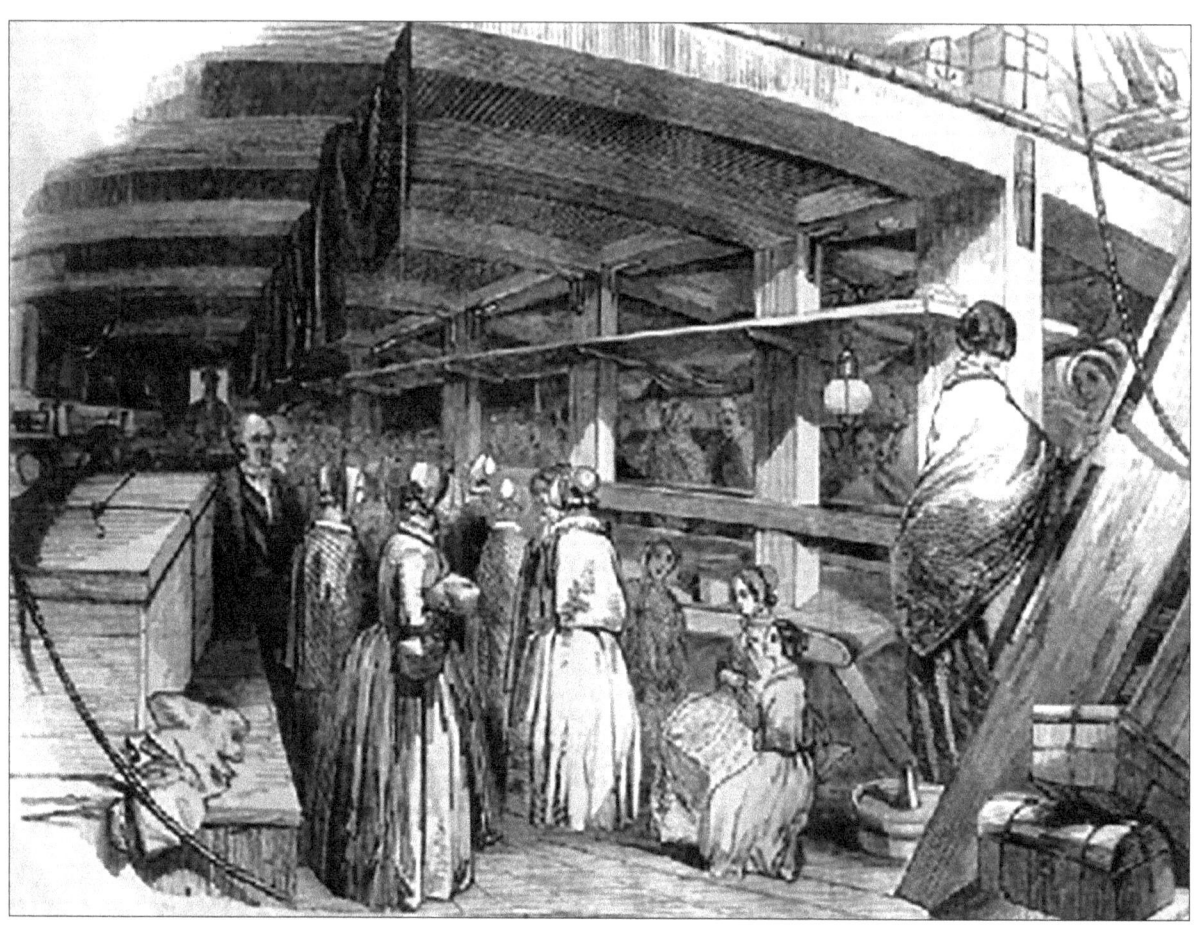

Photo 22: An emigrant ship – between decks, London Illustrated News, *17 August 1850.*

JOHN AND MARGARET MOORE'S LIFE TOGETHER

Living At Springfield

When John Moore married Margaret Considine in Goulburn on 3 September 1839, not only did he marry the mother of an 18 month old infant boy fathered by William Pitt Faithfull, but his new wife was some three months pregnant at the time of the marriage. It appears likely that Faithfull was also the father of Margaret's unborn child.[231] On 9 March 1840, Margaret gave birth to a girl. The child was named Matilda Margaret Moore. On 28 March 1840, she was christened as an Anglican in Goulburn. John and Margaret Moore were recorded as being her parents.[232] Like her older brother Henry, Matilda was raised in John and Margaret's family as a Moore.[233]

Following their marriage, John and Margaret Moore continued to live on *Springfield* for a number of years; with John, and perhaps Margaret, continuing in the service of the Faithfulls. In his later years on *Springfield*, John was said to have been employed on that property as an overseer (or manager). On or about 16 January 1843, Margaret gave birth to a second son in Goulburn. The child was named John Moore after his father; and, in March 1843, like Henry and Matilda, was baptised an Anglican in St Saviour's Church, Goulburn.[234]

---

231 See Coates, *op. cit.* See also the *Faithfull Family Tree: Matilda Margaret Moore Faithfull* (https://tinyurl.com/3x24t33x) (at 11 October 2023).

232 See *Ancestry – Australia, Birth Index, 1788 - 1922: Matilda M Moore* (https://tinyurl.com/2mksvkdn) (at 11 October 2023).

233 It is noteworthy that both Henry and Matilda are listed as members of John and Margaret Moore's family at the front of a Moore Family Bible currently in the possession of Judy Field in Wangaratta: see footnote 65 above.

234 See *FamilySearch – Australia, Births and Baptisms, 1792 – 1981: John Moore* (https://tinyurl.com/54z9remf) (at 11 October 29023). See also *WikiTree – John Moore (1843 – 1899)* (Jnr.) (https://tinyurl.com/359yhf4z) (at 11 October 2023).

It has been asserted by John Faithfull and Jim Lewis that in the second half of 1845, John Moore Snr. was sent by William Pitt Faithfull to act as overseer of the latter's *Ten Mile Hollow* squatting run located on the right bank of the King River in what was then known as the Port Phillip District of New South Wales – later to become the Colony of Victoria.[235] Unfortunately, Faithfull and Lewis have failed to provide any authority for their contention that John and his family made this move in 1845. In reality, there are good grounds for concluding that the move in fact occurred in 1843 and not in 1845.

In the first place, when running for office on the Wangaratta Borough Council in August 1876, John placed an election manifesto in the *Ovens and Murray Advertiser* in which he observed in part:

> "If elected, my object shall always be the advancement of the town in which I have been resident 33 years, and in which my sole interest is staked."[236]

John's stated years of local residence, if indeed accurate, would put his arrival in the area in 1843.

In the second place, John's Death Certificate in August 1891 stated that having been born in England, he had lived 5 years in New South Wales and 48 years in Victoria.[237] That chronology would again put his arrival in Victoria in 1843.[238]

The Faithfulls And North East Victoria.

The association of William Pitt Faithfull and his brother, George Faithfull, with what was to become the north-east of Victoria extended back to 1838. In that year, New South Wales was in the grip of a serious and protracted drought.[239] The Faithfull brothers were undoubtedly under pressure to find fresh pasture for their cattle and sheep. They had been aware for some years that fine land was to be had in the Port Phillip District. In a letter to Lieutenant Governor La Trobe dated 8 September 1853, George Faithfull wrote:

---

235 See Faithfull and Lewis, *op. cit.*, p 147.

236 See the *Ovens and Murray Advertiser*, Tuesday, 8 August 1876, p. 3.

237 See *Deaths in the District of Wangaratta in the Colony of Victoria – John Moore (Snr.)* (https://tinyurl.com/bdds44s2).

238 See also *WikiTree – John Moore (1816 – 1891)* (https://tinyurl.com/p7m48bsu) (at 11 October 2023).

239 See James Gormly, *Exploration and Settlement of Australia* (1921), p. 379; and Kenneth Cox, *Angus McMillan: Pathfinder* (1973), p. 35.

"It was in February 1838, that I first determined to remove my stock from the colony of New South Wales to the famed land of Port Phillip.

It was known for years prior to this time that much fine land lay in this neighbourhood, and extended from the Murrumbidgee to the Bay of Port Phillip. Hume and Hovell were the first discoverers of this fine country, but Sir Thomas Mitchell, some years afterwards in tracing down the Darling, opened up the great country to the westwards, which gave the stimulus to the proprietors of stock in New South Wales to migrate with their flocks and herds from a land at that time suffering from severe drought 'unto a land which is the glory of all lands'."[240]

Early in 1838, George persuaded his brother to accompany him south across the Murray River.

The Faithfull brothers set out from *Springfield* for the Port Phillip District in February 1838 with servants, horses, cattle and sheep. George Faithfull reached the Ovens River with most of the men and stock in early April. William Pitt Faithfull apparently lagged a little behind. George was aware from Hume's account that good grazing lands, the Oxley Plains, lay upstream between the Ovens and King Rivers. He decided to take his cattle to the plains, sending a party of men with his brother's sheep on southwards.[241]

The Faithfulls' advance party reached the Broken River near present day Benalla on 6 and 7 April 1838. There, on 11 April, they were attacked by a party of Taungurong (or Daungwurrung) and Waveroo aborigines. Eight of the 18 Faithfull men then at the Broken River and one aborigine were killed in the attack, which subsequently became known as the *Faithfull Massacre*.[242]

Following the *Faithfull Massacre*, the Faithfull brothers initially moved to establish a squatting run downstream on the Ovens River on the Bontharambo Plains. However, further skirmishes with local aborigines saw them move back upstream to the Oxley

---

240 See Thomas Bride (ed.), *Letters from Victorian Pioneers* (Republished 1983), p. 218.

241 See Bride, *op. cit.*, p. 219.

242 *Ibid.* See also Judith Bassett, "The Faithfull Massacre at the Broken River, 1838" in (2009) 13:24 *Journal of Australian Studies*, pp. 18 – 34. In an article published in the *Wangaratta Chronicle* on Saturday, 4 November 1922, a man identified in the article only as "Old Timer" provided the following account of the *Faithfull Massacre*:

"It was from Oxley Plains Station that a party set out to settle country near Euroa, but were massacred (at what is now known as Faithfull's Creek) by the blacks, it was alleged through some of the party taking a gin; only one man escaped and got back to Wangaratta, being followed practically all the way by the infuriated blacks. He was a well known identity of Benalla, known as Sawyer BROWN. It was a marvel to many how he stayed the distance, as he was a short stout man. When the news got about that the party had been murdered, men gathered from all the stations and started out in pursuit of the tribe. It was easy to trace them, as they had taken a cross-cut saw belonging to the party, and wherever they went they were trying it on logs and trees. When the party of pursuing horsemen came up to the tribe, they practically wiped them out."

See *Kaye's Greta, Myrrhee and Winton Webpages: Newspaper articles – Pioneer stories* (https://tinyurl.com/2rzcmuc9) (at 11 October 2023). Though replete with inaccuracies, the "Old Timer's" reminiscences nonetheless touch both on the probable cause of the *Faithfull Massacre* and on the terrible consequences for the aborigines seemingly involved.

Plains in July 1838. There, they jointly established a 92,00 acre squatting run which they call *Oxley Plains*.²⁴³ This was subsequently divided by them into two equal sized runs, with the northern run (which retained the name *Oxley Plains*) passing to George Faithfull alone and the southern run (originally called *Ten Mile Hollow*, the later *Hedi* and later still *Edi*, on the King River, going to William Pitt Faithfull on his own. Although George Faithfull lived the rest of his life in the Wangaratta region, William Pitt Faithfull soon returned to *Springfield*.²⁴⁴ It was in this context that William Pitt Faithful sent John Moore to manage what was then called the *Ten Mile Hollow* run.

The Moore Family At Ten Mile Hollow

In John Moore's obituary published in the *Wangaratta Despatch* on 5 August 1891, it was observed of John that:

> "he was deputed by the late Mr Faithfull to come to the line of country in the King district afterwards known as the Hollow station, and take the management. The country about that time was inundated by heavy floods, and the project was temporarily relinquished, Mr Moore taking charge of the Little River cattle station where he remained for many years."²⁴⁵

Interestingly, in its obituary for Margaret Moore, published some four years later on 20 July 1895, the *Ovens and Murray Advertiser* repeated this observation word for word.²⁴⁶

This account of the Moore family's movement to "the Little River cattle station" is highly suspect. In the first place, there is no independent support to be found for it. Secondly, although there are many "Little Rivers" in both Victoria and New South Wales,²⁴⁷ it would seem that neither of the Faithfull brothers occupied a property known as *Little River*, or a property going by another name on one of the streams bearing the name "Little River". Finally, and as will be seen in more detail below, at least two of John and Margaret Moore's children were born on *Hedi* station in November 1845.²⁴⁸

The journey undertaken by the Moore family in 1843 from *Springfield* to the *Ten Mile*

---

243 See *The Argus,* Tuesday, 25 July 1848, p. 1.
244 See Bassett, *op. cit.*, p. 32. See also Robert Spreadborough and Hugh Anderson, *Victorian Squatters* (1983), pp. 47 and 66; Faithfull and Lewis, *op. cit.*, p. 147; and the King River Squatting Map below.
245 See the *Wangaratta Despatch*, Wednesday, 5 August 1891.
246 See the *Ovens and Murray Advertiser*, Saturday, 20 July 1895, p. 6.
247 See *Wikipedia – Little River* (https://tinyurl.com/4s84ytfh) (at 12 October 2023).
248 See footnote 252 and its accompanying text below.

Hollow run would have been arduous for Margaret Moore, who would no doubt have borne the primary responsibility along the way for the care of the three young children – Henry, Matilda and John Jnr.

After reaching the *Ten Mile Hollow* run, the Moore family probably occupied a slab hut with a bark roof close to the right bank of the King River at or near to where the present day settlement of Edi is located. Living as they did on the fringe of white settlement in the north-east of the Port Phillip District, life would not have been easy for John and Margaret Moore and their children. It might also have been dangerous. John Moore's relations with local aborigines is not now known. However, his interactions with those aborigines could well have been tense, and perhaps violent. Significantly in this context, George Faithfull is on record as having written of the aborigines after his move to *Oxley Plains* that:

> "I and my men were kept for years in a perpetual state of alarm."[249]

Unfortunately, but perhaps unsurprisingly, Faithfull did not elaborate on the precise circumstances in which aboriginal activities engendered his "perpetual state of alarm", or his responses to that alarm.

James Walsh, the son of an overseer employed by George Faithfull on *Oxley Plains* in about 1846, was more forthcoming. In an article published in the *Wangaratta Chronicle* on Saturday, 13 June 1908, he reminisced:

> "There were not many blacks about when we went to the station; but the owner had had several encounters with them prior to that, and one severe engagement on the King River, near the Home Station [the *Oxley Plains* homestead area]. I heard of one close shave while I was there. One of the shepherds had been out on the run, and was chased by blacks. One spear passed through his hat and pinned it quivering to a tree that was just in front of him. When we were at Mr CHISHOLM's Myrrhee Station [across the King River from the *Oxley Plains* run], Mr BROADRIBB, overseer, had a very narrow escape. He was returning to the station when he caught sight of two blacks shadowing him. He turned and faced them, and they took cover. He then walked backwards half a mile, they following, until he came within hearing of the station, when he gave a long 'Coo-ee'. The men came running out from the station, and one had a gun. The blacks were

---
249 See Bride, *op. cit.*, p. 219.

just preparing for a rush nearer, when each got a bullet that ended his career. Mr FAITHFULL made a very determined stand against the blacks, and they gave the place a wide berth latterly."[250]

James Howard, an old man who had been employed as a shepherd by George Faithfull on the *Oxley Plains* run, and whose story was published in *The Argus* on Thursday, 13 September 1883, was even more graphic in his account of the fate of local aborigines in about the early 1840s. According to *The Argus*, Howard:

"was a shepherd on Faithfull's run, Oxley Plains, when a terrible slaughter of the blacks took place about 42 years ago. Faithful had crossed over from the Sydney side, and had taken up land about Euroa and Oxley. Four of his stockmen were murdered by the blacks near Euroa – just on the spot on Faithfull's Creek where the station which was stuck up by the Kelly gang now stands. The blacks then crossed over to the Oxley or King River plains and played sad havoc with Faithfull's cattle and sheep there, whereupon the stockmen, shepherds and hut keepers turned out, mounted and armed, to the number of about 18, fell upon the blacks in camp on the bank of the King above Oxley, and massacred them. About 200 were killed on the spot, and the others were pursued for miles up the river, until all, with one or two exceptions, were exterminated. Howard is extremely reticent as to who were actually engaged in the slaughter, and when first questioned on the subject said, 'Don't you know there were seven men hanged in Sydney for killing a gin? It is not for me to say who was there.' He, however, vouchsafed the following summary of the proceedings:- 'In 1841, the blacks here were very bad. They were spearing the cattle on the plains, and the poor beasts were running about by the score with spears sticking in them. They also rounded 400 or 500 sheep up, and rushed them into the King River, and walked over them as on a bridge. Faithfull's men had then to go out to protect the stock and the shepherds. Of course a slaughter followed. There were some 300 blacks, and we came upon them on the Oxley Plains. We followed them up the river, and only three of them escaped. The dead bodies were left for the crows to pick'."[251]

---

250 See *Kaye's Greta, Myrrhee and Winton webpages: Newspaper articles – Pioneer articles* (https://tinyurl.com/2rzcmuc9) (at 13 October 2023).

251 See *The Argus*, Thursday, 13 September 1883, p. 9. The aborigines referred to by Howard who were apparently massacred on the King River are likely to have been members of the Pallangan-middang clan or local group: see Jacqui Durrant, "Who were the Aboriginal people of Beechworth? A historical perspective" in *Life on Spring Creek* (https://tinyurl.com/yc668utv) (at 28 October 2023); and Jacqui Durrant, "Mysterious Mogullumbidj – First People of Mount Buffalo" in *Life on Spring Creek* (https://tinyurl.com/yc8x6tna) (at 28 October 2023). The contempt with which the

If James Howard's account of the timing of the massacre of aborigines on the King River in which he participated is accurate, it would have occurred some two years prior to the Moore family's arrival at the *Ten Mile Run*. However, Howard was clearly somewhat confused as to the location and circumstances of what was undoubtedly the *Faithfull Massacre*, so that the King River massacre may have in reality occurred a few years before or after 1841. One can therefore not completely exclude the possibility that John Moore participated in it. In the more likely event that he did not, there would still have been ample reason for John and Margaret Moore to have been wary of an aboriginal attack on them in the years immediately following their arrival at the run.

On 23 November 1845, Margaret Moore gave birth on the *Ten Mile Hollow* run (which by then was seemingly referred to as the *Hedi* run) to twin boys: William Moore and George Moore.[252] The twins were baptised on 10 April 1848 by the Reverend A. C Thomson, an Anglican chaplain for the Port Phillip District and the incumbent of St. James' Church in Melbourne.[253] The baptisms could well have occurred in or near to Wangaratta rather than in Melbourne; perhaps in, or on the banks of, the Ovens River. The Reverend Thomson apparently travelled widely around Victoria on horseback performing baptisms, marriages and funerals.

In 1847, Margaret apparently gave birth to a further unnamed child of unspecified sex, who was either stillborn or died in very early infancy.[254]

For Margaret Moore, life on the *Hedi* run would presumably have been particularly hard in light of the young ages of her children, her pregnancies and her likely lack of nearby female support and companionship. However, virtually nothing is now know of how she managed in the isolated circumstances she was confronted with.[255]

---

white populace regarded the surviving aborigines can be seen in one of a number of articles authored anonymously under the pseudonym "An Imported Article" and published in the *Ovens and Murray Advertiser*. In the article, the author recounted that:

"Towards the end of 1856 a remnant of the Barwidgee blacks were in existence, King Billy, their leader, being a familiar character. He was adorned with a brass plate suspended from his neck with his name engraved on it, which he was very proud of. They held a corroboree on the site where Mr. S. H. Rundle's residence is situated. The moon was at its full. They were painted with white lines that gave them the resemblance of skeletons, and danced around a fire, while two old gins kept up a tatoo with sticks and made a droning kind of noise. There was no melody in it, but the time was perfect. They were a lazy, listless kind of beings, begging for food and drink, which was the means of terminating their existence. The Darwinian theory is 'the survival of the fittest'. It is quite evident they were not."

See the *Ovens and Murray Advertiser*, Saturday, 20 October 1906, p. 8.

252 See *WikiTree – William Moore (1845 – 1908)* (https://tinyurl.com/ybzx549h) (at 13 October 2023); and *WikiTree – George Moore (1845 – 1875)* (https://tinyurl.com/y7zherzr) (at 13 October 2023).

253 See the 1848 baptismal records for William and George Moore held in St. James Old Cathedral in Melbourne.

254 See the *Moore Considine Family Website – Margaret Considine* (https://tinyurl.com/j33nctz: access code - seemoore) (at 13 October 2023).

255 Graham Robb has pertinently observed that:

"In the remnants of a vanished society, the smallest fragment of a woman's life is worth a fortune, but the details have to be teased out of a mass of masculine detail. The published sources have very little to say about women."

See Graham Robb, *The Debatable Land* (2018), p. 130.

Whilst living and working on the *Hedi* run, John Moore may have first become acquainted with the "Father of Wangaratta", William Henry Clark. Clark held the *Whitfield* run, located on the left bank of the King River opposite the *Ten Mile Hollow/ Hedi/Edi* run on the right bank, between 1845 and July 1853.[256] Both men had been born in Kent. Two of John's sons were to marry two of William's daughters; with John Moore Jnr marrying Elizabeth Clark on 1 February 1864 in Wangaratta,[257] and William Moore marrying Alice Rebecca Clark on 1 May 1872 in Benalla.[258]

The Move To Whorouly

In early 1849, John and Margaret Moore and their family left the *Hedi/Edi* run and went to live on Dr George Mackay's *Whorouly* squatting run on the Ovens River. The run, of some 10,000 acres, was also known as *Glencooty*. John secured new employment as Mackay's overseer on this run. What caused him to leave William Pitt Faithfull's employ is not now known. Perceived unsuitability of the accommodation available for the growing family on *Hedi/Edi* may have been a factor. Remoteness from Wangaratta may also have played a part; as could some now forgotten dispute between John and William Pitt Faithfull. Alternatively, Mackay may have offered John better remuneration than William Pitt Faithfull was prepared to pay him.

George Mackay was born in 1811 at Thurso, Caithness in Scotland. He graduated in medicine from Edinburgh University in 1834 and emigrated from Scotland to Australia soon afterwards. He initially took up the *Myrrhee* run on the King River in early 1838. However, he abandoned that run for *Whorouly* in September 1838. He held the latter run until January 1855. In 1853, Mackay also acquired the *Tarrawingee* squatting run to the north of *Whorouly* and across the Ovens River.[259]

Margaret Moore must have been pregnant when the Moore family moved on to *Whorouly*. On 25 August 1849, she gave birth of a son. He was duly christened Charles Moore, and was said to have been born at "Ovens River".[260] As was the case when they lived on *Hedi/Edi*, the Moore family probably again occupied a slab hut with a bark roof whilst living on *Whorouly*. The hut would almost certainly have been located on or close to the left bank of the Ovens River.

---

256 See Spreadborough and Anderson, *op. cit.*, p. 78. See also the King River Squatting Map below.
257 See *WikiTree – John Moore (1843 – 1899)* (https://tinyurl.com/359yhf4z) (at 14 October 2023).
258 See *WikiTree – William Moore (1845 – 1908)* (https://tinyurl.com/ybzx549h) (at 14 October 2023).
259 See Faithfull and Lewis, *op. cit.*, p. 147. See also the King River Squatting Map below
260 See the *Moore Considine Family Website – Charles Moore* (https://tinyurl.com/j33nctz: access code - seemoore) (at 14 October 2023).

John Moore worked for a number of years on *Whorouly*. Margaret's next child, who was baptised as Harriet Jane Moore, was born on that run on 16 August 1851.[261] John may also have worked for a time on *Tarrawingee* for George Mackay. If the author of John's obituary published in the *Wangaratta Despatch* is to be believed, both William Pitt Faithfull and George Mackay:

"entertained the greatest respect for him as an upright, honest and thoroughly good man, and held his ability as a manager in high esteem."[262]

Tenterfield

On a date not presently ascertained, but likely as early as 1854, John left his employment with George Mackay and moved with his family to a property he had purchased closer to the Wangaratta township. The land so purchased straddled One Mile Creek to the west of the township; with frontages to what are now Appin Street, Williams Road, Phillipson Street and the Yarrawonga Road. The property had an area of approximately 100 acres.[263]

John Moore named his property *Tenterfield*.[264] Why he did so is something of a mystery. There is, of course, a town of Tenterfield in northern New South Wales. However, John Moore had no known connection with it. It seems to be likely that his choice of the name stems from his early associations with the ancient town of Tenterden in Kent. A "limb" of the Cinque Ports city of Rye, Tenterden was the market town closest to the West Ashford area in which John was raised.[265] He would undoubtedly have visited it on many occasions in his youth. Perhaps Tenter**field** for John was a pastoral "echo" of Tenter**den**.

John and Margaret Moore and their family were probably living on *Tenterfield* when Margaret's penultimate child, Sarah Moore, was born on 20 May 1854. Unfortunately,

---

261 See the *Moore Considine Family Website – Harriet Jane Moore* (https://tinyurl.com/j33nctz: access code - seemoore) (at 14 October 2023).
262 See the *Wangaratta Despatch*, Wednesday, 5 August 1891.
263 See Faithfull and Lewis, *op. cit.*, pp. 147 – 148. See also the Tenterfield Location Plan and photo 23 below.
264 See Faithfull and Lewis, *op. cit.*, pp. 147 – 148 and 151.
265 See *Wikipedia – Tenterden* (https://tinyurl.com/32u6rnx2) (at 15 October 2023). It is interesting to note that one of John and Margaret Moore's grand-daughters, Jemima ("Mimmie") Moore, lived from about 1928 until her death in 1962 in a house at 16 Templeton Street, Wangaratta called *Tenterfield*. This house is still extant: see Faithfull and Lewis, *op. cit.*, p. 151; and photo 24 below.

Sarah died as an infant on 1 June 1854.[266] On 28 December 1856, Margaret gave birth to her last child, Thomas Moore, while living with her family on that property.[267]

John Moore grazed stock and farmed on *Tenterfield* for the balance of his life. Furthermore, he almost certainly owned and/or leased other rural land in the Wangaratta district. According to his obituary in the *Wangaratta Chronicle*:

> "He became a successful farmer, and owned, at one time, a considerable quantity of land."[268]

Particulars of his further land dealings are presently only partially known.[269] In addition to grazing stock on his lands, he very likely used at least part or parts of his lands to grow hay and other crops. Some of the hay so grown would have been cut for chaff to feed his stock as and when necessary.

John Moore's Community Activities

In addition to working his lands, John Moore took an active interest in local community affairs. Despite having married Margaret according to Catholic rites, he was a committed Anglican. He was described in his obituary published in the *Wangaratta Despatch* as having been:

> "a prominent member of the Church of England ever since its establishment in this district...."[270]

As a freehold landowner, John was registered on Victoria's electoral roll in 1856. In that year, he was one of a number of registered electors who published in *The Argus* newspaper a request to a James Stewart to stand as a candidate for the Eastern Province in the forthcoming Victorian elections.[271] William Henry Clark, John's friend and the

---

266 See *Deaths in the District of Wangaratta in the Colony of Victoria – Sarah Moore* (https://tinyurl.com/5n8tvmyp) (at 15 October 2023); and the *Moore Considine Family Website – Sarah Moore* (https://tinyurl.com/j33nctz: access code - seemoore) (at 15 October 2023).

267 See the *Moore Considine Family Website – Thomas Moore* (https://tinyurl.com/j33nctz: access code - seemoore) (at 15 October 2023)

268 See the *Wangaratta Chronicle*, 5 August 1891, p. 151.

269 John Moore devised five allotments of land to beneficiaries by his Will: see footnote 287 and its accompanying text below.

270 See the *Wangaratta Despatch*, Wednesday, 5 August 1891.

271 See *The Argus*, Saturday, 6 September 1856, p. 6.

father-in-law of two of John's sons, was also a signatory to the request. James Stewart was a Melbourne wine merchant and a pastoralist. He succeeded in being one of five Members elected for the Eastern Province in 1856 at the first bicameral election conducted in the Colony under its 1855 Constitution. He served as a Member for the Eastern Province until his early death in 1863.[272]

In 1858, John Moore was recorded as being a member of the Board of Local Patrons of the Wangaratta National School.[273]

As mentioned above, John stood for election to the Wangaratta Borough Council in August 1876.[274] He was one of six candidates standing for three positions on the Council in an election conducted on 10 August 1876. In an election manifesto he placed in the *Ovens and Murray Advertiser* on 8 August 1876, he asserted that:

> "**To the Ratepayers of the Borough of Wangaratta.**
>
> LADIES and GENTLEMEN, - Having been requested by a large number of my fellow ratepayers to allow myself to be nominated as a Candidate for a seat on your Council, I have, after mature deliberation, consented.
>
> If elected, my object shall always be the advancement of the town in which I have been resident 33 years, and in which my sole interest is staked. The judicious expenditure of the revenue I consider of primary importance, yet where the interests of the borough can be promoted at any time by exceeding the usual limits, I shall endeavour to act liberally though cautiously.
>
> It has been stated that I have come forward for election to serve party interests. I need hardly say that such is not the case, and I feel certain that few if any will credit the assertion.
>
> Should you do me the honor of returning me, I shall endeavour faithfully to serve you to the utmost of my ability.
>
> I have the honor to be,
>
> Yours faithfully,
>
> JOHN MOORE."[275]

---

272   See Parliament of Victoria, *About Parliament; Re-Member (Former Members) – James Stewart* (https://tinyurl.com/ydb65wfe) (at 15 October 2023); and Jenny Coates, "1856 Politics Wangaratta Style" in *Conversations with Grandma* (https://tinyurl.com/ydyozygn) (at 15 October 2023).

273   See Parliament of Victoria, *Sixth Report of the Commissioners of National Education for the Colony of Victoria for the Year 1858*, pp.58 – 59 (https://tinyurl.com/36jpa43c) (at 15 October 2023).

274   See footnote 236 and its accompanying text above.

275   See the *Ovens and Murray Advertiser*, Tuesday, 8 August 1876, p. 3.

In the event, John Moore was unsuccessful in the election; securing three less votes than John Johnston, who was duly elected to fill the third position on the Council.[276]

Some two years after his election loss, on 2 August 1878, John seriously injured one of his hands in a chaff-cutting machine while at work on Tenterfield. The *Ovens and Murray Advertiser* reported this occurrence as follows:

> "While working a chaff-cutting machine, Mr Moore unthinkingly put his hand where the cutters descend, the consequence being that the second finger of one of his hands came in contact with the cutter, which nearly severed it from the second joint, leaving it hanging by the skin. Dr Hutchinson sewed it up, but it is very doubtful whether amputation will not yet have to be resorted to. Mr Moore is one of the oldest residents in this district, and is universally respected."[277]

It is not presently known whether it ultimately did prove necessary to amputate John's badly injured finger.

The Death Of John Moore

John Moore died on Monday, 3 August 1891 in Wangaratta after what his obituary in the *Wangaratta Despatch* described as a "a comparatively short illness".[278] The obituary went on to state that:

> "although the deceased gentleman had for a considerable time past been a martyr to rheumatism, otherwise he was wonderfully hale, cheerful and active, and although 76 years of age, looked fresher than most men ten years his junior."[279]

John was in fact 75 years old when he died. A now missing photo of him is said to have shown an old John Moore as being wiry, slightly stooped, with well-defined muscles in his arms and what looked like rheumatism in his knuckles. Although the provenance

---

276   See the *Ovens and Murray Advertiser*, Saturday, 12 August 1876, p. 5.

277   See the *Ovens and Murray Advertiser*, Saturday, 3 August 1878, p. 7.

278   See the *Wangaratta Despatch*, Wednesday, 5 August 1891. John's Death Certificate records that he died of pleurisy, congestion of the lungs and colic: see *Deaths in the District of Wangaratta in the Colony of Victoria – John Moore* (1891/12661) (https://tinyurl.com/bdds44s2).

279   *Ibid.*

of photo 25 below is uncertain, as is the man shown in it, it may well be a copy of the missing photo of John Moore, taken in old age at *Tenterfield*.[280]

According to his obituaries, John was well-regarded. The *Wangaratta Chronicle* observed that:

> "he was a very kind and quiet, unassuming man, and was highly respected for his integrity and manly character."[281]

His obituary in the *Wangaratta Despatch* was somewhat more effusive:

> "A God-fearing man, he was ever ready and willing to do his friend, his neighbour, or a stranger who came in his way, a good turn, and that in such a pleasant manner that it immensely enhanced to the recipients of his kindness the value of his good natured acts. All who had the pleasure of Mr Moore's acquaintance (and the number was very large), will agree with us, in paying our journalistic tribute to his memory, when we assert that our departed friend would have come closely up to the poet Burns' delineation of the noblest work of God – 'an honest man', for he possessed that virtue in the strictest sense. Beloved by all who knew him, for his many sterling qualities, peacefully he lived and peacefully he passed away."[282]

John Moore was buried on Wednesday, 5 August 1891 in the Church of England section of the Wangaratta Cemetery. The Reverend John Kaye Hall officiated at the burial service.[283] John was buried in the same grave in which his son, George Moore (the twin brother of William Moore), had been interred following George's early death from typhoid fever on 4 July 1875.[284]

John Moore was a modest and hardworking man who successfully rose from humble English beginnings to a successful pioneering life in colonial Victoria. Moore Street in Wangaratta commemorates that life.

---

280   The details of the missing photo are so described in the anonymous document referred to in footnote 64 above. See also photo 25 below.
281   See the *Wangaratta Chronicle*, Wednesday, 5 August 1891.
282   See the *Wangaratta Despatch*, Wednesday, 5 August 1891.
283   *Ibid.*
284   See Jenny Coates, "On This Day In Wangaratta – 4th July 1875" in *Conversations with Grandma* (https://tinyurl.com/qhqcmbf) (at 15 October 2012). See also photos 26 and 27 below.

John Moore's Will

John Moore died leaving a Will executed by him on 6 January 1888. By his Will, he appointed two of his sons, John Moore Jnr and William Moore, together with one of his sons-in-law, Francis Heach,[285] to be his Executors and Trustees. Probate of the Will was granted in the Supreme Court of Victoria on 3 September 1891.[286]

After payment of John's debts, funeral and testamentary expenses; pecuniary legacies of £20 to his widow, Margaret Moore, and £20 to his youngest surviving daughter, Harriet Marum (née Moore); and the provision of £53.4.8 to be held in trust for his grandson, George Earl Moore,[287] until the latter reached the age of 21 years; the Will left the residue of John's estate in trust for the use and benefit of his widow during the balance of her life.

John's Will went on to provide that after Margaret's death, the land comprised in the residue of his estate was to be divided as follows:

- Allotment 3, Section 6, Parish of Wangaratta to his son, Charles Moore.

- Allotments 1 and 2, Section 6, Parish of Wangaratta to his son, John Moore.

- Allotment 4, Section 6, Parish of Wangaratta to his son, William Moore.

- Allotment 13, Section 6, Parish of Wangaratta to his daughter, Harriet Marum.

- Allotment 12, Section 6, Parish of Wangaratta to his son, Thomas Moore.

Lastly, the personal property comprised in the residue of John's estate was to be divided equally between his sons, Charles, John, William and Thomas Moore, and his daughter, Harriet Marum.[288]

It is interesting to note that John Moore left nothing by his Will to either Matilda Heach (née Moore) or Henry Faithfull (in his earlier days known as Henry Moore). He did not disclose in the Will why they had been excluded. However, it could well be that

---

285 Francis Heach had married Margaret Moore's eldest daughter (who was baptised as Matilda Margaret Moore but likely fathered by William Pitt Faithfull rather than John Moore: see footnotes 231, 232 and 233, together with their accompanying texts, above) on 20 July 1857: see the *Moore Considine Family Website – Francis Heach* (https://tinyurl.com/j33nctz: access code - seemoore) (at 15 October 2023).

286 See *Public Records Office of Victoria ("PROV")*, VPRS 28/P0, Unit 580; VPRS 28/P2, Unit 316; and VPRS 7591/P2, Unit 181.

287 George Earl Moore was the son of John Moore's son, George Moore, who predeceased John: see footnote 283 and its accompanying text above.

288 See footnote 286 and its accompanying text above.

he felt that he had no responsibility to benefit either of them by virtue of the fact that both were seemingly fathered by William Pitt Faithfull. In Matilda's case, John may also, or alternatively, have considered that her husband, Francis Heach, was affluent enough to provide for her. In Henry's case, John's decision not to benefit him may have been influenced by reason of the facts that Henry had been materially aided in life by William Pitt Faithfull, and had come to adopt the latter's surname.

Margaret Moore's Later Years And Death

Margaret Moore remained living on *Tenterfield* until her death. She lived long enough to see all her children bar the youngest, Thomas Moore, married. As Jenny Coates has observed, Margaret's two surviving daughters can be said to have "married well". Matilda Moore had married Francis Heach, a wealthy Wangaratta businessman and hotelier, on 20 July 1857.[289] Harriet Moore had married Thomas Marum, a Wangaratta pharmacist, on 28 May 1871.[290] Two of Margaret's sons, John Moore Jnr and William Moore, had married daughters of William Clark, a local squatter, hotelier and landowner.[291]

On the other hand, Margaret had the misfortune to lose three offspring during her lifetime. An unnamed child was either stillborn or died very soon after birth in 1847.[292] Margaret's daughter, Sarah Moore, died on 1 June 1854 after only 11 days of life.[293] Finally, one of her adult sons, George Moore, died of typhoid fever on 4 July 1875 when only 29 years of age.[294]

Margaret Moore survived her husband by a little less than four years. Despite their different religious faiths, Margaret's marriage to John was apparently a happy one. Little is known of her last years. Although of uncertain provenance, photo 28 below may have been taken of her in old age.[295]

Margaret Moore died on Wednesday, 10 July 1895 after a short bout of influenza.[296] According to her obituary in the *Ovens and Murray Advertiser*, she had been in delicate

---

289 See footnote 285 and its accompanying text above.

290 See the *Moore Considine Family Website – Harriet Jane Moore* (https://tinyurl.com/j33nctz: access code –seemoore) at 16 October 2023).

291 See footnotes 257 and 258, together with their accompanying texts, above.

292 See footnote 254 and its accompanying text above.

293 See footnote 266 and its accompanying text above.

294 See footnote 284 and its accompanying text above. See generally here Jenny Coates, "Margaret Considine (c.1818 – 1895)" in *Conversations with Grandma* (https://tinyurl.com/52apm3p3) (at 16 October 2024).

295 See photo 28 below. See also footnote 253 above.

296 See *Deaths in the District of Wangaratta in the Colony of Victoria – Margaret Moore* (No. 1895/11408) (https://tinyurl.com/yfwkew4u) (at 16 October 2023); and the *Moore Considine Family Website – Margaret Considine* (https://tinyurl.com/j33nctz: access code - seemoore) (at 16 October 2023).

health for some time, but passed peacefully away.[297] After a Catholic funeral conducted by the Very Reverend Dean Timothy Murphy, Margaret was interred not in her late husband's grave, but in her own grave in the Catholic section of the Wangaratta Cemetery on Thursday, 11 July 2023.[298] Her grave was unmarked for many years. A headstone has now been erected over it by two of her great-granddaughters, Eileen Bartlett and Mary Parker, and by one of her great-great-grandsons, John Smith.[299]

In its obituary, the *Wangaratta Chronicle* noted of Margaret:

"Her death has removed a fine specimen of the old pioneers of the colony."[300]

Earlier in the obituary, the newspaper had observed:

"She had many interesting reminiscences of the early days, during which time she was exceedingly useful to the settlers by reason of her kindness of heart and skill in the treatment of sickness. Many lives were prolonged by her aid, and her services were always freely and immediately given at a time when medical advice could not be easily obtained."[301]

Margaret's obituary in the *Ovens and Murray Advertiser* was no less glowing. That newspaper asserted that:

"the district loses one of the very earliest pioneers and one whose kind and gentle nature has brought relief and comfort to many a sad and distressed family. All who had the pleasure of her acquaintance will mourn the loss of Mrs. Moore, as her amiable manner won golden opinions from all with whom she came in contact."[302]

In addition to possessing the character and traits outlined in her obituaries, Margaret Moore was clearly a hardy, adventurous and resourceful woman: a worthy Australian matriarch.

---

297 See the *Ovens and Murray Advertiser*, Saturday, 20 July 1895, p. 6.
298 See the *Wangaratta Chronicle*, Saturday, 13 July 1895, p. 2.
299 See photo 29 below.
300 See the *Wangaratta Chronicle*, Saturday, 13 July 1895, p. 2.
301 *Ibid.*
302 See the *Ovens and Murray Advertiser*, Saturday, 20 July 1895, p. 6.

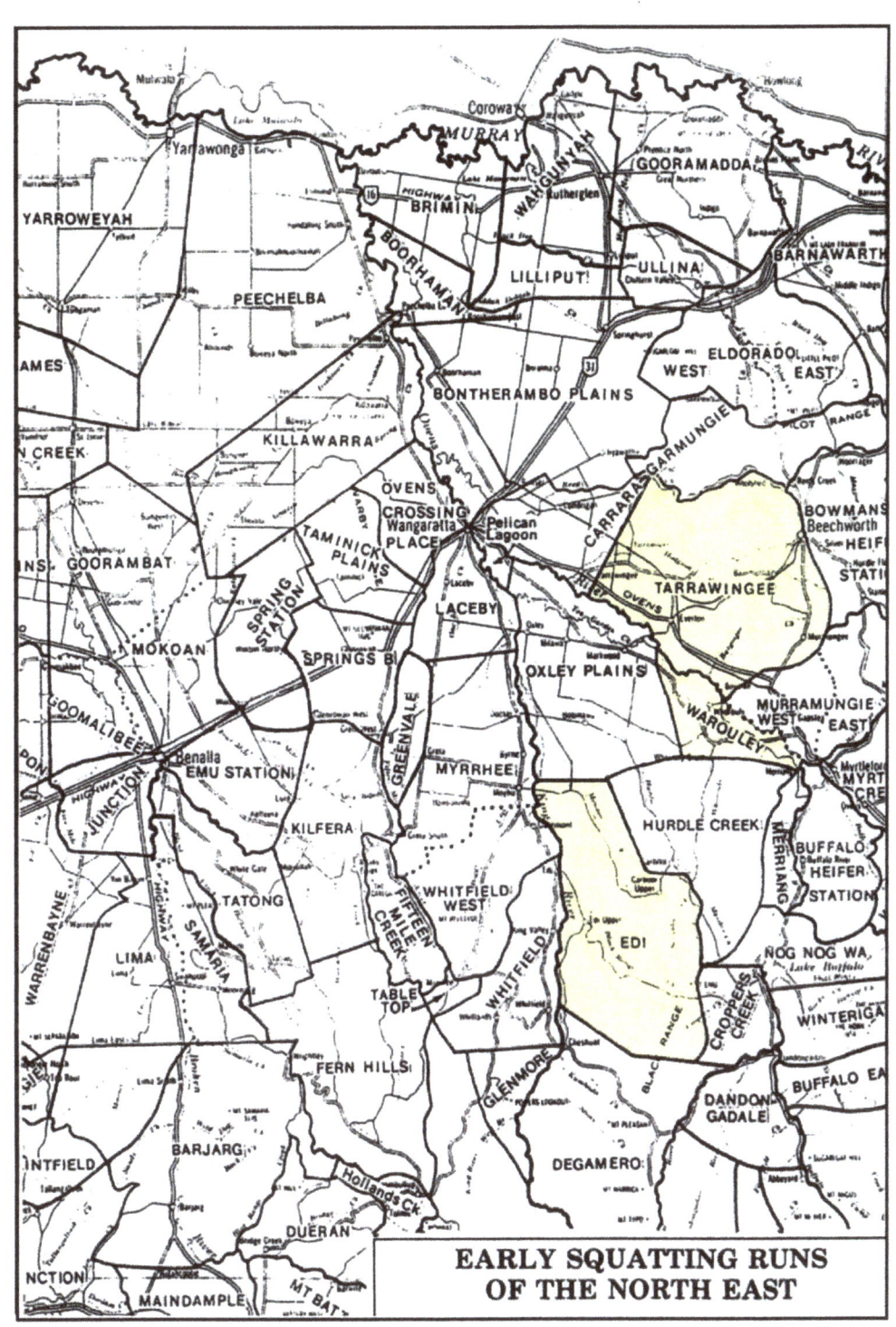

King River Squatting Map.

Henry Moore Born March 5 1838
Matilda Moore Born March 9 1840
John Moore Born January 16 1843
William Moore Born November 25 1845
George Moore Born November 25 1845
Charles Moore Born August 25 1849
Harriet Moore Born August 16 1851
Thomas Moore Born December 27 1857

Page from the Family Bible of John and Margaret Moore, listing their surviving children.

Tenterfield Location Plan.

Photo 23: Farm buildings on John Moore's Tenterfield property. The man standing on the right is Charles Bertram Moore, a grandson of John and Margaret Moore.

Photo 24: "Tenterfield", 16 Templeton Street, Wangaratta.

Photo 25: A possible photo of John Moore in old age.

Photo 26: John Moore's Grave in the Wangaratta Cemetery.

Photo 27: A close up of John Moore's Gravestone inscription in the Wangaratta Cemetery.

Photo 28: A possible photo of Margaret Moore in old age.

Photo 29: Margaret Moore's Grave in the Wangaratta Cemetery.

JOHN AND MARGARET MOORE'S SURVIVING CHILDREN

Margaret Moore gave birth to ten children. Her first child, Henry Faithfull, was indisputably fathered by William Pitt Faithfull. Faithfull was very likely the father of her second child, Matilda Margaret Moore. John Moore was the father of Margaret's remaining eight children. As may be seen above, one of those eight children was either stillborn or died very soon after birth in 1847 without being named.[303] A further child, Sarah Moore, survived for only 12 days after her birth on 20 May 1854.[304]

In the remaining part of this book, I propose to trace the lives of the eight children of Margaret Moore who reached adulthood.

Henry Faithfull

Henry Faithfull was born on 5 March 1838; the illegitimate son of William Pitt Faithfull and Margaret Considine.[305] He was around 18 months old when his mother married John Moore on 3 September 1839.[306] Although in no doubt as to the identity of Henry's father, John Moore appears to have fully accepted Henry and to have given him the Moore surname.[307]

Henry was around 5 years of age when John and Margaret Moore brought him

---

303 See footnote 254 and its accompanying text above.
304 See footnote 266 and its accompanying text above.
305 See footnote 191 and its accompanying text above
306 See footnote 153 and its accompanying text above.
307 See footnote 65 and its accompanying text above.

overland in 1843 from *Springfield* near Goulburn to William Pitt Faithfull's squatting run, *Ten Mile Hollow*, on the King River in the Port Phillip District, where Faithfull had appointed John to be overseer. Accompanying the party were two younger children of Margaret Moore: Matilda Margaret Moore, who was about 3 years old and likely the child of William Pitt Faithfull; and John Moore Jnr, John Moore Snr's son and but an infant at the time of the journey.

Whilst living on *Ten Mile Hollow*, Margaret Moore gave birth to three further children. William and George Moore were twins born on 23 November 1845.[308] An unnamed child, born in 1847, was either stillborn or died soon after birth.[309]

In early 1849, the Moore family moved from *Ten Mile Hollow* (by then known as *Hedi*, and later as *Edi*) to Dr George Mackay's *Whorouly* run on the Ovens River; where John Moore was again employed as overseer. On *Whorouly*, two more children were born to John and Margaret Moore: Charles Moore, born on 25 August 1849;[310] and Harriet Jane Moore, born on 16 August 1851.[311]

Henry Faithfull would likely have lived with the growing Moore family in bark-roofed slab huts on both the *Ten Mile Hollow* and *Whorouly* runs. It is unlikely that he would have received any formal education while living on either run. The two properties were then simply too remote from schools. However, he may have been taught basic reading, writing and arithmetic by John Moore. Undoubtedly, John would have taught Henry how to ride a horse.

In about 1854, the Moore family moved from the *Whorouly* run and on to a property John Moore had purchased, straddling One Mile Creek to the west of Wangaratta township, which John named *Tenterfield*. John and Margaret Moore's last two children were born on this property. Sarah Moore was born on 20 May 1854, but died on 1 June 1854;[312] and Thomas Moore was born on 28 December 1856.[313]

It is unclear what sort of a relationship Henry had with John Moore as Henry grew into maturity. What is clear is that Henry was aware before he reached adulthood that William Pitt Faithfull, and not John Moore, was his biological father. By the time of his marriage in 1857 at the latest, he was calling himself, and being referred to as, Henry Faithfull rather than Henry Moore.

---

308 See footnote 252 and its accompanying text above.
309 See footnote 254 and its accompanying text above.
310 See footnote 260 and its accompanying text above.
311 See footnote 261 and its accompanying text above.
312 See footnote 266 and its accompanying text above.
313 See footnote 267 and its accompanying text above.

In a Catholic service conducted on 19 January 1857, Henry Faithfull, still a month and a half shy of his 19th birthday, married his first cousin, Alice Faithfull. Henry might have been christened an Anglican, but his new wife (like his mother) was a Catholic. Although the marriage was registered in Beechworth, it may well have taken place in Wangaratta. In 1857, the Reverend Father John Kennedy, who was stationed at Beechworth, performed marriages throughout the north-east of Victoria – including in Wangaratta.[314]

Alice Faithfull was born on 15 January 1841, making her just 16 years old when she married Henry.[315] She was the illegitimate daughter of William Pitt Faithfull's younger brother, George Faithfull (who had settled after 1838 on the *Oxley Plains* run beside the King River[316]), and Jane McKenzie.

Jane McKenzie was born at Parramatta in 1821. She was the daughter of Charles and Hannah McKenzie, both ex-convicts. Although Irish by birth, Charles had been transported from England to New South Wales in 1816. His wife, Hannah, whom he married in about 1813, was transported from England to New South Wales in 1817.[317] It is unclear what happened to Charles McKenzie, but in about 1825, Hannah entered into a de facto relationship in Sydney with George Gray. The latter was another Irish ex-convict who had been transported to Australia in 1797. Hannah went on to have three children with George Gray: Mary Gray, Edward (Ned) Gray and George Grey Jnr.[318]

George Gray Snr and his family (including Jane McKenzie) moved from Sydney to the north-east of Victoria in February 1839, where George took up the 12,000 acre *Pelican Lagoon* run immediately to the north-west of *Oxley Plains*.[319] In 1851, Jane McKenzie's

---

314 See *Australian Christian Church Histories: Australian Christian Church and Clergy Database – Reverend John Joseph Hyland Kennedy* (https://tinyurl.com/2xfehxxf) (at 17 October 2023).

315 See the *Moore Considine Family Website – Alice Faithfull* (https://tinyurl.com/j33nctz: access code - seemoore) (at 17 October 2023); and Bienvenu, *op. cit.*, p. 10.

316 See footnote 244 and its accompanying text above. By 1848, George Faithfull also occupied the *Buffalo River Station*, a 25,000 acre squatting run located at the junction of the Ovens and Buffalo Rivers: see Bienvenu, *op. cit.*, p. 8; and *The Argus*, Tuesday, 25 July 1848, p. 1.

317 See *Australian Royalty – Charles McKenzie 1781* (https://tinyurl.com/3pwry3je) (at 17 October 2023); and *Australian Royalty – Hannah McIntosh 1790 – 1864* (https://tinyurl.com/svmc4ka) (at 17 October 2023). See also John Grenville, *Sedition, Treason & Other Pastoral Pursuits* (1997), pp. 13 – 17.

318 See Australian Royalty – George Gray 1755 – 1853 (https://tinyurl.com/28w4h4x4) (at 17 October 2023); Bienvenu, *op. cit.*, p. 10; Grenville, *op. cit.*, pp. (i), 3, 18 and 22; and Ian Stapleton, *From Drovers to Daisy-Pickers: Colourful Characters of the Bogongs* (2006), p. 64.

319 See Stapleton, *op. cit.*, pp. 64 – 65; and Grenville, *op. cit.*, p. 26. In September 1839, Assistant Surveyor Thomas Townsend noted that:

"Grey [sic] has a station…upon the left bank [of the Ovens River], and Faithfull about seven miles further up on that side."

See D. M. Whittaker, *Wangaratta* (1963), p. 23; and Grenville, *op. cit.*, p. 28. George Gray Snr died at the advance aged of 98 years on 15 June 1853. It is uncertain where he was interred. However, his grave stone was found in June 1901 buried under the stables of the Royal Hotel (now the Pinsent Hotel) in Wangaratta, which was then owned by one of his sons-in-law, John Crisp: see the *Ovens and Murray Advertiser*, Saturday, 22 June 1901, p. 2; *Australian Royalty – George Gray 1755 – 1853* (https://tinyurl.com/28w4h4x4) (at 17 October 2023); and Grenville, *op. cit.*, pp. 32 and 47.

half-brothers, Ned Gray and George Gray Jnr, acquired the *Cobungra Station* run in the Victorian High Country to the west of Omeo.[320]

Jane McKenzie very probably met George Faithfull while she was living with her family on *Pelican Lagoon*. Although she was named on her daughter Alice Faithfull's marriage record in 1857 as Jane McKenzie, she appeared in Alice's baptismal record in 1841 as Jane Faithfull. Thus, it is quite likely that Jane lived with George Faithfull on *Oxley Plains* as husband and wife for at least several years around the time of Alice's birth without ever formalising their relationship.[321] It is also likely that Alice Faithfull was born either on *Oxley Plains* or on *Pelican Lagoon*.

George Faithfull died in Wangaratta on 22 October 1855 at the age of 41 years. He died both unmarried and intestate, with his estate being consequentially inherited by his brother, William Pitt Faithfull.[322]

Four years after George Faithfull's death, Jane McKenzie married James ("Jim") Brown in Wangaratta on 31 August 1859.[323] It is interesting to note that at the time of his marriage to Jane, Jim Brown was a stockman working for the Grays on *Cobungra Station*. Brown and another stockman working on *Cobungra Station*, Jack Wells (who was married to Jane McKenzie's sister, Alice Wells (née McKenzie)[324]), in 1851 were likely the first Europeans to make their way up onto the Bogong High Plains. Whilst on the High Plains, they named a number of features; including Mt Feathertop, the Razorback, Mt Fainter, Mt Jim, Rocky Valley and Pretty Valley. JB Plain and JB Hut, both near Mt Hotham, are both named after Jim Brown.[325]

Henry and Alice Faithfull had a total of nine children prior to Alice's untimely death in childbirth on 16 April 1882.[326] Six of their children were born in the Wangaratta district, one at Cobungra and the remaining two in Omeo. The children were:

- William Henry Faithfull, born in Wangaratta on 19 December 1859.

- Emily Blanche Faithfull, born in Wangaratta on 15 December 1860.

---

320 See Stapleton, *op. cit.*, p. 66. On 5 September 1851, George Gray Jnr was formally granted a lease of the *Cobungra Station*: see Grenville, *op. cit.*, p. 45.

321 See Bienvenu, *op. cit.*, pp. 10 - 11. George Faithfull, like his brother William Pitt Faithfull, was an Anglican and it seems likely that Jane McKenzie's Catholic faith played at least a part in inhibiting George from marrying Jane.

322 See Bienvenu, *op. cit.*, p. 8.

323 See Bienvenu, *op. cit.*, p. 10.

324 See Australian Royalty – Alice McKenzie 1815 – 1854 (https://tinyurl.com/2p9hm2kj) (at 17 October 2023).

325 See Stapleton, *op. cit.*, p. 30; and Grenville, *op. cit.*, pp. 30, 42 and 45.

326 See the *Moore Considine Family Website – Alice Faithfull* (https://tinyurl.com/3j33nctz: access code - seemoore) (at 17 October 2023).

- Florence Matilda Faithfull, born in Wangaratta in about 1862.

- Lily Jane Faithfull, born on Pelican Lagoon on 18 December 1865.

- Frank Heach Faithfull, born in Oxley in 1867.

- Ada May Faithfull, born at Oxley on 16 April 1869.

- Rose Gray Faithfull, born at Cobungra in 1871.

- Frederick George Faithfull, born in Omeo on or shortly prior to 23 June 1874.

- Alicia (or Alice) Georgina Faithfull, born in Omeo on 16 April 1882.[327]

In 1865, Henry Faithfull played a part in the death of one of Victoria's worst (if not its most notorious) outlaw bushrangers: "Mad Dog" Daniel ("Dan") Morgan.

Daniel Morgan was born in about 1830 in Appin, New South Wales. In 1854, he was sentenced to 12 years hard labour for highway robbery at Castlemaine in Victoria. Released from prison in 1860,. Morgan quickly returned to theft and robbery under arms. Unstable and violent, he terrorised the eastern Riverina, the western slopes of New South Wales and north-east Victoria. After the commission of a number of atrocities, Morgan was proclaimed an outlaw under the provisions of the *Felons Apprehension Act 1865* (NSW). This authorised any and all to shoot him on sight in the Colony.[328]

On the evening of Saturday, 8 April 1865, "Mad Dog" Morgan bailed up the occupants of the *Peechelba* squatting run of Ewen MacPherson at gunpoint. Later that evening, one of MacPherson's servants, Alice Keenan, managed to slip away and alert a neighbour to what was happening. In turn, the neighbour sent word to inform the police in Wangaratta. On learning of Morgan's location and circumstances, Senior Constable Evans rounded up a party of Wangaratta armed volunteers, including Henry Faithfull, and rode for *Peechelba*. On reaching that run, they spread out in hiding to await Morgan's

---

327 *Ibid*. See also Bienvenu, *op. cit.*, p. 11. It is noteworthy that the middle name of Florence Matilda Faithfull was clearly taken from the first name of Henry Faithfull's sister, Matilda Margaret Heach (née Moore). Similarly, the first and second names of Frank Heach Faithfull were clearly inspired by the names of Matilda Heach's husband, Frank Heach. Finally Henry and Alice Faithfull used the Gray surname of Alice's common law step-father and his family in providing a middle name for Rose Gray Faithfull. It may be significant that neither John nor Margaret Considine's fist names were given to any of Henry and Alice Faithfull's children.

328 See John McQuilton, "Morgan, Daniel (Dan) (1830 – 1865)" in *Australian Dictionary of Biography* https://tinyurl.com/ycy85d3u) (at 17 October 2023). See also "Manuscript: Re Daniel Morgan Bushranger" in *The La Trobe Journal*, No. 5, April 1970 (https://tinyurl.com/jt8zwkd) (at 17 October 1970).

exit. Morgan came out of the *Peechelba* homestead at about 8.00 am on Sunday, 9 April 1865. He was immediately shot without warning through the shoulder and throat by a *Peechelba* employee, John Quinlan. Morgan died some six hours later and is buried in the Wangaratta Cemetery.[329]

As Ian Stapleton has remarked, Henry Faithfull "tried his hand" at many things during his life, "mostly it appears with not much success".[330] It is, perhaps, not insignificant that his working life was, in a sense, "bookended" by two brushes with the law.

On 1 July 1864, Henry found himself before the Wangaratta Police Court defending a civil complaint brought against him for the wrongful detention of a horse. In the event, the Court found against him, and he was ordered to deliver up the horse to the complainant or to pay the latter its value.[331]

Henry Faithfull's second brush with the law was at least potentially more serious. In April 1886, he was charged by police with stealing a cow. On 14 April 1886, and after a lengthy committal hearing in the Omeo Magistrates Court, Henry was committed to stand trial in the Court of General Sessions in Bairnsdale on 10 May 1886. Following the committal hearing, he was released on his own bail in the sum of £50, with a surety of a further £50. The cow allegedly stolen by Henry was said to have belonged to "Messrs Parslow and Hodgkins". Interestingly, a James Parslow was one of the purchasers of the lease of *Cobungra Station* from George Gray Jnr in 1859.[332] Notwithstanding his committal, there appears to be no record that Henry was ever tried on the charge in Bairnsdale or elsewhere. It seems likely that the charge was either withdrawn or the prosecution abandoned it before trial.

In the record of his marriage to Alice on 19 January 1857, Henry Faithfull's occupation was said to be that of a butcher. Interestingly, it has been asserted that his sister Matilda Margaret Moore's husband-to-be, Frank Heach, owned a butcher's shop in Wangaratta.[333] This gives rise to the possibility that Henry was working in Frank Heach's butcher's shop at the time of his wedding to Alice.

---

329 See *The Age*, Thursday, 13 April 1865, p. 6; and *The Argus*, Thursday, 13 April 1865, p. 5, See also photo 30 below. Morgan's body may have been buried in the Wangaratta Cemetery, but his head wasn't. He was decapitated in Wangaratta after death, and his head sent to the Professor of Anatomy at Melbourne University for phrenological studies: see McQuilton, *op. cit*. Interestingly, one of Ewen MacPherson's daughters, Christina MacPherson, who was an infant in the *Peechelba* homestead during Morgan's occupation, later went on in 1894 to play a Scottish tune on her zither which inspired Banjo Paterson to compose the lyrics of *Waltzing Matilda* and set them to the tune. The Scottish tune was originally known as *Bonnie Wood O'Craigielee*: see *Waltzing Matilda: Lyrics, Meaning, History – Christina MacPherson* (https://tinyurl.com/4u74f7m2) (at 18 October 2023).

330 See Stapleton, *op. cit.*, p. 144.

331 See the *Ovens and Murray Advertiser*, Thursday, 7 July 1864, p. 2.

332 See *The Argus*, Thursday, 15 April 1866, p. 7. See also Stapleton, *op. cit.*, p. 67; and Grenville, *op. cit.*, pp. 50 – 51.

333 See Bienvenu, *op. cit.*, p. 12.

Henry may have been working as a butcher in 1857 at the time of his marriage. However, it is clear that he did not pursue that trade for much longer. Instead, he turned from the town back to the land. Henry is thought to have worked at various times over the remained of his working life as a grazier, an overseer and as a drover.

Fred and Diana Bienvenu have noted in *Faithfulls of Omeo* that:

> "Speculation abounds that Henry – known as Harry, was 'set up' by his father's family in Goulburn on various properties in the Wangaratta area, including the Dandongadale (or Dandongetta) station. Apparently, none of these ventures succeeded."[334]

It appears that Henry Faithfull did indeed occupy the *Dandongadale* run from August 1858 until November 1861.[335] However, it does not seem to have been a successful venture, and Henry is on record as "not paying his dues" on the run in 1860.[336]

Henry Faithfull's working life may have reached its nadir in 1866. On 30 June 1866, he was insolvent and declared bankrupt by the Supreme Court of Victoria. In a press report of the bankruptcy proceeding, Henry was described as the "overseer of a station". He apparently attributed his insolvency to:

> "Increased price of supporting self and family caused by the high prices being the effect of the present protective duties, also from having been long out of employment, also from bad debts, also from pressure of creditors."

He was said in the report to then have assets worth £21.14s. and liabilities of £177.15s.4d.[337]

At some time between 1869 and 1871, Henry moved with his family from the Wangaratta district to Cobungra, where his second last child, Rose Gray Faithfull was born in 1871.[338] It might safely be assumed that he moved to Cobungra to work on *Cobungra Station*, the High Country run established by Alice Faithfull's half-brothers, Ned and George

---

334 *Ibid.*
335 See Spreadborough and Anderson, *op. cit.*, p. 45; and the King River Squatting Map below.
336 See Tor and Jane Holth, *Cattlemen of the High Country: The Story of the Mountain Cattlemen of the Bogongs* (2008, 2nd ed.), p. 213.
337 See *The Argus*, Monday, 2 July 1866, p. 6.
338 See footnote 327 and its accompanying text above.

Gray Jnr.³³⁹ By the time of Henry Faithfull's move to Cobungra, *Cobungra Station* was wholly owned by James Parslow.³⁴⁰

By 1874, Henry Faithfull had apparently moved again with his family; travelling further east from Cobungra to the Omeo district, where his youngest son, Frederick George Faithfull, was born on 23 June 1874.³⁴¹

Little appears to be known about Henry Faithfull's life in Omeo. However, it was marked by tragedy when, on 16 April 1882, Alice Faithfull died in childbirth. Although given the name Alicia (or Alice) Georgina Faithfull, the infant girl died on or about 28 April 1882.³⁴² What is known is that Henry was granted a cattle run on the Bogong High Plains in 1887. He only held the run for around two years.³⁴³

Unlike his wife Alice, Henry Faithfull did not die in Omeo. He died in Wangaratta on 3 February 1896 of an unknown cause.³⁴⁴ By the time of his death, his surviving daughters had married and moved away from Omeo.³⁴⁵ However, the reason for his return to Wangaratta prior to his death has not been ascertained. Henry was buried not with his wife in the Omeo Cemetery, but in the Catholic section of the Wangaratta Cemetery in the grave of his mother, who had died some six months earlier on 10 July 1895.³⁴⁶ Henry's burial in his mother's grave is not recorded on the gravestone.

Henry Faithfull's youngest son, Frederick George Faithfull, was killed in action in France during the First World War a little after 27 August 1917.³⁴⁷ This left only Henry's oldest son, William Henry Faithfull, to carry on the Faithfull name in the Omeo district.³⁴⁸ And carry on the Faithfull name in the Omeo district William Henry Faithfull certainly did!

---

339   See footnote 320 and its accompanying text above.

340   See footnote 332 and its accompanying text above. See also Grenville, *op. cit.*, p. 51.

341   See footnote 327 and its accompanying text above. See also Grenville, *op. cit.*, p. 51.

342   See footnote 327 and its accompanying text above; and the *Moore Considine Family Website – Alice Faithfull* (https://tinyurl.com/j33nctz: access code - seemoore) (at 18 October 2023)

343   See Stapleton, *op. cit.*, p. 115. It might be noted that a number of Henry Faithfull's descendants subsequently obtained grazing rights on the Bogong High Plains. In about 1962, some of them constructed a mountain cattlemen's hut on the High Plains at Buckety Plain. The hut is still known as *Faithfull Hut*: see *Flickr – Faithfull Hut* (https://tinyurl.com/yb224p4t) (at 18 October 2023).

344   See the *Moore Considine Family Website – Henry Faithfull* (https://tinyurl.com/j33nctz: access code - seemoore) (at 18 October 2023).

345   See Stapleton, *op. cit.*, p. 115. It is of interest to note that one of Henry and Alice Faithfull's daughters, Ada May Faithfull, married James Witterick Elliott on 6 December 1892. In turn, one of Ada and James Elliott's sons, Frank Elliott, married Anita Dorman. One of Frank and Anita Elliott's sons was John Dorman Elliott – a Melbourne business and political identity. He died on 23 September 2021: see *Wikipedia – John Elliott (businessman)* (https://tinyurl.com/bdd7wwrd) (at 18 October 2023). One of John Elliott's sons is Tom Elliott – a Melbourne radio personality: see *Wikipedia – Tom Elliott (radio personality)* (https://tinyurl.com/3ph5ec8e) (at 18 October 2023).

346   See footnotes 296 and 298, together with their accompanying texts, above. See also Bienvenu, *op. cit.*, p. 12.

347   See *Their Duty Done – Frederick George Faithfull* (https://tinyurl.com/yc2ttxvt) (at 18 October 2023); *The AIF Project – Frederick George Faithfull* (https://tinyurl.com/2n23j72h) (at 18 October 2023); and "Soldiers from the Snowline" in (2015) 38 *Voice of the Mountains* at p. 48 (https://tinyurl.com/3ex2bw2z) (at 23 October 2023).

348   See Stapleton, *op. cit.*, p. 115.

On 5 February 1883, William Henry Faithfull married Louisa Jane Jones in a Catholic marriage ceremony celebrated in Omeo by the Reverend Father Patrick O'Donoghue.[349] Louisa had been born in Omeo on 26 July 1863 on the banks of the Livingstone Creek, and had grown up in difficult circumstances.[350]

William and Louisa Faithfull went on to raise 11 children, and each of these in turn had large families. In the words of Ian Stapleton:

> "There sure are an awful lot of Faithfull around Omeo. Their family tree is a mind-boggling document."[351]

Matilda Margaret Moore

On 9 March 1840, and while still living on *Springfield*, the newly married Margaret Moore (née Considine) gave birth to her second child and first daughter. The infant girl was given the name Matilda Margaret Moore.[352] On or about 28 March 1840, she was christened by the Reverend William Sowerby in the original St. Saviour's Anglican Church in Goulburn. John and Margaret Moore were recorded as being her parents.[353]

Matilda grew up in the Moore family as an accepted child of her named parents.[354] However, although John Moore was named in the official documentation as Matilda's father, it seems highly likely that her biological father was William Pitt Faithfull.

William Pitt Faithfull never acknowledged that Matilda was his daughter. Although he seems to have materially assisted her older brother, George Faithfull, in life, William Pitt Faithfull apparently bestowed no material benefits on Matilda. Nonetheless, there a number of factors pointing to Faithfull being Matilda's biological father.

As Jenny Coates has persuasively observed:

---

349 See Bienvenu, *op. cit.*, p. 18.

350 See Stapleton, *op. cit.*, p. 115. Louisa's mother was a sister of Jack Riley. The latter is reputed to have been an inspiration, if not the inspiration, for Banjo Paterson's *The Man From Snowy River*: *ibid*. See also *The Man From Snowy River – Reality or Myth?* (https://tinyurl.com/hlcpkvd) (at 18 October 2023).

351 See Stapleton, *op. cit.*, p. 112. Ian Stapleton went on to quote the words of an old High Country identity, Jack Batty, as follows:
"They were always wonderful breeders, them Faithfulls. By Christ they were. Bred like Catholic rabbits. Must have been something in the water at Bingo that got 'em going. They used to say in Omeo that Benambra's got the Penders [Pendergasts], Omeo's got the Faithfulls, and 'The Creek's' [Swift's Creek] got bloody rabbits."
Ibid.

352 With respect to the possible origin of Matilda Margaret Moore's first name, see footnote 188 above.

353 See *Ancestry – Australia, Birth Index, 1788 – 1922: Matilda M Moore* (https://tinyurl.com/2mksvkdn) (at 19 October 2023).

354 Matilda was listed as a "Moore" in the Family Bible referred to in footnote 65 above.

"Curiously, a Matilda Faithfull began to appear as a witness at Faithfull weddings and baptisms in later years, including the marriage of Henry Faithfull, Margaret Considine's first child. No record of any other Matilda Faithfull can be found so it seems likely that when representing the Moore side of the family Matilda used Moore as her surname and Faithfull when at Faithfull family events. An examination of these signatures supports this contention as the signatures of Matilda Faithfull and Matilda Moore are almost identical. Perhaps out of respect for the man who raised her, or for her mother, Matilda Moore seemed careful never to openly declare her father as a Faithfull, preferring instead to name John Moore as her father, including at her marriage to Frank Heach."[355]

Jenny Coates went on to observe that:

"in 1938 one of William Pitt Faithfull's legitimate daughters, Constance Mary [Faithfull] died intestate in England. Henry and Alice Faithfull's daughter, Ada Mary Elliott, lodged a claim against the estate and in an effort to prove Henry's paternity an enquiry was made to the Registrar of the Bishop's Registry, Diocese of Wangaratta. His reply amongst other matters stated in relation to Matilda Heach (née Moore), 'While I cannot state any *facts* about Mrs. Heach's parentage, I can say quite definitely that I was informed by my late partner and always understood that she was an illegitimate daughter of George Faithfull'. This response suggests that the fact that John Moore was not Matilda's biological father was known and widely accepted." [356]

Jenny Coates further noted that neither Matilda nor Henry Faithfull had been named as a child of either John or Margaret Moore on John and Margaret's respective Death Certificates even though Matilda and Henry were still alive and John and Margaret's oldest son, John Moore Jnr, registered the deaths in both cases.[357]

It would appear that Matilda Moore continued to live as part of John and Margaret

---

[355] See Jenny Coates, "Margaret Considine (c. 1818 – 1895)" in *Conversations with Grandma* (https://tinyurl.com/ykmpz453) (at 19 October 2023).

[356] *Ibid.* According to Jenny Coates, the Registrar's letter was dated 7 March 1939, and the original is or was in the possession of Max Elliot: *ibid*, footnote 15. See also the *Faithfull Family Tree: Matilda Margaret Moore Faithfull* (https://tinyurl.com/3x24t33x) (at 19 October 2023).

[357] *Ibid.*

Moore's household until her marriage in 1857. On 20 July 1857, Matilda married Francis ("Frank") Heach in Holy Trinity Anglican Church, Wangaratta.[358]

Frank Heach was born towards the end of 1831 in or near to Upton-upon-Severn, Worcestershire in England to a farmer, Thomas Heach, and the latter's wife, Charlotte Heach. He was baptised in St Nicholas' Church at Queenhall in Worstershire.[359] It is unclear what formal education Frank received. However, in 1851, it would appear that he was living in Bath, Somerset and working as an assistant draper.

Frank Heach did not work for long in England as a draper. In 1853, he took ship from London on board the *Ganges*, bound for Victoria. Frank arrived in Melbourne on 22 June 1853.[360] How long he remained in Melbourne before ultimately moving to Wangaratta is not now known.

Frank Heach was a man of many parts. It appears that he worked for at least a time as a butcher in Wangaratta.[361] However, in the record of his marriage to Matilda Moore, in 1857 his occupation was said to be that of a storekeeper.[362] In 1864, he described himself as being a draper.[363] In time, Frank clearly branched out. By the 1870s at the latest, he was also a grazier and cattle dealer.[364] Further, in 1883, he was the licensee of the *Bull's Head* hotel,[365] and by the following year, of the *North Eastern* hotel[366]; both in Wangaratta. Frank undoubtedly pursued other business interests and investments over time. No doubt Frank's business prowess was one of the reasons why he was appointed one of his father-in-law, John Moore's, Executors and Trustees by the latter's Will.[367]

Frank and Matilda Heach had no issue. Having made a substantial amount of money, Frank and Matilda retired to suburban Melbourne at some time between 1884 and

---

358 See *Ancestry – Australia, Marriage Index, 1788 – 1950: Matilda Moore and Frank Heach* (https://tinyurl.com/wnsnjze4) (at 19 October 2023); and *WikiTree – Matilda Moore (1840 – 1912)* (https://tinyurl.com/2c4t429a) (at 19 October 2023).

359 See *Ancestry – England, Select Births and Christenings, 1538 – 1975: Francis Heach* (https://tinyurl.com/3avxxa59) (at 19 October 2023).

360 See *Victoria, Australia, Assisted and Unassisted Passenger Lists, 1839 – 1923 for F. Heach* (https://tinyurl.com/mrcnbkhr) (at 19 October 2023); and the *Colonial Times* (Hobart), Tuesday, 5 July 1857, p. 2.

361 See the *Ovens and Murray Advertiser*, Thursday, 10 August 1865, p. 3; Bienvenu, *op. cit.*, p. 12; and footnote 333 and its accompanying text above

362 See *Marriages in the District of Wangaratta – Frank Heach and Matilda Moore* (No. 1857/2754) (https://tinyurl.com/5e5ej3wu) (at 20 October 2023).

363 See the *Ovens and Murray Advertiser*, Saturday, 12 March 1864, p. 4.

364 See *The Australasian*, Saturday, 8 May 1875; the *Ovens and Murray Advertiser*, Saturday, 27 August 2023, p. 1; and Ian Jones, *Ned Kelly: A Short Life* (2008).

365 See the *Ovens and Murray Advertiser*, Saturday, 15 December 1883, p. 1.

366 See the *Ovens and Murray Advertiser*, Saturday, 13 December 1884, p. 7.

367 See footnote 285 and its accompanying text above.

1891. In December 1891, Frank was recorded as living in Nicholson Street, Essendon.[368] However, it would seem that both Frank and Matilda subsequently moved to live at "Powick" 55 Holmes Road, Moonee Ponds.[369]

Matilda Heach died on Sunday, 7 July 1912 at her Moonee Ponds home. She was buried on Tuesday, 9 July 1912 in the Coburg Pine Ridge Cemetery.[370]

Matilda died intestate. Her widower, Frank Heach, authorised the Trustees Executors and Agency Co. Ltd. to apply to the Supreme Court of Victoria for Letters of Administration of her estate. These were granted by the Court's Registrar of Probates on 15 August 1912.

At the time of her death, Matilda owned a five room brick house at 26 Eglinton Street, Moone Ponds. This was subsequently sold by the Administrator of her estate for £530.

Matilda's personal estate consisted of £361.4.4 in a bank account, jewellry and other personal effects valued at £34.2.4, and 480 shares in The Mutual Stores Limited Ltd valued at £708. After payment of debts, estate and administration expenses, the residue of the estate was distributed in accordance with the Victorian laws of intestacy; with Frank Heach receiving half and the balance going to some 19 of Matilda's Moore relatives.[371]

In 1913, Frank Heach married his housekeeper, Mary Elizabeth McCulloch.[372] He died on Saturday, 13 May 1922 at the advanced age of 90 years.[373] He was subsequently buried in Matilda's grave in the Coburg Pine Ridge Cemetery.[374]

Frank Heach died leaving a Will executed by him on 12 December 1921; together with two Codicils to that Will. By his Will, he appointed the Trustees Executors and Agency Co. Ltd. to be his Executor and Trustee. The latter duly secured probate of the Will and the two Codicils.

By his Will, Frank left a legacy of £100 to his widow, Mary Elizabeth Heach (née McCulloch), together with a life interest in his former home at 55 Holmes Street, Moonee Ponds, and in two adjacent properties, 57A and 59 Holmes Street, Moonee Ponds. Upon

---

368   See the *New South Wales Government Gazette* (No. 760), Tuesday, 1 December 1891, p. 9448.

369   See *Australia, Electoral Rolls, 1903 – 1980 for Francis Heach* (https://tinyurl.com/2p8mu6z4) (at 20 October 2023). See also Jenny Coates, "Sepia Saturday 219 – Arches and Significant Buildings" in *Conversations with Grandma* (https://tinyurl.com/unc5f8fs) (at 20 October 2023).

370   See *The Age*, Saturday, 13 July 1912, p. 5; and *Billion Graves – Matilda Heach (Moore)* (https://tinyurl.com/zznnm5xj) (at 20 October 2023).

371   See *Victoria, Australia, Wills and Probate Records, 1841 – 2009 for Matilda Heach* (Supreme Court of Victoria Probate and Administration No. 125502) (https://tinyurl.com/ycy87jxm) (at 22 October 2023).

372   See *Births Deaths and Marriages, Victoria (Marriages) – Francis Heach and Mary Elizabeth McCulloch* (No. 1913/6049) (https://tinyurl.com/2mjfm22d) (at 22 October 2023).

373   See *The Argus*, Wednesday, 17 May 1922, p. 1.

374   See *Billion Graves – Francis Heach* (https://tinyurl.com/mv3yf6tu) (at 22 October 2023). In 1940, Frank's second wife, Mary Elizabeth Heach (née McCulloch), was buried in the same grave; as was the latter's sister, Selina Jane Goulden, after her death in 1953: *ibid*.

her death, his non-monetary estate (including his real property) was to be sold and converted into money. From the residue of his estate then remaining, Frank directed his Executor and Trustee to pay:

- a legacy of £100 to Mrs Florence Hodgson (Henry Faithfull's third child);

- a legacy of £100 to William Henry Faithfull (Henry Faithfull's eldest child);

- a legacy of £100 to the Salvation Army;

- a legacy of £100 to an institution chosen by his Executor and Trustee which benefitted blinded soldiers; and

- a legacy of £200 to the Building Fund of the Wangaratta Atheneum and Public Library.

Following these payments, and the payment of his debts, funeral and testamentary expenses, Frank further directed his Executor and Trustee to invest £1,000 in Government securities; with the annual income from such investments to be paid to the General Funds of the Wangaratta Hospital.

Frank then directed that the balance of his residuary estate was to be paid to the Building Fund of the Church of England Cathedral at Wangaratta; with such monies to be expended as follows:

- £6,000 to be used to complete the Chancel end of the Cathedral (including the Chancel, Sanctuary, Vestries and Organ Chamber), and with a sum of not less than £500 and not more than £800 to be used for the erection in Frank's memory of "a suitable window or windows in such Sanctuary and a suitable tablet";

- in or towards the erection of a tower at the western end of the Cathedral; and

- the balance to be used for the general completion of the Cathedral.[375]

---

375 See *Victoria, Australia, Wills and Probate Records, 1841 – 2009 for Francis Heach* (Supreme Court of Victoria, Probate and Administration No. 183211) (https://tinyurl.com/z8cpsjyd) (at 23 October 2023).

By the first Codicil to his Will dated 29 March 1922, Frank varied his residuary gift to the Building Fund of the Cathedral by providing that in lieu of his direction as to the expenditure of the gifted monies contained in the Will, he wished but did not direct that such monies should be expended in the following manner:

- in the erection of a tower;

- in the purchase and installation in the tower of a peal of bells;

- in the purchase, building and erection of an organ to cost £1,000;

- in the erection in his memory of a suitable window or windows (at a cost of not more than £500) in the Sanctuary, with a suitable inscription; and

- the balance (if any) remaining to be used for the general completion of the Cathedral.[376]

By the second Codicil to the Will dated 5 April 1922, Frank directed his Executor and Trustee to invest out of the residue of his estate a sum not exceeding £3,000, to be known as "The Francis Heach Bequest", and to apply the income therefrom:

> "towards the maintenance and upkeep of the building of such Cathedral and towards the maintenance and upkeep of the Choir and the services of such Cathedral."

In all other respects, he confirmed both his Will and the first Codicil thereto.[377]

It would appear that by his Will and its two Codicils, Frank Heach left around £12,750 to the Anglican Church to be used in connection with the building and operation of the Cathedral.[378] The money was used to assist in paying for the construction of the Cathedral's Chancel and Sanctuary, and in part for the purchase of the Cathedral's organ. A plaque

---

376 *Ibid.*

377 *Ibid.*

378 See *Victorian Heritage Database Report – Holy Trinity Anglican Cathedral Close* (https://tinyurl.com/ksmmcrs) (at 23 October 2023); Colin Holden, *Church in a Landscape: A History of the Diocese of Wangaratta* (2002), p.73; the *Wangaratta Despatch*, Wednesday, 4 June 1924, p. 3; and the *Wangaratta Chronicle*, Saturday, 7 June 1924. See also Jenny Coates, "Sepia Saturday 219 – Arches and significant buildings" in *Conversations with Grandma* (https://tinyurl.com/unc5f8fs) (at 23 October 2023).

was affixed to the wall of the Sanctuary in Frank's memory. According to an address by the Bishop of Wangaratta, Bishop Armstrong, to the Diocesan Synod in 1924, the Rose Window over the High Altar was also dedicated as a special memorial to Frank.[379]

Unfortunately, it would seem that there was insufficient money available from Frank Heach's estate to pay for the construction of a tower for the Cathedral or for the purchase of either an organ or bells.[380] Frank's widow, Mary Heach, apparently complained to the press about the delay in the Cathedral's acquisition of the bells. They were ultimately acquired in 1976, but remained in storage until the Cathedral's timber-clad tower was constructed in 1983.[381]

John Moore Junior

John Moore Jnr was the third child of Margaret Moore (née Considine), and likely the first child fathered by Margaret's husband, John Moore Snr. As mentioned above, he was born in Goulburn on or around 16 January 1843, and baptised in March 1843 in St Saviour's Anglican Church, Goulburn.[382] Later in that year, he accompanied his parents and his mother's two older children from *Springfield* near Goulburn to the King River valley in the Port Phillip District after his father had been appointed as overseer of William Pitt Faithfull's *Ten Mile Hollow* run. John Moore Jnr spent his formative years with his parents' growing family in the valleys of the King and Ovens Rivers and then, in or after about 1854, on the farm acquired by his father known as *Tenterfield* which was situated on the One Mile Creek to the west of Wangaratta.

No doubt John would have been taught by his father to ride, to raise and care for sheep and cattle, and to farm the land. It seems clear that as an adult, he spent most, if not all, his working life as a farmer. [383]

Tracing the life of John Moore Jnr through publicly available documentation presents a number of difficulties. In the first place, such documentation does not always distinguish between John and his father; simply referring to "John Moore" at times when their adult

---

379 See the *Wangaratta Chronicle* (Special Issue), Wednesday, 4 June 1924. See also *Holy Trinity Cathedral Wangaratta 1908 – 2008: Centenary History Booklet*; and photos 31 and 32 below.

380 *Ibid.*

381 See Holden, *op. cit.*, p. 264. The bells were purchased from St George's Anglican Church, Bolton in England. They are the oldest ring of eight bells in Australia, and were cast in 1806 after the battle of Trafalgar. The bells were housed in the Cathedral's tower in 1986: see *Holy Trinity Cathedral Wangaratta: A Short History and Guide*.

382 See footnote 234 and its accompanying text above.

383 John was described as a "Farmer" after his death in the Accounts filed in the Supreme Court of Victoria by his eldest son and administrator of his estate, John George Moore: see *Victoria, Australia, Wills and Probate Records, 1841 – 2009 for John Moore Jnr.* (Supreme Court of Victoria, Probate and Administration No. 72/380) (https://tinyurl.com/29tx4wwv) (at 24 October 2023).

lives clearly overlapped.[384] The context in which the name appears sometimes provides a clue, but not always.[385]

In the second place, it would seem that there were a number of other men bearing the name "John Moore" who were living in the north-east of Victoria contemporaneously with John Moore Jnr. There was a "John Moore" who was a miner living near Yackandandah for one.[386] Perhaps more significantly for present purposes, there was a "John Moore" who worked as a "hairdresser" or barber in Wangaratta during the 1860s and 1870s. In 1868, this "John Moore" was said to be living in Murphy Street, Wangaratta with a shoemaker, Edward Greathead – this at a time some four years after John Moore Junior had married.[387] And in a "sly grog" case heard in the Wangaratta Police Court some two years later in 1870 in which he had been a witness for the accused man, John Moore gave evidence that:

"I have been a hairdresser for 24 years. I have lived in London, Melbourne, and Sandhurst [Bendigo]."[388]

Finally, it would appear that John Moore Jnr did not have much of a public persona; substantially devoting his adult life to his wife, his children and his farming activities.

On 1 February 1864, John married Elizabeth Mary Clark in Holy Trinity Church, Wangaratta.[389] At the time of their marriage, John was 21 years old. His bride was 20 years of age.

Elizabeth Mary Clark was born on 30 June 1843 in the *Hope Inn* on the left bank of the Ovens River, where Wangaratta is now situated.[390] She was likely baptised in or on the bank of the Ovens River on 28 January 1846 by the Reverend A. C. Thomson, the

---

384 See, for example, reports of debts said to be owed by "John Moore" to the Wangaratta Hospital in 1887: see the *Ovens and Murray Advertiser*, Saturday, 23 April 1887, p. 12; and the *Ovens and Murray Advertiser*, Saturday, 19 November 1887, p. 9.

385 By way of example, in July 1879, "John Moore, a farmer at Wangaratta" gave character evidence in a Wangaratta General Sessions criminal trial on behalf of the accused, Maria Elvire Larkins. He deposed that he had known Larkins for 27 years, and "never knew anything against her character before": see the *Ovens and Murray Advertiser*, Tuesday, 15 July 1879, p. 3. If the "John Moore" who gave evidence was John Moore Jnr, then he would have been around nine years old when he first met Ms Larkins. Although this was clearly a possibility, it seems much more likely that it was John Moore Snr who first met Ms Larkins in about 1852.

386 See the *Ovens and Murray Advertiser*, Saturday, 25 September 1873, p. 4; and the *Ovens and Murray Advertiser*, Saturday, 13 October 1883, p. 1.

387 See the *Ovens and Murray Advertiser*, Thursday, 22 October 1868, p. 2. "John Moore the barber" appears to have been something of a wild man. Edward Greathead was giving evidence on behalf of John Moore during the course of a committal hearing in the Wangaratta Police Court in which Moore was facing a charge of assault occasioning grievous bodily harm. Moore was duly committed for trial and released on bail: *ibid*. What eventuated thereafter remains unknown. See also the *Ovens and Murray Advertiser*, Saturday, 16 January 1869, p. 2.

388 See the *Ovens and Murray Advertiser*, Thursday, 12 May 1870, p. 4.

389 See *Ancestry – Victoria, Australia, Marriage Index, 1788 – 1950: John Moore and Elizabeth Mary Clark* (No. 1864/333) (https://tinyurl.com/4vfsfx76) (at 25 October 2023).

390 See *Ancestry – Victoria, Australia, Birth Index, 1788 – 1922: Elizabeth Mary Clark* (Registration No. 14586) (https://tinyurl.com/44acfm8y) (at 25 October 2023).

itinerant incumbent of St. James' Anglican Church in Melbourne.[391] Elizabeth was the third child and second daughter of William Henry Clark and his wife, Elizabeth Clark (née Harris). Henry Clark was a pioneer settler on the Ovens River (arriving there in 1838) and is frequently referred to as "the Father of Wangaratta".[392]

Little appears to be known of Elizabeth Mary Clark's early years. Prior to her marriage to John Clark Jnr, she presumably spent the bulk of her time immersed in family and household duties in the Clark family home. Elizabeth and John went on to have a total of 10 children together. All survived to adulthood, and were as follows:

- Charlotte Margaret Moore, born on the Ovens River at Wangaratta on or slightly before 25 April 1864.

- John George ("Flash Jack") Moore, born at Wangaratta on or a little before 17 June 1866.

- Margaret Sarah Moore, born at Wangaratta on or shortly prior to 20 August 1868.

- Sarah Ann Moore, born at Wangaratta on or slightly prior to 2 September 1870.

- William Clark Moore, born at Wangaratta on or shortly before 18 November 1872.

- Henry Arthur ("Harry") Moore, born at Wangaratta on or a little before 13 September 1875.

- Thomas Edward Moore, born at Wangandary a little to the west of Wangaratta on or slightly before 3 December 1876.

- Elizabeth Mary Moore, born at Wangandary on or a little prior to 29 January 1878.

- Charles Ernest Moore, born at Wangandary on or slightly prior to 21 February 1881.

- Edith Sophia Moore, born at Wangaratta on or shortly before 23 May 1884.[393]

Prior to his marriage to Elizabeth Mary Clark, John was likely engaged in farming and grazing land in the vicinity of Wangaratta. In his early years, the land in question

---

391 *Ibid.* See also footnote 253 and its accompanying text above.

392 See Garry Moore, *The Clark Brothers: Pioneer Squatters in the North East of Victoria* (2023), pp. 91 – 92.

393 See the *Moore Considine Family Website – John Moore Jnr.* (https://tinyurl.com/j33nctz: access code - seemoore) (at 26 October 2023). It may well be that Elizabeth Mary Moore's mother, Elizabeth Clark, delivered most, if not all, of her Daughter's children: see the *Ovens and Murray Advertiser*, Saturday, 13 October 1888, p. 6.

was likely his father's property, *Tenterfield*.³⁹⁴ However, by 1866 at the latest, it appears that he had acquired his own rural land; acquiring it by way of an inter vivos gift from his father-in-law, William Clark. The land gifted consisted of a block in the north-west corner of a parcel of land owned by Clark and referred to on the Victorian cadastre as *Pre-Emptive Section E*, together with some adjacent land.³⁹⁵

Pre-Emptive Section E itself was a section of William Clark's original *Ovens Crossing Place* squatting run. Covering a total of 640 acres, and located in the vicinity of the intersection of what are now Sessions and the Warby Range Roads, *Pre-Emptive Section E* was purchased by Clark from the Victorian Government by way of a Crown Grant in 1858.³⁹⁶

On 24 April 1871, William Clark, the father of John's wife, Elizabeth Mary Moore, died.³⁹⁷ By clause 2 of his Will dated 24 February 1871, he provided:

> "I give and devise to my daughter, Elizabeth Mary, wife of John Moore the younger, and her heirs for her sole and separate use during her life and to her right heirs in fee all those my lands known as and being part of my preemptive section of land for the Ovens Crossing Place run lying between the land of John Moore the younger and the Ovens River which portion of my lands is defined by posts and shown upon a sketch of my preemptive section. And also Allotments one and two of Section 40, Wangaratta."³⁹⁸

Further, and by clause 6 of his Will, William Clark left Elizabeth Mary Moore a share in his residuary estate.³⁹⁹

Although the rural land was left to his wife, there can be little doubt that it was thereafter farmed and grazed by John Moore Jnr. When combined with his own adjacent land, the devise would have given John a substantial property extending to the east to the Ovens River.

It would seem that by 1877, John and Elizabeth had each also acquired adjoining parcels of land on the Ovens River at Wangandary. On or about 5 February 1887, John

---

394 John Moore Jnr may well have been the "John Moore" who participated in a ploughing contest conducted by the Ovens and Murray Agricultural and Horticultural Association on *Bontharambo* on Tuesday, 3 July 1860: see the *Ovens and Murray Advertiser*, Wednesday, 11 July 1860, p. 3.

395 See Faithfull and Lewis, *op. cit.*, p. 102.

396 See Faithfull and Lewis, *op. cit.*, pp. 20, 96 and 98.

397 See the *Deaths Registered in New South Wales – William Clark* (1871) (No. 1872/2828).

398 See *William Clark's Will* (PROV, VPRS 28/P0, Unit 103).

399 *Ibid.*

made an application to the Commissioner of Titles to bring his parcel under the Victorian *Transfer of Land Statute*. The land referred to in the application was described as:

> "Part of Crown pre-emptive section A, known as Wangandary in the Parish of South Wangaratta, County of Moira, commencing at the intersection of the Wangaratta and Bundalong Road and the Ovens River; thence south by that road 6020 links; thence east 3140 links; thence north 1650 links to a swamp; thence northerly by that swamp to the Ovens River; then westerly by that river to the commencing point."[400]

In like manner, Elizabeth made application on or about 27 March 1877 to bring her parcel of land under the *Transfer of Land Statute*. Her land was described as:

> "Part of Crown section A, known as "Wangandary", Parish of South Wangaratta, county of Moira, commencing on the western margin of a lagoon; 3140 links east, from a point 4370 links south from the [401]north-west corner of the said section; thence northerly by that margin to the Ovens River; thence west 4420 links; and thence north 384 links to the commencing point."

On a date a little before 17 June 1879, John Moore Jnr successfully applied for a Crown Grant of 60 acres of land at Wangaratta North.[402] Precisely where this land was situated is not presently known.

How John managed these various parcels of land is likewise currently unknown. However, it seems fair to say that he would no doubt have farmed and/or grazed them all. By 1878 at the latest, he would appear to have moved with his family onto his land at Wangandary.[403]

It might be noted that a "John Moore" was fined 2s 6d in the Wangaratta Police Court for neglecting to send a child to school for the requisite number of days.[404] On 24 August 1881, a "John Moore" was further fined 7s 6d in the same Court for the third instance of that offence.[405] Again, a "John Moore" was fined 2s 6d in the Wangaratta Police Court

---

400 See the *Ovens and Murray* Advertiser, Thursday, 8 February 1877, p. 3. One link equals 0.201 metres.
401 See the *Ovens and Murray Advertiser*, Thursday, 29 March 1877, p. 3.
402 See the *Ovens and Murray Advertiser*, Tuesday, 17 June 1879, p. 2.
403 John and Elizabeth Moore's seventh child and fourth son, Thomas Edward Moore, was said to have been born at Wangandary on or a little before 3 December 1876: see footnote 393 and its accompanying text above.
404 See the *Ovens and Murray Advertiser*, Saturday, 14 August 1880, p. 5.
405 See the *Ovens and Murray Advertiser*, Saturday, 27 August 1881, p. 1.

for the same offence on Tuesday, 5 April 1887.[406] Whether the "John Moore" in all or any of these matters was John Moore Jnr. is currently unascertained.

In the Wangaratta Police Court on 16 June 1887, Constable Dainty summoned a "John Moore" for obstructing the footpath in Rowan Street by allowing a cart to remain thereon. The Defendant admitted the obstruction and stated that he was unloading a dray of wood and was obliged to venture onto the footpath owing to there being no gate. In those circumstances, the Court dismissed the charge.[407] Once more, whether this "John Moore" was John Moore Jnr is not now known. However, given John's rural and farming circumstances, it seems likely the he was the Defendant concerned.

On Monday, 3 August 1891, John Moore Snr died.[408] He left a Will executed by him on 6 January 1888. By that Will, and after the payment of his debts and a number of specific bequests, he left the residue of his estate to be held in trust for his widow, Margaret Moore, for her use during the remainder of her life. Upon her death, the balance of the residuary estate was to be distributed between some, but not all, of his children. Those benefiting included John Moore Jnr. In accordance with the Will, the latter's share was to be the land consisting of Allotments 1 and 2, Section 6, Parish of Wangaratta; together with a share in his father's residuary personal property.[409]

John Moore Snr's widow, Margaret Moore, died on Wednesday, 10 July 1895.[410] Presumably, her death was followed by John Moore Jnr's receipt of the land and personal property left to him by his father's Will. Unfortunately, he would not have had much time to enjoy it.

On Monday, 19 December 1898, Elizabeth Moore died at the Women's Hospital in Melbourne. She had apparently been suffering from colon cancer for nine months, and died from a combination of that disease and exhaustion. She was 55 years old when she died. Elizabeth was buried in the Wangaratta Cemetery on Wednesday, 21 December 1898.[411]

A little over 6 months after Elizabeth Moore's death, John Moore Jnr died in Wangaratta on Tuesday, 4 July 1899. He was 56 years old when he died. His cause of death was recorded as being from "general paralysis" of some two years in duration. Unfortunately, there would appear to be no record as to what was the cause of John's

---

406 See the *Ovens and Murray Advertiser*, Saturday, 9 April 1887, p. 10.
407 See the *Ovens and Murray Advertiser*, Thursday, 18 June 1887, p. 4.
408 See footnote 278 and its accompanying text above.
409 See footnotes 286 and 288, together with their accompanying texts, above.
410 See footnote 296 and its accompanying text above.
411 See *Deaths in the District of Carlton in the Colony of Victoria – Elizabeth Moore* (No. 1898/15508) (https://tinyurl.com/yckfdkkm) (at 29 October 2023).

general paralysis. He was buried on Thursday, 6 July 1899 in his late wife's grave in the Wangaratta Cemetery.[412]

Unlike his father, John Moore Jnr died intestate. On 28 August 1899, Letters of Administration of his estate were granted in the Supreme Court of Victoria by the Registrar of Probates to John's eldest son, John George Moore.[413] In his Inventory filed with the Court, John George Moore declared that the only real property in his late father's estate consisted of the land comprised in Allotments 1, 2 and 3, Section 6, Parish of North Wangaratta, County of Moira; and that his late father left no personal estate.

John George Moore stated in his Inventory that the allotments in his late father's real property contained:

> "19 acres 2 roods 36 perches more or less used for grazing and cultivation; together with the buildings thereon consisting of a four roomed weatherboard cottage with iron roof, stable and hayshed. Municipal assessment £19 per annum. Estimated value £10 per acre - £197.6.0.

This property is subject to a mortgage to James Brien to secure £120 and interest."[414]

On the face of matters, it would appear that John Moore Jnr was virtually insolvent at the time of his death. Given that he was seemingly paralysed for some two years prior to his death, and that his late wife had been suffering from cancer for nine months before she died, it may be that much of his estate had been realised by John to pay medical and like expenses. Alternatively, John may have made a number of bad investment in his later years; years marked by a severe economic depression in Victoria. However, it is also possible that in anticipation of his death, he gave most of his property to his children by way of inter vivos gifts prior to dying to escape death duty.

William Moore

On 23 November 1845, Margaret Moore gave birth at the Moore family's home on William Pitt Faithfull's *Hedi* run beside the King River to twin boys, who were duly

---

412 See *Deaths in the District of Wangaratta in the Colony of Victoria: John Moore (Jnr.)* (No. 1899/11521) (https://tinyurl.com/5cejantp) (at 29 October 2023).

413 See *Ancestry – Victoria, Australia, Wills and Probate Records, 1841 – 2009: John Moore (Jnr.)* (https://tinyurl.com/54nadsjn) (at 29 October 2023).

414 *Ibid.*

named William Moore and George Moore.[415] Although the matter is not entirely free from doubt, the two boys may well have been identical, rather than fraternal, twins.[416] On 10 April 1848, the twins were baptised by the Reverend A. C. Thomson of St. James' Anglican Church, Melbourne.[417]

Like most of their siblings, William and George Moore grew up on the *Hedi* and later the *Whorouly* runs in the King and Ovens River valleys (on which runs their father was successively employed as overseer) and finally the farm known as *Tenterfield* purchased by their father on the One Mile Creek near Wangaratta.

The can be no doubt that William and George would have been taught the skills of farming and grazing by their father on these rural properties. They would also have been taught to ride, handle and care for horses. Equally, there can be no doubt that William, for one, came to love horses; working with them throughout his adult life and acquiring the nickname "Horse".[418]

As an adult, William Moore worked widely with horses in the north-east of Victoria. He worked for some years as a drover for Mr Dominic Farrell on *Edi* station.[419] In addition to driving cattle and horses throughout the district, he apparently gained expertise in horse breaking. It was said in his obituary published in the *Wangaratta Chronicle* on Wednesday, 18 November 1908 that he:

> "was recognised as the most careful and trustworthy drover that the district possessed, while his knowledge of horses and cattle was unlimited. For the handling and breaking in of a young horse he had the confidence of the principal

---

415 See the *Moore Considine Family Website – William Moore* (https://tinyurl.com/j33nctz: access code - seemoore) (at 30 October 2023).

416 Following William Moore's death in 1908, a friend who had known him for 46 years, George Moore, remarked of William in a letter:
"When he and his late twin brother George were young men – that was when they were 17 years of age – when I first knew them, they were so much alike that it was hard to distinguish one from the other."
See the *Ovens and Murray Advertiser*, Saturday, 2 January 1908, p. 15. The letter's author was not related to the two men, emigrating from England to Victoria in 1851: see *The Weekly Times*, Saturday, 9 March 1929, p. 5.

417 See *Baptisms Solemnised in the Parish of St. James Melbourne in the County of Bourke in the Year 1848 – William and George Moore* (https://tinyurl.com/3wpvem6z) (at 31 October 2023). See also footnote 253 and its accompanying text above. It probably says something about the remoteness of the Moore family's homes that it took some three and a half years following their births before it likely became possible to have William and George baptised.

418 In a statement contained in a one page document authored by one of William's grandsons, Albert Edgar ("Bert") Moore, dated 1992 and entitled "RE William & Alice Rebecca MOORE" ("*Albert Moore's 1992 document*"), Bert wrote:
"A National School was opened in 1850 and stood where the present Chisholm Street [Wangaratta] State School [stands] and young William and his brothers may have attended that school".
I have a copy of this document.

419 See William Moore's obituary in the *Wangaratta Chronicle*, Wednesday, 18 November 1908, p. 3. The *Edi* station, formerly in the possession of William Pitt Faithfull and serially known earlier as the *Ten Mile Hollow* and the *Hedi* run, had apparently been inherited by Dominic Farrell from his father, J. J. Farrell: see the *Wangaratta Chronicle*, Saturday, 19 October 1918, p. 2.

horse-owners throughout the Wangaratta district, and for 30 years had broken in horses for Messrs F. G. and J. G. Docker of Bontharambo and Myrrhee."[420]

On Wednesday, 1 May 1872, William Moore married Alice Rebecca Clark in Holy Trinity Church in Benalla. The witnesses to the marriage were Jonathan Harris, Alice's maternal grandfather, and Jemima Maria Clark, one of Alice's younger sisters. Both the bride and the groom were said to be usually resident in Wangaratta but presently residing in Benalla. William was 26 years old at the time of the marriage; Alice was 20 years of age.[421]

Alice Rebecca Moore (née Clark) was born or shortly before 12 December 1851 in her father's *Commercial Inn* at Wangaratta.[422] She was the eighth child and sixth daughter of William Henry Clark and his wife, Elizabeth Clark (née Harris). Her father, and perhaps her mother, had likely been friendly with William Moore's father, and perhaps William's mother, for a number of years prior to the marriage. William Moore older brother, John Moore Jnr, had married Alice's older sister. Elizabeth Mary Clark, on 1 February 1864.[423]

An interesting question arises as to why William and Alice chose to be married in Benalla, although usually resident in Wangaratta according to their marriage record. Given his work with horses, William clearly moved around the north-east of Victoria. His work may have taken him to Benalla at the time of his marriage. If so, it is not presently known where he was living in or around Benalla or who he was working for.

Alice was presumably living with her grandfather in his home at the time of the marriage. It will be recalled that her grandfather was one of the witnesses to the marriage. But what drew her to live in Benalla in the first place? It is possible that the fact that she was the mother of an illegitimate child when she married may have had something to do with her relocation to Benalla from Wangaratta. Alice Rebecca Clark gave birth in Benalla on 8 August 1869 to a daughter who she named Alice Rosetta Clark. The informant for the purposes of the birth record was her maternal grandfather, Jonathan Harris.[424]

It may be that Alice Rebecca Clark travelled to her grandfather's Benalla home for

---

420 See the *Wangaratta Chronicle*, Wednesday, 18 November 1908, p. 3.

421 See *Marriages in the District of Benalla in the Colony of Victoria – William Moore and Alice Rebecca Clark* (https://tinyurl.com/33pprfeu) (at 31 October 2023). Being illiterate, Jonathan signed the Marriage Certificate with an "x". See also photos 33 and 34 below

422 See *Births Registered in the District of Wangaratta in the Colony of Victoria – Alice Rebecca Clark* (https://tinyurl.com/yx2b84yv) (at 31 October 2023); and the *Moore Considine Family Website – Alice Rebecca Clark* (https://tinyurl.com/j33nctz: access code - seemoore) (at 31 October 2023).

423 See footnote 389 and its accompanying text above.

424 See *Births in the District of Benalla in the Colony of Victoria – Alice Rosetta Clark* (https://tinyurl.com/y2dba49t) (at 31 October 2023).

the birth of her first child to avoid ostracism arising from her pregnancy and emanating from her immediate family in Wangaratta or from the wider Wangaratta community; with mother and child remaining in Benalla until Alice Rebecca Clark's marriage to William Moore some three years later. This is, of course, all speculation. The truth of the matter is probably now hidden by the mists of time.[425]

The identity of Alice Rosetta Clark's biological father remains unknown. He could well have been William Moore. Whatever be the case, it is clear that Alice Rosetta Clark was fully accepted into William's household after the marriage; adopting the surname "Moore" seemingly without being formally adopted by William.

Following their marriage, William and Alice returned to Wangaratta. William had apparently acquired land adjacent to, or partly coextensive with, his father's *Tenterfield* property. The land extended to and beyond the junction of Three Mile and One Mile Creeks. William and Alice called the property *The Three Mile*.[426] Near to the junction itself, William built a house on the property in which he and Alice were to live for the balance of their respective lives. Their grandson, Albert Moore wrote this of his grandparents' house:

> "Their home as I remember it:- mostly [built] of slabs and not large. The water available was from a nearby well which was strong tasting and my father described it as 'brackish'."[427]

After William and Alice Moore moved into their Wangaratta home with Alice Rosetta Moore, they had a further nine children together. These were:

- Jemima Emily ("Mimi")Moore, born on or a little before 9 February 1873.

- William Henry Moore, born on or shortly prior to 27 September 1874.

- George Moore, born on or a little before 10 August 1876.

---

425 It might be noted that Alice Rebecca Clark's father, William Henry Clark, died on 24 April 1871: see footnote 379 and its accompanying text above. However, it is difficult to see how his death could have contributed to Alice's stay or stays in Benalla. Unlike her older sister, Elizabeth Mary Moore (née Clark), Alice did not receive any land under her father's Will. However, like her other siblings, she did ultimately receive a share of his residuary estate: see *William Clark's Will* (*PROV*, VPRS 28/P0, Unit 103).

426 This account is contained in a one page document entitled "*William Moore of Three Mile Wangaratta*" apparently typed by Albert Edgar ("Bert") Moore in September 1991 ("*Albert Moore's 1991 document*"). I have a copy of this document.

427 This statement is to be found in *Albert Moore's 1992 document*. At the time he wrote it, Albert Moore was living in St. John's Aged Care Village located on Williams Road, Wangaratta. In his *1992 document*, he further stated:
"I can from the front door of our unit at St. John's Village look out over the Tree Mille Creek onto what was once William's farm and later taken over by my father. Today a very fine State School [the Appin Park Primary School] stands there together with an educational facility for less gifted children [the Wangaratta District Specialist School]."
See footnote 418 above. See also *The Chronicle*, Friday, 24 March 1995, p. 6.

- Albert Arthur ("Bert") Moore, born on or a short time before 10 November 1877.

- Francis Richard Moore, born on or a little before 25 December 1878.

- Mary Elizabeth ("Molly") Moore, born on or shortly before 7 July 1880.

- Alice Ann Cusack Moore, born on or shortly prior to 27 March 1882.

- Frederick Edward Charles Moore, born on or a short while before 8 July 1883.

- James Edgar Gordon ("Gordie") Moore, born on or a little before 11 May 1885.

All of William and Alice's children were born in Wangaratta, save for Alice Ann Cusack Moore, who was born in Oxley. William may have been temporarily working nearby when she was born. Unfortunately she died when less than two month old – also in Oxley. The remaining children all survived into adulthood.[428]

After moving onto *The Three Mile*, William Moore farmed the land. However, he was thereafter mainly engaged in breeding, buying and selling horses and continuing his work as a drover.[429]

Easter Monday in 1878 saw William Moore assaulted in Chisholm Street, Wangaratta by two men: John Jones and John Banks. The circumstances surrounding the assault are somewhat obscure. However, it would seem that William's brother-in-law, Frank Heach, enlisted William's support to gain possession of a hearse and a wagonette from a Mr John Grant. Heach asserted that both he and an unidentified bank had unidentified interests in the hearse and the wagonette, and that he had been authorised by the bank to seize them from Grant. After the two vehicles had been taken out of Grant's property and on to Chisholm Street, William had been grabbed by his whiskers by John Jones. This resulted in hair being pulled out of William's beard. William was subsequently struck with a swingle bar on the back of his head by John Banks. The blow left him in pain for some two weeks. Both Jones and Banks were apparently acting in support of Grant.

The assault case was heard in the Wangaratta Police Court on 20 June 1878. Both Jones and Banks were found guilty by the Court of assaulting William. Jones was fined 10s, with 26s costs. Banks was fined 40s, with 36s costs.[430]

---

428 See the *Moore Considine Family Website – Alice Rebecca Clark* (https://tinyurl.com/j33nctz: access code - seemoore) (at 31 October 2023).

429 See *Albert Moore's 1991 document*. See also photo 35 below.

430 See the *Ovens and Murray Advertiser*, Saturday, 8 June 1878, p. 5; and the *Ovens and Murray Advertiser*, Saturday, 22 June 1878, p. 4. The swingle bar with which Banks struck William on the head was a horizontal bar used to balance the pull of a draught horse when pulling a vehicle.

Two cases heard in 1880 in the Wangaratta County Court saw William Moore in the position of a defendant rather than a claimant. In each case, a James Sloan successfully sued William for goods sold and delivered. In the first case, heard on Wednesday, 1 September 1880, William was ordered to pay Sloan £4.9.0 plus costs.[431] In the second case, heard on Thursday, 9 December 1880, he was ordered to pay Sloan £4.9.1.[432] William does not appear to have defended either case. What the goods sold and delivered by Sloan to William were, and why William had not paid for them prior to the Court cases is not now known. James Sloan was apparently a Wangaratta draper.[433]

On Thursday, 22 May 1890 a young man named John Dowling was sentenced in the Wangaratta Police Court to six months imprisonment in Beechworth Gaol for stealing and cashing a cheque for £15.1.5 made out to William Moore and pocketing the proceeds. William gave evidence that he had received the cheque from Messrs J. H. Teague and Co. but had lost it.[434] It seems that J. H. Teague and Co. were stock agents and auctioneers.[435]

William Moore's father, John Moore, died on 5 August 1891. Under his Will, executed by him on 6 January 1888, John gave his widow, Margaret Moore, a life interest in the residue of his estate. Upon her death, he provided that the property comprised in Allotment 4, Section 6, Parish of Wangaratta, together with a share in his personal property, was to be gifted to William.[436]

On Tuesday, 8 January 1895, William appeared as a witness in the Benalla Court of Petty Sessions in a case in which a James Field sued a Patrick Macauley for wrongfully detention of three horses belonging to Field. William's evidence related to his identification of one of the horses and his knowledge of Field's ownership of it. William deposed that he had first seen the horse in question at Whorouly some four years previously. In the event, the Court ordered that Macauley return two of the horses to Field (the third horse having died) and further pay Field £5.8.8 in costs.[437]

A brief report published in the *Benalla Standard* on Tuesday, 27 January 1903 stated that William had been severely kicked on the back of the hand by a young horse which he was breaking in.[438] It is not known exactly how William came to be kicked by the

---

431 See the *Ovens and Murray Advertiser*, Saturday, 4 September 1880, p. 1.

432 See the *Ovens and Murray Advertiser*, Saturday, 11 December 1880, p. 1.

433 See the *Ovens and Murray Advertiser*, Saturday, 28 February 1885, p. 8.

434 See the *Ovens and Murray Advertiser*, Saturday, 24 May 1890, p. 6; and the *Ovens and Murray Advertiser*, Saturday, 31 May 1890, p. 4.

435 See the *Nagambie Times*, Friday, 26 May 1882, p. 2.

436 See footnote 288 and its accompanying text above.

437 See the *North Eastern Ensign*, Friday, 11 January 1895, p. 2.

438 See the *Benalla Standard*, Tuesday, 27 January 1903, p. 3.

horse or what the consequences of the kick were for William. However, it would seem that he was still breaking in horses notwithstanding that he was then 57 years old.

After his family, horses appear to have been the love of William Moore's life. From 1868 until his death in 1908, William acted as Clerk of the Course at the Wangaratta Racecourse during the many horse racing meetings conducted there.[439] As Charles Moore noted:

> "It was a very responsible position, and one requiring skill and experience in guiding, leading, directing and shepherding the many entrants and their mounts as they took part in the various events, and sometimes having to bring a runaway horse under control."[440]

Charles Moore went on to state that in performing his duties as Clerk of the Course, William:

> "must surely have been an impressive sight; clad in red riding coat, white riding breeches, finishing in "concertina" leggings and riding boots, both highly polished."[441]

On Saturday, 18 January 1902, the *Ovens and Murray Advertiser*, under the sub-heading "A LONG SERVICE RECORD", wrote:

> "It is not many racing officials who can even approach the record achieved by Mr. William Moore, who as Clerk of the Course for the various race meetings at Wangaratta, completed his 34th year of office on the 8th inst., never having missed a single meeting during that period. Mr. Moore has deservedly gained the reputation of having always been courteous and obliging, and it has been suggested that the members of the racing club might mark their appreciation of his services by presenting him with a suitable testimonial."[442]

---

439 See the *Ovens and Murray Advertiser*, Saturday, 18 January 1902, p. 10; William also officiated over many years as Clerk of the Course at the annual Wangaratta Agricultural Show. See also the *North-Eastern Despatch*, Tuesday, 28 April 1908, pp. 3 and 4. Following William's death in 1908, one of his sons, Francis Richard Moore, took over these duties: see *Albert Moore's 1991 document*.

440 See the document authored by Charles Bertram ("Bert") Moore, a grandson of George Moore, and dated 23 February 1987 ("*Charles Bertram Moore's 1987 document*"). I have a copy of this document.

441 Ibid. See also photo 36 below. This photo is of William Moore in his uniform as Clark of the Course. The original is held by the Wangaratta Racing Club in its Club Rooms.

442 See the *Ovens and Murray Advertiser*, Saturday, 18 January 1902. See also photo 37 below.

It is not now known whether William in fact received the suggested testimonial or not. Horses were undoubtedly central to William Clark's work and life. It is sad and ironic that a horse was the cause of his death in Wangaratta on Saturday, 14 November 1908.[443] The circumstances associated with his death were traced in detail in an obituary published in the *Wangaratta Chronicle* on Wednesday, 18 November 1908. The obituary stated that:

> "Perhaps no sudden death that has occurred in the Wangaratta district for many years past occasioned such genuine expressions of sorrow and regret as that which occurred at Wangaratta on Saturday morning last when Mr. William Moore Snr was thrown from his horse and killed almost instantaneously.
>
> Mr. Moore was one of the most widely known identities in the district and his unexpected demise came as a painful shock to his relatives and numerous acquaintances. The sad fatal riding accident occurred on Saturday morning whilst he was following his duties as a drover, but precisely how the accident was brought about no-one can authoritatively explain. Mr. Moore, with Messrs. C. Evans, J. Cowan, R. Tutty and D. Hoban left the Wangaratta Market Yards at about 7 o'clock driving a mob of 32 horses to the One Mile Creek for water prior to taking them to the trucking yards at the Railway Station. Before leaving the sale-yards, Mr. Moore remarked to the owner of the horses that the animal he was riding was rather high spirited and that he would ride a pony that was in the mob if the owner had no objection. The owner consenting, Mr. Moore captured the pony and started off on it. Mr. Tutty and Mr. Evans rode in front of the mob, Mr. Cowan on the left hand side and Messrs Moore and Hoban in the rear. Considerable dust was raised by the horses as they proceeded along Ovens Street, and when at the rear of Mr. D. Kane's private residence, Mr. Cowan observed the animal that Mr. Moore was riding in amongst the mob riderless and he informed Mr. Evans who rode back to ascertain what had happened. Mr. Moore was found lying on the footpath, close to Messrs. Wilson Bros. grain store. By this time, Mr. Kane had arrived to render assistance to the deceased, as a lady next door who saw the man lying on the ground directed his attention to the occurrence. Mr. Moore was lying in a pool of blood and was insensible. He was taken to Miss Dunkley's Private Hospital, where Dr. Henderson saw him and pronounced him to be in a dying state. The doctor considered the base of the skull had been fractured, while other serious

---

443 See *Deaths in the District of Wangaratta in the State of Victoria – William Moore* (https://tinyurl.com/4k3bu64s) (at 2 November 2023).

injuries were also sustained. Mr. Moore expired within half an hour from the time the accident occurred.

Constable Grey inquired into the matter and at the spot where the deceased was killed, he found there was a slight embankment leading up to the culvert over the channel which the horse had evidently struck unobserved in the dense dust and had stumbled, throwing the deceased head foremost onto the hard ground with great violence. The off-side of the horse and saddle were covered with dust, and the deceased's clothing had dust on the right side."[444]

After a burial service conducted by the Reverend A. Law in Holy Trinity Church, William Moore was buried in the Wangaratta Cemetery. A procession of 98 vehicles accompanied the hearse to the Cemetery.[445]

Obituaries in local newspapers were effusive in their praise of William. The *Ovens and Murray Advertiser* observed that:

"The late Mr. Moore, who was more popularly known as "old Billy" Moore, was 63 years of age, and was recognised as one of the best stockmen and horsemen in the district, and indeed was scarcely ever out of the saddle, if so he would be driving in a brake....[A]ll his dealings were marked with honesty and integrity, which won him the confidence and esteem of all who knew him."[446]

In its obituary, the *Border Morning Mail and Riverina Times* wrote of William that:

"He was a splendid man in handling young horses and had been connected with the horse and cattle sales at Wangaratta for many years. Much sympathy is felt for his bereaved family, and quite a gloom was cast over the town when his awfully sudden death became known."[447]

---

444 See the *Wangaratta Chronicle*, Wednesday, 18 November 1908, p. 3. The *Ovens and Murray Advertiser* observed this of the fatal injuries sustained by William:
"Beside a deep cut on the right temple, blood was coming from the ears, and within 20 minutes of the accident Mr. Moore was dead. A formal enquiry was held on Saturday afternoon, when the doctor certified that death was due to a fracture of the base of the skull or neck."
See the *Ovens and Murray Advertiser*, Saturday, 21 November 1908, p. 9. See also *The Age*, Monday 16 November 1908, p. 8; *The Argus*, Monday, 16 August 1908, p. 8; and the *Weekly Times*, Saturday, 21 November 1908, p. 24.

445 See the *Wangaratta Chronicle*, Wednesday, 18 November 1908, p. 3.

446 See the *Ovens and Murray Advertiser*, Saturday, 21 November 1906, p. 9.

447 See the *Border Morning Mail and Riverina Times*, Monday, 16 November 1908, p. 2.

The *Wangaratta Chronicle* stated in its obituary that:

"He was always most courteous and obliging and was respected and esteemed by all who knew him. Much sympathy has been expressed for his bereaved wife and family of six sons and three daughters."[448]

The *North-Eastern Despatch* noted William's "exceptional worth as a stockman" and "his excellent character"; further observing that William:

"was never known to wilfully do an injustice to anyone….[T]he familiar name of 'Billy' Moore will be long remembered as conveying all that is honorable and meritorious in connection with stockriding and droving."[449]

On Saturday, 2 January 1909, the *Ovens and Murray Advertiser* published a letter regarding William sent by George Moore to Thomas Notcutt. George Moore was an old friend of William but not a relative. In his letter, George Moore stated of William:

"He was of the type that constituted the true gentleman….It was always a pleasure for me to meet the late William Moore, and the news of his sad and untimely end was to me a source of great grief. He was in harness to the very last. To further mark my esteem for him, I will give, in his name, and to his memory, £50 towards the building fund of the new library."[450]

Following William's death, a subscription for a monument over his grave was opened by John Sisely, the Mayor of Wangaratta, and Daniel Evans J.P. This led to the erection of an imposing obelisk over the grave which bears the following inscription:

"Erected by his many friends in memory of WILLIAM MOORE who was killed through his horse falling 14th Nov. 1908 aged 62 years.

A native of the district, an accomplished horseman, a kind and generous friend."[451]

---

448 See the *Wangaratta Chronicle*, Wednesday, 18 November 1908, p. 3.

449 Cited in Jenny Coates, "William Moore – death of an 'honorable and meritorious' man" in *Conversations with Grandma* (https://tinyurl.com/4hxsnatw) (at 3 November 2023).

450 See the *Ovens and Murray Advertiser*, Saturday, 2 January 1909, p. 2. See also footnote 416 above.

451 See the *Wangaratta Chronicle*, Wednesday, 18 November 1908, p. 3. See also Jenny Coates, "William Moore – death of an 'honorable and meritorious' man" in *Conversations with Grandma* (https://tinyurl.com/4hxsnatw) (at 3 November

Both William and Alice Moore were committed Anglicans. In a lengthy article in which Albert Moore reminisced about his family history, he stated with respect to Alice:

"His grandmother, who lived with the family after the death of her husband, taught him the Lord's Prayer and encouraged him to attend a bush Sunday school conducted by the Misses Guarda and Doreen Steel in their home on the three Mile Creek.[452]

In 1910, the Moore family donated a stained glass clerestory window depicting St. Alban, which was installed in the Holy Trinity Cathedral in Wangaratta in memory of William Moore[453]

William Moore's widow, Alice Moore lived quietly until her death. She died aged 67 years of influenza on Saturday, 2 August 1919 during the great Spanish Flu pandemic that year. Alice was buried the following day, on 3 August 1919, in her husband's grave in the Wangaratta Cemetery. Subsequently, her name, date of death and age at death were engraved on the obelisk over the grave.[454] Further, Alice's name was added to that of William's on the memorial plaque fixed to the wall below the 1910 St. Alban clerestory window in Holy Trinity Cathedral, and a Bible was donated in her memory for the Lady Chapel in the Cathedral.[455]

Prior to Alice Moore's death, she had executed a Deed and her Will on 1 February 1916. In both the Deed and the Will, she referred to an earlier Deed executed on 9 May 1878 by her, together with William Moore, John Hampton Thomas, Arthur Jennings Smith and Thomas Clark, by which a piece of land was vested in William to be held by him in trust for Alice during her life, and after her death in trust for such of Alice's children as she might appoint by Deed or by her Will.

By her 1916 Deed, Alice executed the power of appointment given to her by the 1878 Deed to surrender her life estate in the piece of land, and directed that a James Maudsley, as her Executor and Trustee, hold an unidentified part of the piece of land in trust for her son, James Edgar Gordon Moore.

By her Will, she directed that the remainder of the piece of land referred to in the 1878

2023); and photos 38 and 39 below.

452 See *The Chronicle*, Friday, 24 March 1995, p. 6. See also *Albert Moore's 1992 document*.

453 See photo 40 below. The window depicts the early English saint, St. Alban. See also the *Albury Banner and Wodonga Express*, Friday, 7 January 1910, p. 2.

454 See the Keir Fisher – Montgomery Moore Family Tree: Alice Rebecca Clark (https://tinyurl.com/2yc4e5bz) (at 3 November 2023). See also photo 41 below.

455 *See Holy Trinity Cathedral Wangaratta 1908 – 2008: Centenary History Booklet.* See also photo 42 below.

Deed be held in trust by Maudsley for her children, other than James Edgar Gordon Moore, as tenants in common:

> "in such shares as that the share of each daughter shall be three times the share of each son but otherwise in equal shares."

She further directed Maudsley to hold the balance of her real and personal estate in trust for her daughters.[456]

None of the lands disposed of by Alice Moore in her 1916 Deed and Will are identified in either document. However the land left to James Edgar Gordon Moore might well have been all or part of his parents' *The Three Mile* property. Why the land was left to him is also not known. Although he was Alice's youngest child, he was 30 years old when Alice executed her 1916 Deed and Will.[457] Finally, it is unclear why Alice seemingly benefitted her daughters more than her sons. Perhaps the sons had benefitted from earlier inter vivos gifts. Again, perhaps Alice thought that the boys were better positioned economically than the girls. These details would now appear to be lost in time.

George Moore

Sadly, William Moore's twin brother, George Moore, led a short life. The twin boys were born on 23 November 1845 at their parents' family home on William Pitt Faithfull's *Hedi* run located on the King River.[458] The two brothers were christened by the Reverend A. C. Thomson of St. James' Anglican Church, Melbourne on 10 April 1848.[459]

George grew up with his parents and siblings on the *Hedi* and then the *Whorouly* runs in the King and Ovens River valley, and then on his father's *Tenterfield* property on the One Mile Creek near Wangaratta. He probably attended school for a time near *Tenterfield*.[460] However, in the main, most of his education was likely of a practical nature. His father, John Moore, almost certainly would have taught him to ride horses, to care for cattle and sheep and to cultivate the land.

---

456 See *Ancestry – Victoria, Australia, Wills and Probate Records, 1841 – 2009 for Alice Moore* (https://tinyurl.com/3585yus6) (at 4 November 2023).

457 See the *Moore Considine Family Website – Alice Rebecca Clark* (https://tinyurl.com/j33nctz: access code - seemoore) (at 4 November 2023).

458 See the *Moore Considine Family Website – George Moore* (https://tinyurl.com/j33nctz: access code - seemoore) (at 4 November 2023).

459 See *Baptisms Solemnised in the Parish of St. James Melbourne in the County of Bourke in the Year 1848 – George Moore* (https://tinyurl.com/4zaardfe) (at 4 November 2023). See also footnote 253 and its accompanying text above.

460 See footnote 418 and its accompanying text above.

On reaching his maturity, George Moore worked for a time on *Tenterfield*. However, it also seems that he may have worked more widely in the north-east of Victoria as a labourer.[461]

On Wednesday, 25 September 1872, George married Mary Jane Armstrong in Holy Trinity Church, Wangaratta. The marriage was performed by the Reverend William Charles Ford. The official witnesses to the ceremony were John Moore Jnr, George's elder brother, and Harriet Marum, George's younger sister.[462] George was 26 at the time of the marriage. His bride was 17 years of age. As Mary was still a minor, her mother, Sarah Ann Montgomery Staton, was required to give her permission to the marriage.[463]

Mary was born in North Melbourne on 16 June 1856. Her father, John Armstrong, had been a mines inspector who died shortly after Mary's birth. When Mary was around two years old, her mother remarried. Sarah's new husband was a Richard ("Dick") Staton. It would seem that he, Sarah and Mary may have lived together for at least a time in Moyhu prior to Mary's marriage to George Moore.[464]

It appears that after their marriage, George and Mary Moore lived together either on, or in close proximity to, George's parents' *Tenterfield* property on One Mile Creek to the north-west of Wangaratta.

George and Mary Jane were to have only the one child together. Their son George Earl Moore, was born in Wangaratta on or a little before Sunday, 1 February 1874.[465] Unfortunately, the child was not to grow up knowing his father. Sadly, and after suffering from the effects of typhoid fever for some four weeks, George Moore succumbed to the illness on Sunday, 4 July 1875.[466] He was 29 years old when he died. George was buried Monday, 5 July 1875 in the Wangaratta Cemetery.[467]

---

461 See the *Moore Considine Family Website – George Moore* (https://tinyurl.com/j33nctz: access code - seemoore) (at 4 November 2023).

462 See *Marriages in the District of Wangaratta in the Colony of Victoria – George Moore and Mary Jane Armstrong* (https://tinyurl.com/msu5wyrk) (at 4 November 2023).

463 See Jenny Coates, "On This Day In Wangaratta – 4th July 1875" in *Conversations with Grandma* (https://tinyurl.com/qhqcmbf) (at 4 November 2023).

464 *Ibid.*

465 See *Births in the District of Wangaratta in the Colony of Victoria – George Earl Moore* (https://tinyurl.com/32w4bt4j) (at 5 November 2023); and the *Moore Considine Family Website – George Earle Moore* (https://tinyurl.com/j33nctz: access code - seemoore) (at 5 November 2023).

466 See *Deaths in the District of Wangaratta in the Colony of Victoria – George Moore* (https://tinyurl.com/4m62h5ca) (at 5 November 2023); and Jenny Coates, "On This Day In Wangaratta – 4th July 1875" in *Conversations with Grandma* (https://tinyurl.com/qhqcmbf) (at 5 November 2023). Typhoid fever is an infection caused by the bacterium *Salmonella typhi*. It is usually spread through contaminated food or water. Once *Salmonella typhi* bacteria are ingested, they multiply and spread into the bloodstream. *Salmonella typhi* lives only in humans. Persons with typhoid fever carry the bacteria in their bloodstream and intestinal tract. Symptoms include prolonged high fever, fatigue, headache, nausea, abdominal pain, and constipation or diarrhoea. Some victims may have a rash. Prior to the development an d use of antibiotics, typhoid fever frequently resulted in death – as in George Moore's case.: see *World Health Organisation – Typhoid* (https://tinyurl.com/4wwwfee7) at 5 November 2023).

467 See *Billion Graves – George Moore* (https://tinyurl.com/2xttezen (at 5 November 2023). George's sister, Harriet Marum

George Moore's parents both survived George. John Moore died on Monday, 3 August 1891.[468] He was buried on 5 August 1891 in the same grave as George.[469] John left a Will dated 6 January 1888. In it he left a bequest of £53.4.8 to be held in trust by his Executors and Trustees for George until he reached the age of 21 years.[470]

On Christmas day 1879, Mary Jane Moore remarried in Beechworth. Her second husband was a James Lonnie Fulton.[471] The son of Scottish immigrants, Fulton was born in 1856 at Woolshed.[472] Following their marriage, Mary Jane and James Fulton apparently lived together in Moyhu, where James Fulton worked as a blacksmith. The two went on to have seven daughters and a son together.[473]

According to Charles Moore, his father, George Earl Moore, went to live with his grandparents, John and Margaret Moore, after his mother's marriage to James Fulton; remaining with them until the 1890s, when he moved to Melbourne.[474] It would also seem that notwithstanding her marriage to James Fulton, Mary Jane Fulton continued to be a part of the Moore family, visiting *Tenterfield* regularly until the 1890s.[475]

James Fulton died at Wangaratta in September 1897. Sadly, like Mary Jane Fulton's first husband, George Moore, Fulton died of typhoid fever. Mary Jane Fulton lived on for a further 38 years. She died in Camberwell on 12 May 1936.[476]

Charles Moore

It might be recalled that in 1847, Margaret Moore gave birth to an unnamed child of unspecified sex, who was either stillborn or died in very early infancy.[477] Her next child, a son, was born close by the Ovens River on the *Whorouly* run, where his father was

---

(née Moore) apparently arranged for the headstone over the grave: see *Charles Bertram Moore's 1987 document*.

468 See footnote 278 and its accompanying text above.

469 See footnote 284 and its accompanying text above. See also *Billion Graves – John Moore* (https://tinyurl.com/2r85rspw) (at 5 November 2023).

470 See footnotes 286 and 288, together with their accompanying texts, above.

471 See *Ancestry – Victoria, Australia, Marriage Index, 1837 – 1950: Mary Jane Moore and James Lonnie Fulton* (https://tinyurl.com/3pjhhhae) (at 5 November 2023).

472 See *WikiTree – James Lonnie Fulton (1856)* (https://tinyurl.com/37d639h4) (at 5 November 2023).

473 See Jenny Coates, "On This Day In Wangaratta – 4th July 1875" in *Conversations with Grandma* (https://tinyurl.com/qhqcmbf) (at 5 November 2023).

474 See *Charles Bertram Moore's 1987 document*.

475 See Jenny Coates, "On This Day In Wangaratta – 4th July 1875" in *Conversations with Grandma* (https://tinyurl.com/qhqcmbf) (at 5 November 2023).

476 *Ibid*.

477 See footnote 254 and its accompanying text above.

employed by Dr. George Mackay as overseer, on 25 August 1849. He was given the name "Charles Moore".[478]

Although Charles Moore was born on *Whorouly*, his childhood years were largely spent on his father's *Tenterfield* property near Wangaratta. He probably attended school nearby for a time.[479] However, it seems likely that he left school early to assist his father and older brothers in farming and grazing work on *Tenterfield* and possibly surrounding properties.

A great deal of Charles' life story appears to be lost. However, he was probably employed as an agricultural labourer over the balance of his working life. As an agricultural labourer, he may well have worked widely around the north-east of Victoria and into the Riverina.

On 19 September 1870, Charles married Jane Molina Dawson in St. Saviour's Anglican Cathedral in Goulburn.[480] He was 21 years old at the time of the marriage. She was 17 years of age. Both were then living in Collector, with Charles no doubt working as a rural labourer nearby. It may well be that Jane's father, Isaac Dawson, was farming in the area.

Jane Dawson was born on 17 December 1852 at Denham Court near Campbelltown in New South Wales; the daughter of Isaac and Isabella Dawson. At the time of Jane's birth, Isaac Dawson was described as being a farmer. Jane was christened in St. Mary the Virgin's Anglican Church, Denham Court on 23 January 1853.[481]

Following their marriage, it would appear that Charles and Jane Moore made their homes in the north-east of Victoria. They probably moved as and when Charles' employment changed. They had the following three children together:

- Isabella Margaret Moore, born at Taminick on or a little prior to 20 October 1871.

- Francis Charles Moore, born at Wangaratta on or shortly before 17 September 1873.

- Richard Isaac Moore, born at Wangaratta in 1875.

Sadly, Richard Isaac Moore only lived a short time; dying in the year of his birth, 1875.[482]

---

478   See footnote 260 and its accompanying text above.

479   See footnote 418 and its accompanying text above.

480   See *Ancestry – Australian Marriage Index, 1788 – 1950 for Jane Dawson* (https://tinyurl.com/ybcjsmox) (at 6 November 2023); and *Ancestry: Jonathan Harris Family Tree – Jane Molina Dawson* (https://tinyurl.com/yxoepm4f) (at 6 November 2023).

481   See *Ancestry – Sydney, Australia, Anglican Parish Registers, 1814 – 2011 for Jane Dawson* (https://tinyurl.com/yydh7jey) (at 6 November 2023).

482   See *Ancestry: Jonathan Harris Family Tree – Charles Moore* (https://tinyurl.com/y5vxa4ly) (at 6 November 2023).

At some point in time prior to 1877, it would seem that George Jarvis Harris began a relationship with Jane Moore. That relationship was to endure until George Harris' death in 1928.[483]

George Jarvis Harris was born on the Goulburn Plains on 19 August 1835 and baptised in St John's Church, Parramatta.[484] He was the sixth and last child of Jonathan Harris and the latter's first wife, Elizabeth Harris (née Baker). During the first half of the 1850s, George moved as a young man to Wangaratta, where his older sister, Elizabeth Clark (née Harris) was living with her husband, William Clark. He married Annie Matilda Brown on 27 August 1856. He was then said to be working as a carrier.[485]

On 16 October 1874, Annie Harris died in the Wangaratta Hospital of tuberculosis.[486] About two years thereafter, it would seem that her widower, George Harris, began cohabiting with Jane Moore. Whether Charles Moore abandoned Jane or Jane left Charles for George Harris remains unclear. In any event, it could well have been that Charles and Jane's separation and/or Jane's new relationship with George precipitated something of a scandal in the Wangaratta community of the day. For whatever cause, Jane and George appear to have left Victoria soon after they began cohabiting. They both spent the rest of their lives in New South Wales.[487]

In New South Wales, Jane became known as Jane Harris. Her *Death Certificate* states that she married George Jarvis Harris in Echuca when she was 28 years of age.[488] If correct, this would mean the marriage would probably have occurred in 1880. However, as the *Moore Considine Family Website* points out, there would seem to be no record of a divorce between Jane and Charles Moore, or of a marriage between Jane and George Jarvis Harris.[489] It seems more likely, therefore, that Jane and George enjoyed a de facto relationship.

---

483 Jane Moore's last child with her husband, Charles Moore, Richard Isaac Moore, was born (and died) in Wangaratta in 1875. Her first child with George Harris, Elizabeth Jane Harris, was born in Wagga Wagga on or a little before 9 July 1877: see *Ancestry: Jonathan Harris Family Tree – Jane Molina Dawson* (https://tinyurl.com/yxoepm4f) (at 6 November 2023). It therefore seems likely that George began cohabiting with Jane in 1876.

484 See *Ancestry – St. John's Church, Parramatta: Baptism Record for George Jarvis Harris* (https://tinyurl.com/y6c63h7t) (at 6 November 2023).

485 See *Marriages in the District of Collingwood in the Colony of Victoria – George Harris and Annie Brown* (https://tinyurl.com/476s6dut) (at 6 November 2023).

486 See *Deaths in the District of Wangaratta in the Colony of Victoria – Annie Harris* (https://tinyurl.com/3sevxdre) at 6 November 2023).

487 See *Ancestry: Jonathan Harris Family Tree – Jane Molina Dawson* (https://tinyurl.com/yxoepm4f) (at 6 November 2023); and *Ancestry: Jonathan Harris Family Tree – George Jarvis Harris* (https://tinyurl.com/yyqhxe4a) (at 6 November 2023).

488 See *New South Wales Death Certificate, 1933 – Jane Harris* (https://tinyurl.com/yyjclabu) (at 6 November 2023). The *Jonathan Harris Family Tree* website also asserts that the marriage may have occurred in Echuca in 1876: see *Ancestry: Jonathan Harris Family Tree – Jane Molina Dawson* (https://tinyurl.com/yxoepm4f) (at 6 November 2023).

489 See the *Moore Considine Family Website – Jane Molina Dawson* (https://tinyurl.com/2vctk4s5) (at 6 November 2023).

Between 1877 and 1896, George and Jane Harris had a total of 10 children together.[490] George died in Sydney on 26 June 1928.[491] Jane Harris also died in Sydney. Her death occurred on 10 December 1933.[492]

It would seem that Charles Moore had no further romantic entanglements following the breakdown of his marriage to Jane. He appears to have lived quietly for the balance of his life. He probably continued to work as an agricultural labourer until he retired. In his father, John Moore's, Will of 1888, Charles was left the land comprised in Allotment 3, Section 6, Parish of Wangaratta, together with a share of his father's residuary estate; all subject to a life interest granted by the Will to his mother. What use, if any, he made of this land when it vested in him on his mother's death in 1895 is not currently known.

Charles Moore died at Edi on the King River on 21 August 1929. He was 80 years old when he died and apparently living in the home of his daughter, Isabella Wright (née Moore), and her husband, Richard Wright.[493] Charles was subsequently buried in the Wangaratta Cemetery.[494]

Harriet Jane Moore

Harriet Jane Moore was the second of John and Margaret Moore's two children born on Dr. George Mackay's *Whorouly* run, where Harriet's father was employed by Dr. Mackay as overseer. Harriet was born on or a little before Saturday, 16 August 1851.[495] In all likelihood, Harriet would have had very little memory of her early life on *Whorouly*, as she moved with her family in about 1854 to the *Tenterfield* property acquired by her father near Wangaratta.

It appears that Harriet Moore lived on *Tenterfield* until her marriage in 1871. She would no doubt have assisted her mother and father with domestic and family duties and other duties on the property.

On 28 May 1871, Father Thomas Egan married Harriet Moore and Thomas Marum in St Patrick's Catholic Church in Wangaratta. Thomas Marum was 35 years old at the time of the marriage. As Harriet was only 20 years of age, her mother, Margaret Moore,

---

490 See *Ancestry: Jonathan Harris Family Tree – Jane Molina Dawson* (https://tinyurl.com/yxoepm4f) (at 6 November 2023).

491 See *Ancestry: Jonathan Harris Family Tree – George Jarvis Harris* (https://tinyurl.com/yyqhxe4a) (at 6 November 2023).

492 See *Ancestry: Jonathan Harris Family Tree – Jane Molina Dawson* (https://tinyurl.com/yxoepm4f) (at 6 November 2023).

493 See the *Moore Considine Family Website – Charles Moore* (https://tinyurl.com/mszxntyn) (at 6 November 2023); and *Ancestry: Jonathan Harris Family Tree – Charles Moore* (https://tinyurl.com/y5vxa4ly) (at 6 November 2023). See also the *Ovens and Murray Advertiser*, Saturday, 12 October 1901, p. 11.

494 See *Billion Graves – Charles Moore* (https://tinyurl.com/yak3zvn4) (at 6 November 2023).

495 See the *Moore Considine Family Website – Harriet Jane Moore* (https://tinyurl.com/4s76x9zj) (at 7 November 2023).

was required to provide written consent to the marriage.[496] Harriet and Thomas were to have no children together.

Thomas Marum was born on or a little before 18 June 1835 to farming parents, Pierce and Alacia Marum, at Newpark on the northern outskirts of Kilkenny in Ireland.[497] Particulars of his life in Ireland are not presently known. He emigrated from Ireland to Australia with his parents and some of his siblings in the early 1840s; with the family settling in Beechworth.[498] It appears that he later lived in Chiltern, Wangaratta and Benalla; ultimately working as a druggist (that is, a chemist) in each these towns.

In 1866, and then resident in Chiltern, Thomas Marum subscribed to five shares in the Chiltern All Nations Quartz Mining Company, which was seeking registration under the provisions of *The Mining Companies Limited Liability Act 1864* (Vic.) in order to mine for gold at the Skeleton Lead near Chiltern.[499] There would seem to be no record that this company's endeavours were ever profitable.

In 1867, Marum was one of a number of men in different towns in the north-east of Victoria who were said in a series of advertisements published in the *Albury Banner and Wodonga Express* to be local agents for the sale of "Weston's Wizard Oil"; alleged to be a great American remedy for "rheumatism, neuralgia, gout, sprains, headache. etc."[500]

Marum appears to have been community spirited during his time in Chiltern. In 1869, he was appointed as a member of the Committee of Management of "the land set apart for racecourse and recreation purposes at Chiltern".[501]

By the time of his marriage to Harriet Moore in May 1871, it would seem that Thomas Marum had severed his ties with Chiltern and was both resident in Wangaratta and working there as a druggist.[502]

It appears that within months of his marriage to Harriet Moore, Thomas Marum had relocated from Wangaratta to Benalla. However, he did not last long in Benalla. On 16 November 1871, an advertisement published in the *Ovens and Murray Advertiser* announced a mortgagee's auction to be conducted on 18 November 1871 Marum's shop

---

496 See *Marriages in the District of Wangaratta in the Colony of Victoria – Thomas Marum and Harriet Moore* (https://tinyurl.com/mr4y92hd) (at 7 November 2023).Margaret Moore was, of course, a Catholic. Her husband was a committed Anglican. However, as he was married to Margaret in a Catholic ceremony, he is unlikely to have objected to Harriet marrying a Catholic man: see footnote 153 and its accompanying text above.

497 See *Find a Grave – Thomas Marum* (https://tinyurl.com/29m6jahk) (at 7 November 2023).

498 See *Find a Grave – Pierce Marum* (https://tinyurl.com/4ezm6tzs) (at 7 November 2023).

499 See the *Ovens and Murray Advertiser*, Saturday, 3 March 1866, p. 3.

500 See, for example, the *Albury Banner and Wodonga Express*, Saturday, 7 September 1867, p. 4.

501 See *The Argus*, Saturday, 18 December 1869, p. 5.

502 See *Marriages in the District of Wangaratta in the Colony of Victoria – Thomas Marum and Harriet Moore* (https://tinyurl.com/mr4y92hd) (at 7 November 2023)

in Bridge Street, Benalla. To be auctioned were all of Marum's stock-in-trade; including "bottles, jars, drugs, shop fittings, etc.", together with a brown gelding horse.[503]

What happened to Thomas Marum after the dissolution of his Benalla business appears to be unclear. However, it would seem that he eventually moved to Sydney, where he obtained the position as a dispenser at Darlinghurst Gaol.[504] Whether Harriet went to Sydney with Thomas is not known. It is possible that their relationship had broken down, with Harriet instead returning to live with her parents in *Tenterfield*.

In any event, Thomas Marum died in Sydney on 12 December 1879 at the age of 44 years. He was buried in Sydney's Rookwood Catholic Cemetery on 14 December 1879.[505]

After some 16 years living as a widow in the Wangaratta area, Harriet Marum finally remarried on 1 January 1896. Her new husband, John Jones, was a widower around 26 years older than she was. Harriet's second marriage ceremony was an Anglican one, performed by the Reverend John Kaye Hall in Holy Trinity Church, Wangaratta.[506]

John Jones was born in the village of Blagdon in Somerset, England; the son of Thomas Jones, a labourer, and his wife, Mary Jones (née Parnell).[507] His birth date is uncertain. According to the registration particulars he provided at the time of his marriage to Harriet Marum, he was then 66 years old.[508] This would have given him a birth date of around 1830. However, his grave stone asserts that he was 89 years old at the time of his death in 1913.[509] This would give about 1824 for the year of his birth.

In 1856, John Jones was apparently engaged as a labourer in the construction of tramways and railways in the vicinity of Sebastopol for the British Army during the later stages of the Crimean War. Leaving the Crimea shortly before the War ended, he arrived in Sydney a little later in 1856. After working for a time on railway construction in the Hunter Valley, he moved to Victoria, where he initially spent time in Ballarat and Bendigo. He then travelled to Gippsland, where he married his first wife, Margaret

---

503   See the *Ovens and Murray Advertiser*, Thursday, 16 November 1871, p. 3.

504   See Jenny Coates, "George Clark and his unfortunate end" in *Conversations with Grandma* (https://tinyurl.com/5dv93su7) (at 7 November 2023).

505   See *Find a Grave – Thomas Marum* (https://tinyurl.com/29m6jahk) (at 8 November 2023). Interestingly, the Informant for the purposes of Marum's Death Certificate was "Mary Ann Casey, Sister-in-Law" and not Harriet Marum.

506   See *Marriages in the District of Wangaratta in the Colony of Victoria – John Jones and Harriet Marum* (https://tinyurl.com/2spu49jr) (at 8 November 2023).

507   See *Wikipedia – Blagdon* (https://tinyurl.com/2ad8c9k4) (at 8 November 2023).

508   See *Marriages in the District of Wangaratta in the Colony of Victoria – John Jones and Harriet Marum* (https://tinyurl.com/2spu49jr) (at 8 November 2023).

509   *Ibid.* See also *Billion Graves – John Jones* (https://tinyurl.com/4ar8na7n) (at 8 November 2023).

Murtaugh, in Alberton on 16 November 1858.[510] John and Margaret Jones were to have at least one child, Mary Ann Hammersley (née Jones).[511]

John and Margaret Jones arrived in Wangaratta in the early 1860s. John initially worked on the construction of roads and bridges. He then took up farming on a portion of the *Waldara* run near Wangaratta, which he later sold to Joseph Trotman. John thereafter became a commission agent for a Melbourne financier, invested in a series of businesses and acquired interests in a number of properties, including the *Vine Hotel*, Wangaratta. He was a one point said to be worth £40,000. However, he also suffered heavy losses through unsuccessful investments in Indigo.

John Jones ultimately acquired the *Bontharambo Hotel* at Boorahman. Although he and his wife, Margaret Jones, lived at the Hotel, their daughter, Mary Ann Hammersley (née Jones) came to manage it as its licensee. On 9 July 1895, Margaret Jones was seated alone by an open fire at the *Bontharambo Hotel*. As she leaned forward towards the fire, she possibly fainted, hit her head on a log of wood and was burned to death.[512]

Following Margaret's death, John Jones moved to Wangaratta. It is likely that after his move, Harriet Marum became his housekeeper. Less than six months after that death, on 1 January 1896 Harriet and John were married.[513] It is interesting to note that at around the time of this second marriage for both parties, John transferred a lease of land held in his name at Boorhaman to Harriet.[514] Was this land transfer intended to be some form of consideration for her marrying him, or was it simply a tax or an estate planning measure on his part?

John Jones died on 12 December 1913 at his home at 16 Templeton Street, Wangaratta.[515] An obituary published in the *North Eastern Despatch* the following day said this of him:

> "He was always a quiet unassuming man who took little or no part in public affairs, business matters fully occupying his time of late years, and although generally credited with a desire for keenness in a bargain there are many who had need to know that beneath this characteristic of his business dealings there was a disposition to extend a helping hand where it was felt to be deserved. He had no

---

510 See *Marriages in the District of Tarraville in the Colony of Victoria – John Jones and Margaret Murtaugh* (https://tinyurl.com/5be4kkme) (at 8 November 2023).

511 See the *Ovens and Murray Advertiser*, Saturday, 13 July 1895, p. 5.

512 See *The Argus*, Tuesday, 9 July 1895, p. 6; and the *Ovens and Murray Advertiser*, Saturday, 13 July 1895, p. 5.

513 See footnote 506 and its accompanying text above.

514 See the *Ovens and Murray Advertiser*, Saturday, 29 February 1896, p. 3. The land in question comprised 319 acres, 3 roods and 18 perches: *ibid*.

515 See the *Moore Considine Family Website – John Jones* (https://tinyurl.com/52nn33js) (at 9 November 2023)

ostentation, and his good deeds were not made known....For the past five years his health had failed considerably, and his death came at the last as the happy termination of a long period of incapacity, during which he was carefully tended by his wife and his medical attendant, Dr. Boyes."[516]

He was buried on 13 December in the Wangaratta Cemetery.[517]

Harriet Jones died at the age of 76 years at her home at 16 Templeton Street, Wangaratta on Saturday, 21 July 1928. She was buried shortly afterwards in her second husband's grave in the Wangaratta Cemetery.[518]

Harriet left a Will executed by her on 31 March 1926.[519] By it, she appointed Henry Alexander Murdoch, a Wangaratta Solicitor, to be her Executor and Trustee. Harriet directed Murdoch to pay her debts, funeral and testamentary expenses from her estate. She further bequeathed legacies ranging between £100 and £50 to her surviving brother, Charles Moore; to Mary Moore, the widow of her brother Thomas Moore; and to a number of her nephews. The principal beneficiaries under Will were two of her nieces: Jemima Moore, the daughter of her brother William Moore; and Isabella Wright (née Moore), the daughter of her brother, Charles Moore. To Jemima Moore, she left her home at 16 Templeton Street, Wangaratta. To Isabella Wright, she left the land on One Mile Creek to be found in Allotments 4 and 13, Section 6, Parish of Wangaratta North. Harriet left the residue of her estate to be divided equally between Jemima Moore and Isabella Wright.[520]

Thomas Moore

Thomas Moore was the last of John and Margaret Moore's children to be born. He first saw light of day at *Tenterfield* on or shortly before Sunday, 28 December 1856. Like his older brothers and sisters, he probably had a fairly short formal education. From his father he would have learned how to ride and handle horses. From a comparatively young age, he would have assisted his father and older brothers with the work associated with grazing and farming *Tenterfield* and other properties in the possession of his father.

---

516   See the *North Eastern Despatch*, Saturday, 13 December 1913, p. 2.
517   See *Billion Graves – John Jones* (https://tinyurl.com/csd9wzy8) (at 9 November 2023).
518   See the *Moore Considine Family Website – Harriet Jane Moore* (https://tinyurl.com/4s76x9zj) (at 9 November 2023); and *Billion Graves – Harriet Jones* (https://tinyurl.com/5bhh36yz) (at 9 November 2023).
519   See *PROV*, VPRS 7591, P0002, 225/736.
520   *Ibid.* By the Will, Harriet left her brother Charles Moore £50 "to be paid to him by my Executor and Trustee in sums of one pound per week until the whole amount has been paid to him". Could it be that Charles was a heavy drinker, and that Harriet wanted to ensure that he didn't spend all the money at once on a binge? See also footnote 493 and its accompanying text above.

Like his older brother, William Moore, Thomas Moore came to work as a drover. He also acquired and worked land on his own behalf.

On Wednesday, 19 December 1883, Thomas Moore and Mary Ann Brennan were married by the Reverend Edwin Rodda in the Parsonage of Holy Trinity Anglican Church, Benalla. Thomas was 26 years old at the time. Mary Ann was aged 24 years. Whilst Thomas was said to be ordinarily resident in Wangaratta, Mary Ann was recorded as being usually resident in Benalla.[521] While Mary Ann's usual residence may explain the location of the marriage, it doesn't explain why the marriage occurred in Holy Trinity Church's Parsonage, rather than in the Church itself. It may be that the reason lies in the fact that although Thomas was an Anglican, Mary Ann had been christened a Catholic.

Mary Ann Brennan was born on or a little prior to 21 October 1858 in Woodford; a village a little north of Warrnambool in Western Victoria.[522] Her father, Patrick Cavanagh Brennan, was an Irish farmer who immigrated to Australia in around 1833. After marrying Mary Ann's mother, Anastasia Brennan (née Murphy), he farmed land and managed a hotel at Terang. Patrick later acquired the *Emu* property near Benalla. Patrick and Anastasia Brennan subsequently retired to Portarlington. After Anastasia died in May 1912, Patrick went to live with a daughter in Melbourne. He died in Wangaratta on 18 August 1913.[523]

Following their marriage, Thomas and Mary Ann Moore returned to live their married life in Wangaratta.[524] They had a total of nine children together; all born in Wangaratta. The children were as follows:

- Frederick Francis Moore, born in 1884.

- Lucy Maude Moore, also born in 1884.

- Percy Michael Moore, born in 1886.

- William Moore, born in 1887.

- Mary Florence Moore, born on or a little before 27 December 1889.

- Rupert James Cavanagh Moore, born in 1892.

---

521 See *Marriages in the District of Benalla in the Colony of Victoria – Thomas Moore and Mary Ann Brennan* (https://tinyurl.com/3ujcsjwr) (at 12 November 2023).

522 See the *Lowe Tree – Mary Ann Brennan* (https://tinyurl.com/36drfw4f) (at 12 November 2023).

523 See the *North Eastern Despatch*, Wednesday, 20 August 1913, p. 2.

524 See photo 43 below.

- Ruby Anastasia Moore, born in 1895.

- Cyril Thomas Moore, born in 1895.

- Grace Margaret Moore, born on or slightly prior to 20 November 1899.[525]

Frederick Francis Moore and Lucy Maude Moore, both born in 1884, may have been twins. It would further seem that both Lucy Maude Moore and William Moore died in infancy.[526] Ruby Anastasia Moore and Cyril Thomas Moore were probably also twins.

Following his father's death in 1891, Thomas Moore was left the land Allotment 12, Section 6, Parish of Wangaratta, together with a share in John Moore's residuary estate under John's Will. This gift was subject to a life interest provided to John's widow, Margaret Moore, who died in 1895[527] Thomas presumably used this land, along with other land he acquired in the vicinity of Wangaratta, for grazing purposes.

On Wednesday, 25 November 1903, tragedy struck Thomas and Mary Ann Moore's family when their oldest surviving son, Percy Michael Moore, drowned while swimming with friends in the Ovens River. Percy was 16 years old when he died.[528]

About three years later, on Tuesday, 16 October 1906, another of Thomas and Mary Ann's sons, Rupert Moore, sustained a broken arm after being thrown from a horse he was riding. It seems that a dog rushed out towards the horse, causing it to shy.[529] Rupert was about 13 years old when the incident occurred.

During 1907, Thomas Moore was caught up in a protracted court case. A James Delloro was charged with stealing and taking away two heifers belonging to Thomas. After a two day trial which commenced on Thursday, 8 August in the Wangaratta Court of General Sessions before Judge Box, the Jury were deadlocked and unable to reach a verdict. The Judge then ordered that the matter be reheard at the Beechworth Court of General Sessions in October, 1907.

Delloro was retried in Beechworth in a trial which commenced before Judge Chomley on Thursday, 3 October 1907. Thomas Moore gave evidence to the Court that he was the owner of two heifers, each two years old and each ear-marked and branded "TM". The two heifers disappeared from the Wangaratta Common on 16 December 1916. On 21 March

---

525 See the *Moore Considine Family Website – Thomas Moore* (https://tinyurl.com/mb88kwde) (at 12 November 2023).
526 *Ibid*.
527 See footnote 288 and its accompanying text above.
528 See the *Ovens and Murray Advertiser*, Saturday, 5 December 1903, p. 3. See also *The Argus*, Friday, 27 November 1903, p. 6.
529 See *The Age*, Wednesday, 17 October 1906, p. 8.

1907, Thomas attended the Wangaratta Market where he saw Delloro endeavouring to sell the heifers. Thomas enlisted the support of Police Inspector Canny and publicly claimed the cattle in the presence of Delloro. Notwithstanding denials and protests by Delloro, the heifers were handed over to Thomas. He kept them in one of his paddocks for 10 days. They were then transferred to the Police Paddock, where they remained for a further week. They then suddenly disappeared and were never seen again. The Crown contended that the cattle had been stolen on both occasions and that Delloro was the thief.

After a two day trial, the Jury in the Delloro case returned a verdict of guilty. Judge Chomley then remanded Delloro for sentencing.[530] On Tuesday, 8 October 1907, the Judge sentenced Delloro to eighteen months imprisonment.[531]

On Saturday, 4 July 1908, Thomas Moore sustained nasty wounds. These occurred as he started to cross a timber footbridge at the corner of Mackay and Templeton Streets in Wangaratta leading from the roadway towards the Railway Hotel. As he stepped onto the footbridge, a plank on the end of which he stepped sprang up. The plank struck him on the head. This left him with a significant gash on his forehead. He further suffered cuts to one of his hands. Bleeding profusely, Thomas attended a Dr. Boyes, who inserted three or four stitches into his forehead. In addition to the physical discomfort he sustained, it would seem that Thomas was required to postpone for a week a droving engagement which he had previously entered into.[532]

It appears that the ends of the planks of the footbridge each extended about 11 inches beyond the two cross-beams to which they were nailed. Thomas seemingly placed one of his feet towards the outside edge of the plank in question. The plank had not been nailed securely to the far cross-beam. Thomas' weight caused the plank to come free and spring up and strike him.[533]

In due course, Thomas Moore claimed the sum of £10 from the Wangaratta Borough Council as compensation for his injuries, loss and suffering. Councillors were informed that Thomas was the fourth person to suffer injuries in consequence of the state of the footbridge. They were further informed that the Council's foreman denied being aware of the dangerous condition of the footbridge prior to Thomas's claim.[534] Unfortunately, there does not appear to be any extant information regarding the outcome of the claim.

On Thursday, 15 October 1908, Thomas Moore was brought before the Wangaratta

---

530 See the *Ovens and Murray Advertiser*, Saturday, 5 October 1907, p. 8
531 See the *Border Morning Mail and Riverina Times*, Wednesday, 9 October 1907, p. 2.
532 The *North Eastern Despatch*, Thursday, 9 July 1908, p. 2; and the *Ovens and Murray Advertiser*, Saturday, 11 July 1908, p. 7.
533 See the *North Eastern Despatch, Tuesday,* 7 July 1908, p. 2.
534 See the *North Eastern Despatch*, Thursday, 23 July 1908, p. 3.

Police Court to face four charges of failing to send his child to school on four separate occasions contrary to the provisions of the *Education Act*. In his own defence, Thomas stated that he had done his best to get the boy to go to school, but that he had "played truant". The Court was advised that Thomas had been convicted of similar charges on nine occasions. I convicted him on the four new counts; fining him two shillings on each count.[535]

Thomas' truant son could have been either Rupert Moore or Cyril Moore. Rupert would have been about 16 years old at the time of the Court case. Cyril would have been aged around 13. It seems likely that Cyril was the son in question.

By 1910, Thomas Moore was the owner of allotments of land on Swan Street, Wangaratta. The allotments had frontages on One Mile Creek. For a reason or reasons now lost in time, he decided to sell 18 of these allotments as building blocks. The allotments to be sold were apparently auctioned on Saturday, 15 October 1910 by Phillipson, Newman & Co.[536] How many of the allotments were sold at the auction, and at what prices, is also not now known.

On Saturday, 13 July 1918, Thomas and Mary Ann Moore's son, Rupert Moore, paid the supreme sacrifice while fighting in Frances during the First World War. He was around 26 years old when he died.[537]

Rupert joined the printing department of *The Wangaratta Chronicle* newspaper in Wangaratta as a printer in about 1909. He was said by the *Wangaratta Chronicle* to have been a proficient skater who:

> "was always foremost at skating carnivals, where he frequently won prizes for the best poster costume, or most original costume; he also took part in fancy dress processions and successfully represented Charlie Chaplin on several occasions."[538]

Prior to his enlistment in the Australian Army, he lived with his parents in the house in Faithfull Street, Wangaratta.

Rupert Moore enlisted on 6 February 1917. His fellow employees at the *Wangaratta Chronicle* presented him with a wrist watch on his enlistment. He was assigned to the 22nd Infantry Battalion, 19th Reinforcement. He embarked with his Unit from Melbourne on board HMAT A11 *Ascanius* bound for England on 11 May 1917. In England, he was

---

535 See the *North Eastern Despatch*, Saturday, 17 October 1908, p. 3.
536 See the *North Eastern Despatch*, Saturday, 8 October 1910, p. 2.
537 See *Find a Grave – Pvt Rupert James Cavanagh Moore* (https://tinyurl.com/mrxt9uh5) (at 13 November 2023).
538 See the *Wangaratta Chronicle*, Saturday, 27 July 1918, p. 3. See also footnote 529 and the accompanying text above.

assigned to the 3rd Machine Gun Battalion as a machine gunner. He travelled with his Unit to France in March 1918. He was gassed in France, but apparently recovered and returned to the front line, where he was shot and killed on the Somme Front on 13 July 1918.[539]

Rupert Moore lies buried in the Daours Communal Cemetery Extension, Daours, Departement de la Somme, Picardie, France.[540]

Rupert's father, Thomas Moore, died of heart failure and associated dropsy (now known as oedema) in the Wangaratta Hospital on Tuesday, 8 June 1920. He was 63 year old when he died.[541] He was buried in the grave of his father-in-law, Patrick Cavanagh Brennan, in the Wangaratta Cemetery on Thursday, 10 June 1920.[542]

Mary Ann Moore survived her late husband by 24 years. She died in Northcote on 27 June 1944 at the age of 85 years.[543] She was buried in the Melbourne General Cemetery.[544]

---

[539] See *Commonwealth War Graves Commission – Private Rupert James Cavanagh Moore* (https://tinyurl.com/5y36vmp6) (at 13 November 2023); *Virtual War Memorial – Moore, Rupert James Cavanagh*, (https://tinyurl.com/3x4wss4f) (at 13 November 2023); UNSW Canberra, *The AIF Project – Rupert James Cavanagh Moore* (https://tinyurl.com/bdftbha4) (at 13 November 2023); the *Wangaratta Chronicle*, Saturday, 11 May 1918, p. 3; and the *Wangaratta Chronicle*, Saturday, 27 July 1918, p. 3. What became of his wrist watch is not presently known. See also photo 44 below.

[540] See *Find a Grave – Pvt Rupert James Cavanagh Moore* (https://tinyurl.com/mrxt9uh5) (at 13 November 2023). See also photo 45 below.

[541] See the *Moore Considine Family Website – Thomas Moore* (https://tinyurl.com/mb88kwde) (at 13 November 2023); and the *Benalla Standard*, Friday, 11 June 1920, p. 4. See also photo 46 below.

[542] See *Billion Graves – Thomas Moore* (https://tinyurl.com/as7zf2f4) (at 13 November 2023).

[543] See *Deaths in the District of Prahran in the State of Victoria – Mary Ann Moore* (https://tinyurl.com/2kt4cte3) (at 13 November 2023). See also the *Lowe Tree – Mary Ann Brennan* (https://tinyurl.com/36drfw4f) (at 13 November 2023).

[544] See *Find a Grave – Mary Ann Moore* (https://tinyurl.com/ypvjdju5) (at 13 November 2023).

Photo 30: The body of "Mad Dog" Daniel Morgan, the bushranger, at Peechelba, Victoria.

Photo 31: The plaque on the wall in the Chancel of the Holy Trinity Cathedral, Wangaratta in memory of Frank Heach.

Photo 32: The Rose Window in the Holy Trinity Cathedral, Wangaratta dedicated to Frank Heach.

Photo 33: William Moore as a young man.

Photo 34: Alice Rebecca Moore (née Clark) as a young woman.

Photo 35: William Moore as a young man on horseback at The Three Mile.

Photo 36: An older William Moore in his uniform as Clerk of the Course at the Wangaratta Racecourse.

Photo 37: William Moore (seated in the centre) as an older man.

Photo 38: The memorial obelisk over William Moore's grave in the Wangaratta Cemetery.

Photo 7:

Photo 39: The memorial inscription for William Moore on his obelisk in the Wangaratta Cemetery.

Photo 40: The St. Alban stained glass clerestory windows in memory of William and Alice Moore in the Holy Trinity Cathedral, Wangaratta.

Photo 41: The memorial inscription for Alice Moore on William Moore's obelisk in the Wangaratta Cemetery.

Photo 42: The plaque fixed to a pillar below the St. Alban window in the Holy Trinity Cathedral, Wangaratta.

Photo 43: Thomas and Mary Moore's house in Wangaratta.

Photo 44: Private Rupert Moore (seated) with First World War comrades.

Photo 45: Private Rupert Moore's Grave, Daours Communal Cemetery Extension, Daours, Departement de la Somme, Picardie, France.

Photo 46: Thomas Moore as a mature man.

 # CONCLUSION

As can be seen above, there were eight surviving children in John and Margaret Moore's family and many grandchildren. The members of subsequent generations descended from John and Margaret are legion. These descendants are spread across Australia and beyond its shores.

John and Margaret escaped both poverty and constrained opportunities in England and Ireland respectively. In the north-east of Victoria, they lived lives that rewarded them for their hard work. Although neither of them rose to any social heights, they earned the respect and admiration of their peers.

They proved themselves to be worthy white settlers in their new land. Although their time and times are now long past, they deserve to be remembered.

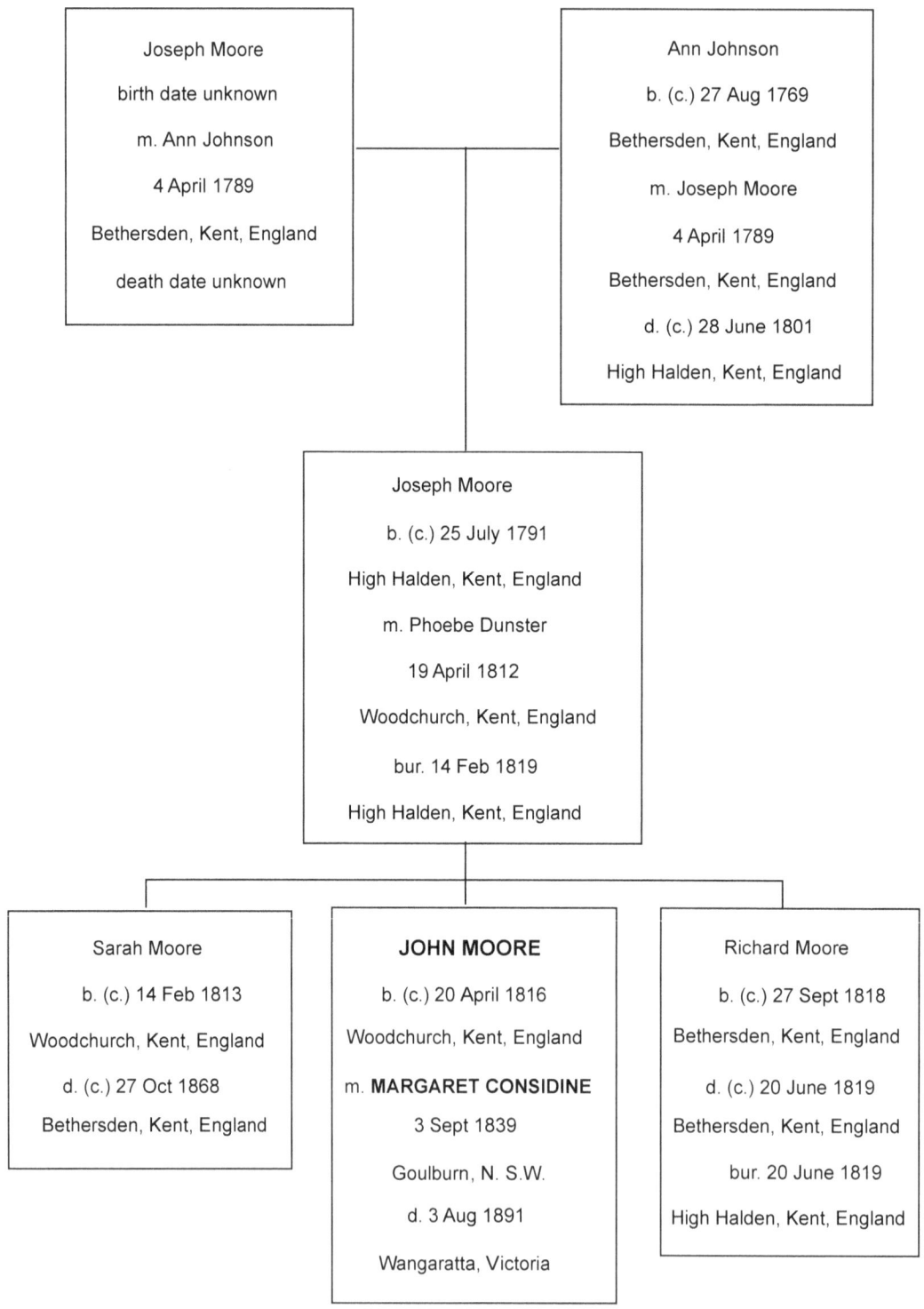

Joseph Moore's proximate family tree

Genealogical Charts

```
┌─────────────────────────────┐         ┌─────────────────────────────┐
│      Francis Dunster        │         │   Sarah Burt (née Barman)   │
│    b. (c.) 1 Oct 1759       │         │    b. (c.) 1 Oct 1750       │
│   Tenterden, Kent, England  │─────┬───│  Woodchurch, Kent, England  │
│ m. Sarah Burt (née Barman)  │     │   │     m. Francis Dunster      │
│       26 March 1780         │     │   │       26 March 1780         │
│  Woodchurch, Kent, England  │     │   │  Woodchurch, Kent, England  │
│    d. (c.) 27 Jan 1828      │     │   │    d. (c.) 14 Dec 1828      │
│  Woodchurch, Kent, England  │     │   │  Woodchurch, Kent, England  │
└─────────────────────────────┘     │   └─────────────────────────────┘
                                    │
                        ┌───────────┴───────────┐
                        │    Phoebe Dunster     │
                        │  b. (c.) 17 March 1793│
                        │ Woodchurch, Kent, England│
                        │    1 m. Joseph Moore  │
                        │     19 April 1812     │
                        │ Woodchurch, Kent, England│
                        │   2 m. Thomas Buckman │
                        │      11 Aug 1821      │
                        │ Bethersden, Kent England│
                        │   d. (c.) 20 Aug 1865 │
                        │ Bethersden, Kent England│
                        └───────────────────────┘
```

Phoebe Dunster's Children with Joseph Moore

```
┌──────────────────────────┐  ┌──────────────────────────┐  ┌──────────────────────────┐
│      Sarah Moore         │  │       JOHN MOORE         │  │      Richard Moore       │
│   b. (c.) 14 Feb 1813    │  │   b. (c.) 20 April 1816  │  │   b. (c.) 27 Sept 1818   │
│ Woodchurch, Kent, England│  │ Woodchurch, Kent, England│  │ Bethersden, Kent, England│
│   d. (c.) 27 Oct 1868    │  │   m. MARGARET CONSIDINE  │  │    d. (c.) 20 June 1819  │
│ Bethersden, Kent England │  │       3 Sept 1839        │  │ Bethersden, Kent, England│
│                          │  │     Goulburn, N.S.W.     │  │      bur. 20 June 1819   │
│                          │  │      d. 3 Aug 1891       │  │ High Halden, Kent, England│
│                          │  │    Wangaratta, Victoria  │  │                          │
└──────────────────────────┘  └──────────────────────────┘  └──────────────────────────┘
```

Phoebe Dunster's proximate family tree (1)

Phoebe Dunster's children with Thomas Buckman

```
                    Elizabeth Buckman                          Mahala Buckman
                    b. 1823                                    b. 14 July 1828
                    Bethersden, Kent, England                  Bethersden, Kent, England
                    d. 1884                                    bap. 29 June 1851
                    Isle of Thanet, Kent, England              m. Alfred Law
                                                               5 Oct 1851
                                                               Sevenoaks, Kent, England
                                                               d. 1884
                                                               Isle of Thanet, Kent, England

                    George Buckman                             Eliza Buckman
                    b. 1831                                    b. 1833
                    Bethersden, Kent, England                  Bethersden, Kent, England
                    Bap. 24 April 1853                         m. Walter Heathfield
                    Bethersden, Kent, England                  27 June 1858
                    m. Rebecca Reeves                          Sevenoaks, Kent, England
                    3 Nov 1853                                 d. 1894
                    Bethersden, Kent, England                  Smarden, Kent, England
                    d. 1909
                    Stockbridge, New York, U.S.A.

                                    Sophia Buckman
                                    b. 1835
                                    Bethersden, Kent, England
                                    m. John Clinch
                                    6 April 1868
                                    Hastings, Sussex, England
                                    d. 1922
                                    Stockbridge, New York, U.S.A.
```

Phoebe Dunster's proximate family tree (2)

Genealogical Charts

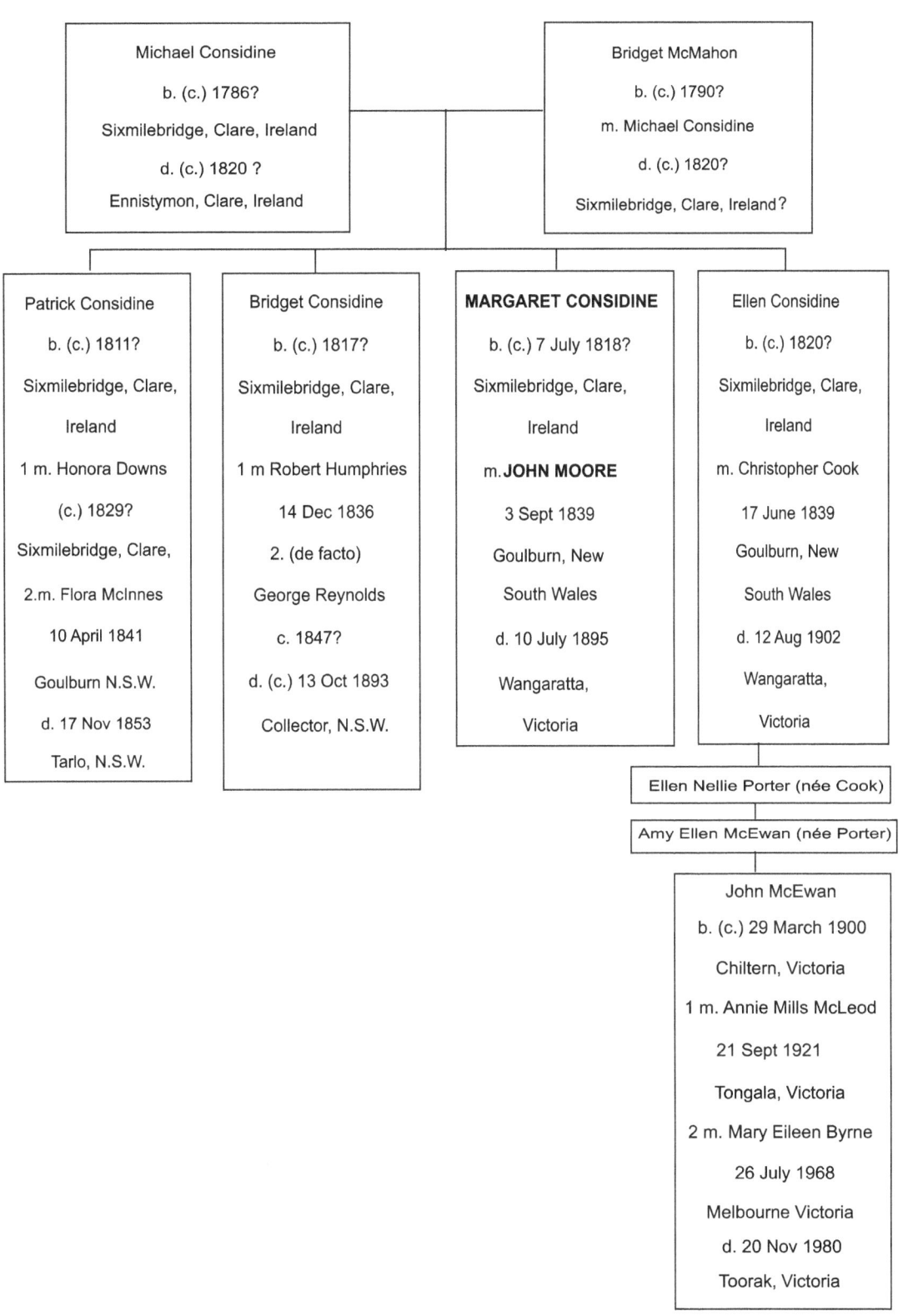

Michael Considine and Bridget McMahon's proximate family tree

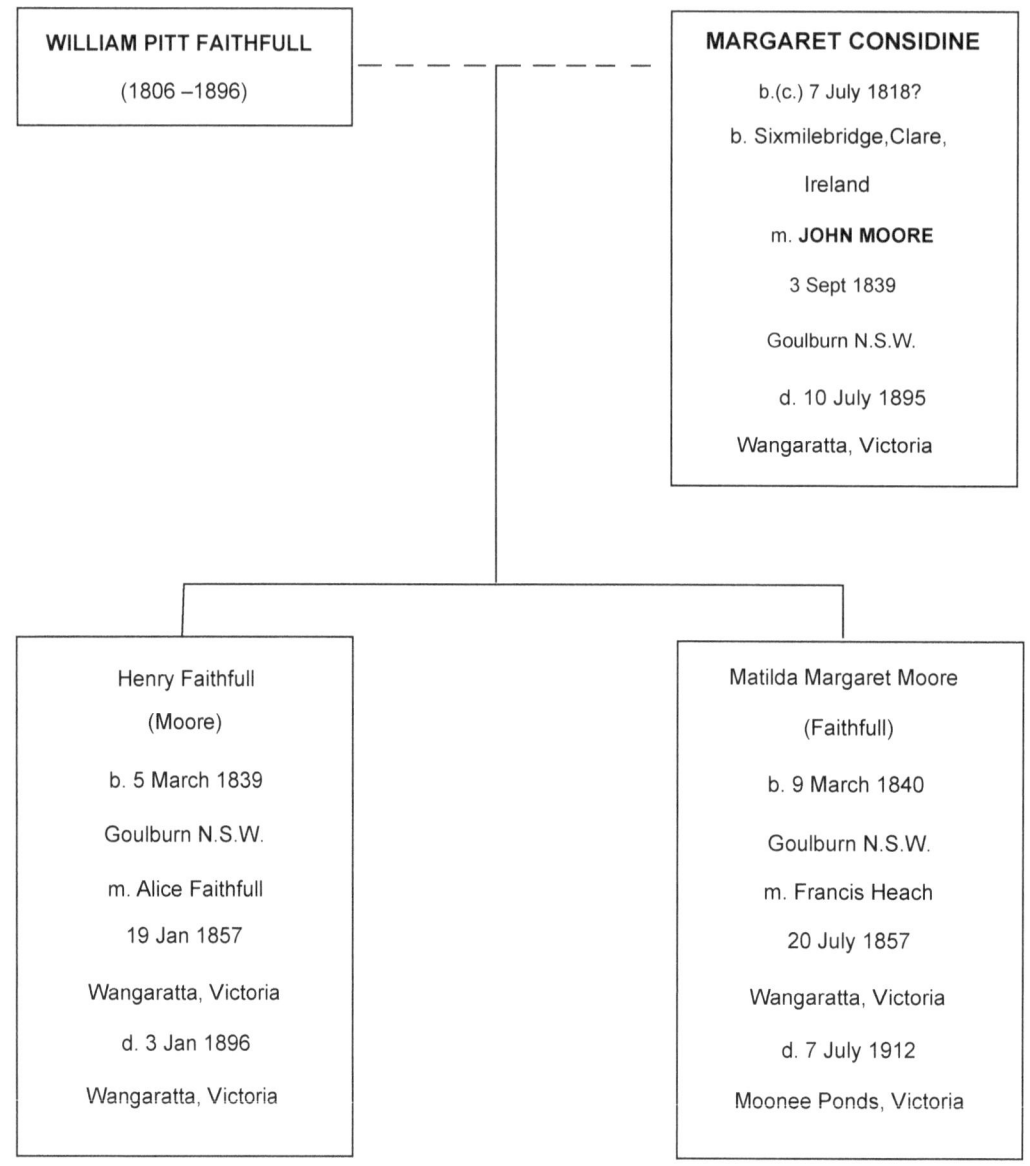

Margaret Considine and William Pitt Faithfull's proximate family tree

Genealogical Charts

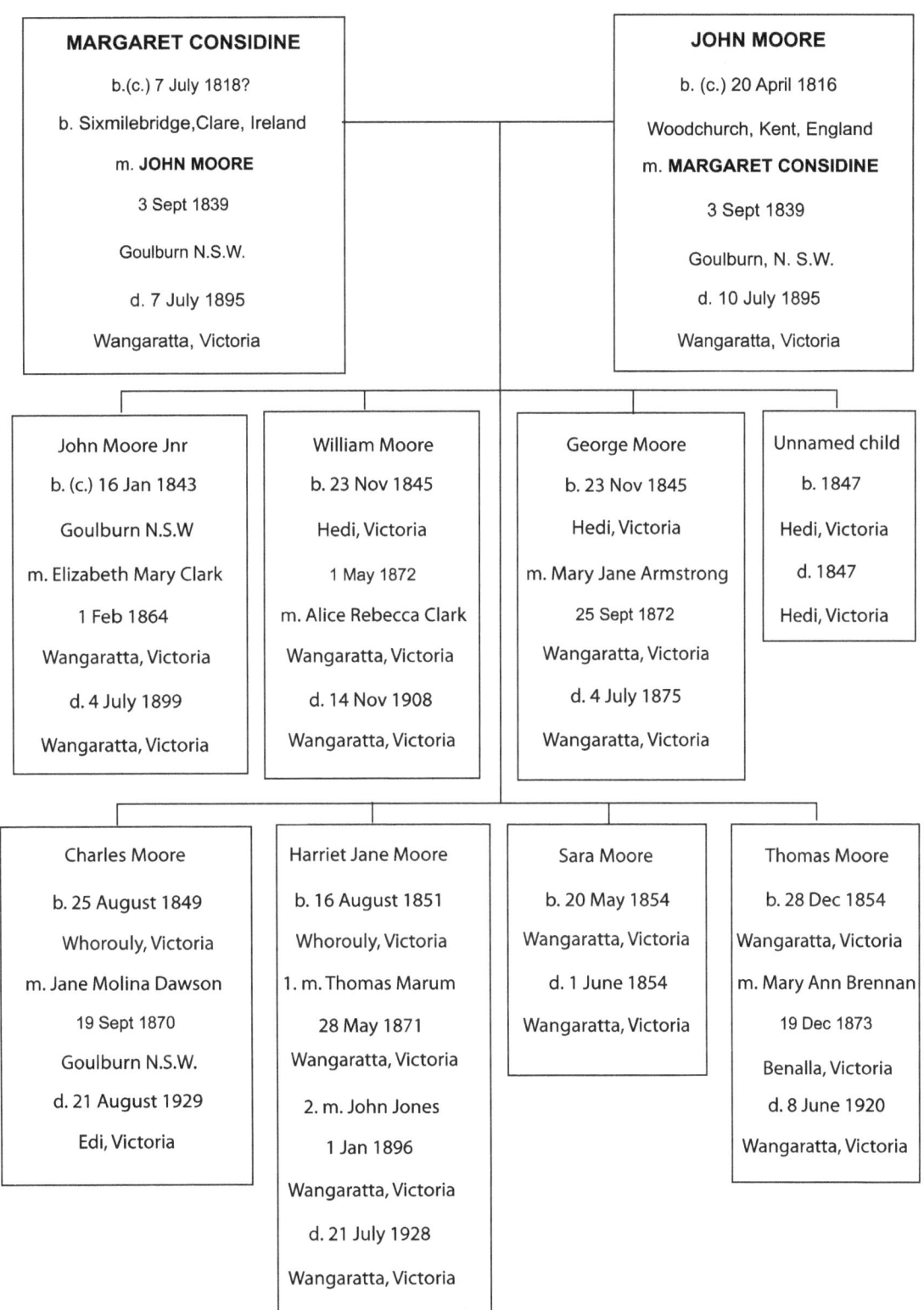

Margaret Considine and John Moore's proximate family tree

BIBLIOGRAPHY

Books

Andrews, Arthur: *First Settlement on the Upper Murray, 1835 – 1845* (1920).

Bienvenu, Fred and Diana: *Faithfulls of Omeo* (1963).

Bride, Thomas (ed.): *Letters from Victorian Pioneers* (Republished 1983).

Cox, Kenneth: *Angus McMillan: Pathfinder* (1973).

Duffy, Seán (ed.): *Medieval Dublin XVI – Proceedings of Clontarf 1014 – 2014* (2017).

Ellis, Malcolm Henry: *John Macarthur* (1963).

Faithfull, John and Lewis, Jim: *From 16,000 to 5* (2003. 2nd ed.).

Frankopan, Peter: *The Earth Transformed: An Untold History* (2023).

Gleig, George: *The Chronicles of Waltham* (1835).

Gormly, James: *Exploration and Settlement of Australia* (1921).

Grenville, John: *Sedition, Treason & Other Pastoral Pursuits* (1997).

Hobsbawm, Eric and Rudé, George: *Captain Swing* (1969).

Holden, Colin: *Church in a Landscape: A History of the Diocese of Wangaratta* (2002).

Holth, Tor and Jane: *Cattlemen of the High Country: The Story of the Mountain Cattlemen of the Bogongs* (2008, 2nd ed.).

Holy Trinity Cathedral Wangaratta: A Short History and Guide.

Holy Trinity Cathedral Wangaratta 1908 – 2008: Centenary History Booklet.

Jones, Ian: *Ned Kelly: A Short Life* (2008).

Lewis, Samuel: *A Topographical Dictionary of Ireland* (1837, Vol. 2).

Mallory, J. P.: *The Origins of the Irish* (2015).

Moore, Garry: *The Clark Brothers: Pioneer Squatters in the North East of Victoria* (2023).

Noone, Val: *Hidden Ireland in Victoria* (2012).

Robb, Graham: *The Debatable Land* (2018).

Rushen, Elizabeth: *Colonial Duchesses: The Migration of Irish Women to New South Wales Before the great Famine* (2014).

Sockett, Thomas: *Emigration: A Letter to a Member of Parliament* (1834, 2nd ed.).

Spreadborough, Robert and Anderson, Hugh: *Victorian Squatters* (1983).

Stapleton, Ian: *From Drovers to Daisy-Pickers: Colourful Characters of the Bogongs* (2006).

Whittaker, D. M.: *Wangaratta* (1963).

Wood, Gillen D'Arcy: *Tambora: The Eruption That Changed The World* (2014).

Articles

Australian Christian Church Histories: Australian Christian Church and Clergy Database –

Reverend John Joseph Hyland Kennedy (https://tinyurl.com/2xfehxxf).

Australia's Early Immigration Schemes: The Bounty Scheme (https://tinyurl.com/yd2gegpa).

Bassett, Judith: "The Faithfull Massacre at the Broken River, 1838" in (2009) 13:24 *Journal of Australian Studies* 18.

Bean, Christine: *From Tradesman to the Poor House (Gransden Family Website)* (https://tinyurl.com/y7z2xkx4).

Bloy, Marjorie: "Causes of Discontent and Distress, 1812 – 1822" in *A Web of History: The Age of George 111* (https://tinyurl.com/4aw7vfyy).

Chaplin, John and Gardiner, Pauline: "Introduction" in Woodchurch Ancestry Group (eds.),

Leaving Woodchurch: Emigration from Woodchurch since the Seventeenth Century (2011).

Chown, Robert A.: "The Population of Woodchurch and Emigration" in Woodchurch Ancestry Group (eds.), *Leaving Woodchurch: Emigration from Woodchurch since the Seventeenth Century* (2011).

Coates, Jenny: "1856 Politics Wangaratta Style" in *Conversations with Grandma* (https://tinyurl.com/ydyozygn).

Coates, Jenny: "George Clark and his unfortunate end" in *Conversations with Grandma* (https://tinyurl.com/5dv93su7).

Coates, Jenny: "Margaret Considine (c. 1818 – 1895)" in *Conversations with Grandma* (https://tinyurl.com/52apm3p3).

Coates, Jenny: "On This Day in Wangaratta – 4th July 1875" in *Conversations with Grandma* (https://tinyurl.com/qhqcmbf).

Coates, Jenny: "Sepia Saturday 219 – Arches and Significant Buildings" in *Conversations with Grandma* (https://tinyurl.com/unc5f8fs).

Coates, Jenny: "William Moore – death of an 'honorable and meritorious' man" in *Conversations with Grandma* (https://tinyurl.com/4hxsnatw).

Comerford, Patrick: *The Old Bridges, Mills and Ducks on the River at Sixmilebridge* (https://tinyurl.com/yckz2372).

Cook, James: *A Journal of the Proceedings of His Majesty's Bark Endeavour, 1770* (https://tinyurl.com/m89enu5d).

Durrant, Jacqui: "Mysterious Mogullumbidj – First People of Mount Buffalo" in *Life on Spring Creek* (https://tinyurl.com/yc8x6tna).

Durrant, Jacqui: "Who were the Aboriginal people of Beechworth? A historical perspective" in *Life on Spring Creek* (https://tinyurl.com/yc668utv).

Flickr – Faithfull Hut (https://tinyurl.com/yb224p4t).

Greek Origins of Mac Considine from Constantine (https://tinyurl.com/yd3bawut).

Griffin, Carl J.: "Parish farms and the poor law: a response to unemployment in rural southern England, c. 1812 – 1825" in (2011) 59 *Agricultural History Review* 176.

Heritage Genealogy: Immigration Indexes (https://tinyurl.com/y9m7tqfk).

Historic England, 4 – 8 Batemans Corner (https://tinyurl.com/39k8df9h).

Historical Records of Australia, Series 1, Volume 1, p. 664.

Historical Records of New Zealand, *Crew of Lieutenant Cook's Ship Endeavour, 1770* (https://tinyurl.com/5n7rurts).

Kelly Gang and friends, *Adjie* (https://tinyurl.com/2u8h7yzt).

Lambert, Tim: *A History of Life Expectancy in Britain* (https://tinyurl.com/h2mzho7).

Light, Jenny: "Overseers of the Poor and the Vestry Meeting (1757 – 1850)" in Woodchurch Ancestry Group (eds.), *A Social History of Woodchurch: The People* (2014).

Linder, Marc: "The Joint Employment Doctrine: Clarifying Joint Legislative – Judicial Confusion" in (1989) 10(2) *Hamlin Journal of Law and Public Policy* 321.

Lloyd, C. J.: "McEwan, Sir John (1900 – 1980)" in *Australian Dictionary of Biography* (https://tinyurl.com/2avhu9hp).

Mackie, Josie: "Riot in Woodchurch: A Summer of Discontent" in (2019) 1 *Scuppets & Scutchell* 60.

Mackie, Josie: "Social Conditions and Agriculture" in Woodchurch Ancestry Group (eds.), *Leaving Woodchurch: Emigration from Woodchurch since the Seventeenth Century* (2011).

"Manuscript: Re Daniel Morgan Bushranger" in *The La Trobe Journal*, No. 5, April 1970 (https://tinyurl.com/jt8zwkd).

McQuilton, John: "Morgan, Daniel (Dan) (1830 – 1865)" in *Australian Dictionary of Biography* (https://tinyurl.com/ycy85d3u).

Newton, R. J. M.: "Manning, John Edye (1783 – 1870)" in *Australian Dictionary of Biography* (https://tinyurl.com/y6v2q57j).

Oppenheimer, Clive: "Climatic, environmental and human consequences of the largest known historic eruption: Tambora volcano (Indonesia) 1815" in (2003) 27(2) *Progress in Physical Geography* 230.

Ozships: Australian 1788 – 1968: Arrivals: James Pattison – 11 December 1838 (https://tinyurl.com/y83da271).

Paterson, James: "Protection of the Body against Want and Destitution" in *Commentaries on the Liberty of the Subject and the Laws of England Relating to the Security of the Person* (1877).

Ratbag Encyclopedia: *Researching a Convict Ship* (https://tinyurl.com/4sbpn37x).

Sewell, Robert: *Monypenny of Pitmilly* (https://tinyurl.com/ycky8kdx).

Sixmilebridge Historical Background (https://tinyurl.com/y8kfkp8x).

"Soldiers from the Snowline" in (2015) 38 *Voice of the Mountains* 48.

The AIF Project – Frederick George Faithfull (https://tinyurl.com/2n23j72h).

Their Duty Done – Frederick George Faithfull (https://tinyurl.com/yc2ttxvt).

The Man From Snowy River – Reality or Myth? (https://tinyurl.com/hlcpkvd).

The Peerage: Person Page 31884 – William Deedes (https://tinyurl.com/yxapd3gd).

Victorian Heritage Database Report – Holy Trinity Anglican Cathedral Close (https://tinyurl.com/ksmmcrs).

Waltzing Matilda: Lyrics, Meaning, History – Christina MacPherson (https://tinyurl.com/4u74f7m2).

Wikipedia – Blagdon (https://tinyurl.com/2ad8c9k4).

Wikipedia – Colac, Victoria (https://tinyurl.com/pf3vjfsb).

Wikipedia – Colac Colac, Victoria (https://tinyurl.com/7v9b74w6).

Wikipedia – Delcassians (https://tinyurl.com/yamgmb4b).

Wikipedia – Dunster (https://tinyurl.com/y8jfnalw).

Wikipedia – James Pattison (1828 ship) (https://tinyurl.com/2jwtuyzu).

Wikipedia – John Elliott (businessman) (https://tinyurl.com/bdd7wwrd).
Wikipedia – Little River (https://tinyurl.com/4s84ytfh).
Wikipedia – Swing Riots (https://tinyurl.com/n9gry8t).
Wikipedia – Tenterden (https://tinyurl.com/32u6rnx2).
Wikipedia – Thomas Law Hodges (https://tinyurl.com/bd2kpnke).
Wikipedia – Tom Elliott (radio personality) (https://tinyurl.com/3ph5ec8e).
WikiTree – Bounty Immigrant Voyages to Australia, Arrivals in New South Wales – Strathfieldsaye 26 January 1838 (https://tinyurl.com/2xytysb3).
Windeyer, Victor: "A Birthright and Inheritance" in (1961) 1 *Tasmania University Law Review* 635.
Woodchurch Ancestry Group, *Facebook Posts Page*, Entry for 9 July 2018 (https://tinyurl.com/ybnlg4q6).
World Health Organization, *Typhoid* (https://tinyurl.com/4wwwfee7).

Genealogical Materials

All Canadian Passenger Lists, 1865 – 1935: George Buckman (https://tinyurl.com/y5o77zzy).
Ancestry – Australia, Births and Baptisms, 1792 – 1821: Henry Concidine [sic] (FHL Film No. 993952) (https://tinyurl.com/5f7vrp37).
Ancestry – Australia, Birth Index, 1788 – 1922: Matilda M Moore (https://tinyurl.com/2mksvkdn).
Ancestry – Australia, Marriage Index, 1788 – 1950: Jane Dawson and Charles Moore (https://tinyurl.com/ybcjsmox).
Ancestry – Australia, Marriage Index, 1788 – 1950: Matilda Moore and Frank Heach (https://tinyurl.com/wnsnjze4).
Ancestry – England, Select Births and Christenings, 1538 – 1975: Francis Heach (https://tinyurl.com/3avxxa59).
Ancestry – Jonathan Harris Family Tree: Charles Moore (https://tinyurl.com/y5vxa4ly).
Ancestry – Jonathan Harris Family Tree – George Jarvis Harris (https://tinyurl.com/yyqhxe4a).
Ancestry – Jonathan Harris Family Tree: Jane Molina Dawson (https://tinyurl.com/yxoepm4f).
Ancestry – Bridget McMahon (https://tinyurl.com/ya9jhc6n).

Ancestry – St. John's Church, Parramatta: Baptism Record for George Jarvis Harris (https://tinyurl.com/y6c63h7t).

Ancestry – Sydney, Australia, Anglican Parish registers, 1814 – 2011 for Jane Dawson (https://tinyurl.com/yydh7jey).

Ancestry – Victoria, Australia, Marriage Index, 1788 – 1950: John Moore and Elizabeth Mary Clark (https://tinyurl.com/4vfsfx76).

Ancestry – Victoria, Australia, Marriage Index, 1837 – 1950: Mary Jane Moore and James Lonie Fulton (https://tinyurl.com/3pjhhhae).

Ancestry – Victoria, Australia, Wills and Probate Records, 1841 – 2009 for Alice Moore (https://tinyurl.com/3585yus6).

Ancestry – Victoria, Australia, Wills and Probate Records, 1841 – 2009 for John Moore (Jnr.) (https://tinyurl.com/54nadsjn).

Australia, Electoral Rolls, 1903 – 1980 for Francis Heach (https://tinyurl.com/2p8mu6z4).

Australian Convict Transportation Registers: Other Fleets and Ships, 1791 – 1868: Robert Humphries (https://tinyurl.com/zhvu8j3k).

Australian Royalty – Alice McKenzie 1815 – 1854 (https://tinyurl.com/2p9hm2kj).

Australian Royalty – Charles McKenzie 1781 (https://tinyurl.com/3pwry3je).

Australian Royalty – George Gray 1755 – 1853 (https://tinyurl.com/28w4h4x4).

Australian Royalty – Hannah McIntosh 1790 – 1864 (https://tinyurl.com/svmc4ka).

Baptisms Solemnised in the Parish of St. James Melbourne in the County of Bourke in the Year 1848 – William and George Moore (https://tinyurl.com/3wpvem6z).

Billion Graves – Charles Moore (https://tinyurl.com/yak3zvn4).

Billion Graves – Christopher, Ellen and William Cook (https://tinyurl.com/266axe25).

Billion Graves – Francis Heach (https://tinyurl.com/mv3yf6tu).

Billion Graves – George Moore (https://tinyurl.com/2xttezen).

Billion Graves – John Jones (https://tinyurl.com/4ar8na7n).

Billion Graves – John McEwan (https://tinyurl.com/ntffsn8j).

Billion Graves – John Moore (https://tinyurl.com/2r85rspw).

Billion Graves – Matilda Heach (Moore) (https://tinyurl.com/zznnm5xj).

Billion Graves – Thomas Marum (https://tinyurl.com/nhcxv38m).

Billion Graves – Thomas Moore (https://tinyurl.com/as7zf2f4).

Births, Deaths and Marriages, Victoria (Marriages) – Francis Heach and Mary Elizabeth McCulloch (https://tinyurl.com/2mjfm22d).

Births in the District of Benalla in the Colony of Victoria – Alice Rosetta Clark (https://tinyurl.com/y2dba49t).

Births in the District of Wangaratta in the Colony of Victoria – Alice Rebecca Clark (https://tinyurl.com/yx2b84yv).

Births in the District of Wangaratta in the Colony of Victoria – George Earl Moore (https://tinyurl.com/32w4bt4j).

Certificate of Marriage – Christopher Cook and Ellen Considine (https://tinyurl.com/5eddp5k2).

Commonwealth War Graves Commission – Private Rupert James Cavanagh Moore (https://tinyurl.com/5y36vmp6).

Death Certificate – Margaret Moore (https://tinyurl.com/yfwkew4u).

Deaths in the District of Carlton in the Colony of Victoria – Elizabeth Moore (https://tinyurl.com/yckfdkkm).

Deaths in the District of Prahran in the State of Victoria – Mary Ann Moore (https://tinyurl.com/2kt4cte3).

Deaths in the District of Wangaratta in the Colony of Victoria – Annie Harris (https://tinyurl.com/3sevxdre).

Deaths in the District of Wangaratta in the Colony of Victoria – George Moore (https://tinyurl.com/4m62h5ca).

Deaths in the District of Wangaratta in the Colony of Victoria – John Moore (Snr.) (https://tinyurl.com/bdds44s2).

Deaths in the District of Wangaratta in the Colony of Victoria – John Moore (Jnr.) (https://tinyurl.com/5cejantp).

Deaths in the District of Wangaratta in the Colony of Victoria – Margaret Moore (https://tinyurl.com/yfwkew4u).

Deaths in the District of Prahran in the Colony of Victoria – Mary Ann Moore (https://tinyurl.com/2kt4cte3).

Deaths in the District of Wangaratta in the Colony of Victoria – Sarah Moore

Deaths in the District of Wangaratta in the State of Victoria – William Moore (https://tinyurl.com/4k3bu64s).

(https://tinyurl.com/5n8tvmyp).

Deaths Registered in New South Wales – Bridget Humphries (https://tinyurl.com/2da79mmw).

Deaths Registered in New South Wales – William Clark (No. 2828/ 1872).

England and Wales, Civil Registration Death Index, 1837 – 1915: Eliza Heathfield (https://tinyurl.com/2f586pxm).

England and Wales, Civil Registration Death Index, 1837 – 1915: Elizabeth Buckman (https://tinyurl.com/y4p3ntgc).

England and Wales, Civil Registration Death Index, 1837 – 1915: Mahala Law (https://tinyurl.com/y5n4ognh).

England, Births and Christenings, 1538 – 1975: Anne Johnson – 1769 (https://tinyurl.com/jcca631).

England, Births and Christenings, 1538 – 1975: George Buckman – 1853 (https://tinyurl.com/4w9htr7t).

England, Births and Christenings, 1538 – 1975: Joseph Moore – 1763 (https://tinyurl.com/gtjz3hd).

England, Births and Christenings, 1538 – 1975: Joseph Moore – 1791 (https://tinyurl.com/4exsd8xp).

England, Select Deaths and Burials, 1538 – 1991: Sarah Moore – 1868 (https://tinyurl.com/4mkabkyx).

England, Select Marriages, 1538 – 1973: John Buckman and Sarah Reeves – 1863 (https://tinyurl.com/2szsy4jn).

England, Select Marriages, 1538 – 1973: Joseph Moore and Anne Johnson – 1789 (https://tinyurl.com/bdeeawck).

England, Select Marriages, 1538 – 1973: Joseph Moore and Phoebe Dunster – 1812 (https://tinyurl.com/hknrauk).

England, Select Marriages, 1538 – 1973: Sophia Buckman and John Clinch – 1868 (https://tinyurl.com/y4y20656).

Faithfull Family Tree – Matilda Margaret Moore Faithfull (https://tinyurl.com/3x24t33x).

Family Search – Australia, Births and Baptisms, 1792 – 1981: John Moore (https://tinyurl.com/54z9remf).

Find a Grave – Mary Ann Brennan (https://tinyurl.com/ypvjdju5).

Find a grave – Pierce Marum (https://tinyurl.com/4ezm6tzs).

Find a Grave – Pvt. Rupert James Cavanagh Moore (https://tinyurl.com/mrxt9uh5).

Find a Grave – Thomas Marum (https://tinyurl.com/29m6jahk).

Find a Grave Memorial – Alice Ellen Clinch LaBarr (1870 – 1958) (https://tinyurl.com/ydk99h2r).

Find a Grave Memorial – George Buckman (1831 - 1909) (https://tinyurl.com/yxfacgqy).

Find a Grave Memorial – John Clinch (1840 - 1912) (https://tinyurl.com/2ep6f3z8).

Find a Grave Memorial – LaVerne Judson LaBarr (1870 – 1958)
   (https://tinyurl.com/bdf67y6t).

Find a Grave Memorial – Sophia Buckman Clinch (1835 - 1922)
   (https://tinyurl.com/32r8peh8).

FreeREG Baptism Entry – George Buckman (https://tinyurl.com/y62ldgnv).

FreeREG Baptism Entry – John Moore (https://tinyurl.com/ycwajrq2).

FreeREG Baptism Entry – Mahala Buckman (https://tinyurl.com/y8wbuw3c).

FreeREG Baptism Entry – Mahala Law (https://tinyurl.com/yxo7y7sd).

FreeREG Baptism Entry – Phoebe Dunster (https://tinyurl.com/yd6bzk4o).

FreeREG Baptism Entry – Richard Moore (https://tinyurl.com/ycmdzzlo).

FreeREG Baptism Entry – Sarah Moore (https://tinyurl.com/y974x83y).

FreeREG Burial Entry – Francis Dunster (https://tinyurl.com/3rmm6rmv).

FreeREG Burial Entry – Phoebe Buckman (https://tinyurl.com/y9swkvsc).

FreeREG Burial Entry – Richard Moore (https://tinyurl.com/yagekwpb).

FreeREG Burial Entry – Sarah Dunster (https://tinyurl.com/y55raanw).

FreeREG Burial Entry – Thomas Buckman (https://tinyurl.com/ybnkalcv).

FreeREG Marriage Entry – Francis Dunster and Sarah Burt
   (https://tinyurl.com/yxf2u6k7).

FreeREG Marriage Entry – George Buckman and Rebecca Reeves
   (https://tinyurl.com/y5a8hk6e).

FreeREG Marriage Entry – Phoebe Moore and Thomas Buckman
   (https://tinyurl.com/yc6znkuj).

Geni – Bridget McMahon (https://tinyurl.com/4yw3kxut).

Geni – Margaret Moore (Considine) (1818 – 1895) (https://tinyurl.com/4erxud4w).

Geni – Michael Considine (https://tinyurl.com/yabvj7g2).

Immigration Record – Patrick Considine (https://tinyurl.com/4kx2cf6u).

Immigration Series: Entitlement Certificates for Persons on Bounty Ships, 1832 – 1842:
   John Moore (AONSW 4/4830) (https://tinyurl.com/4334fnhc).

Ireland, Catholic Parish Registers, 1655 – 1915 for Joannes (John) Considine
   (https://tinyurl.com/3579p72s).

Ireland, Catholic Parish Registers, 1655 - 1915 for Michael Considine
   (https://tinyurl.com/4ej9ahp7).

Ireland, Catholic Parish Registers, 1655 – 1915 for Patritius Considen
   (Patrick Considine) (https://tinyurl.com/2kx2yb2c).

Kaye's Greta, Myrrhee and Winton Webpage – Newspaper articles: Pioneer stories (https://tinyurl.com/2rzcmuc9).

Keir Fisher – Montgomery Moore Family Tree: Alice Rebecca Clark (https://tinyurl.com/2yc4e5bz).

Keir Fisher – Montgomery Moore Family Tree: Patrick Considine (https://tinyurl.com/4j7erfz6).

Kent, England, Church of England Baptisms, Marriages and Burials, 1538 – 1914: Mahala Buckman) (https://tinyurl.com/3wdhefwv).

Kent, England, Church of England Baptisms, Marriages and Burials, 1538 – 1914: Eliza Buckman (https://tinyurl.com/22bvmrze).

Lamb – McInnes Family Tree – Bridget McMahon (https://tinyurl.com/2p8r6hf2).

Lamb – McInnes Family Tree – Michael Considine (https://tinyurl.com/y83sb3gr).

Lowe Tree – Mary Ann Brennan (https://tinyurl.com/36drfw4f).

Manwaring Family History Website – Bridget Considine (https://tinyurl.com/9mpba2np).

Marriages in the District of Benalla in the Colony of Victoria – Thomas Moore and Mary Ann Brennan (https://tinyurl.com/3ujcsjwr).

Marriages in the District of Benalla in the Colony of Victoria – William Moore and Alice Rebecca Clark (https://tinyurl.com/33pprfeu).

Marriages in the District of Collingwood in the Colony of Victoria – George Harris and Annie Brown (https://tinyurl.com/476s6dut).

Marriages in the District of Tarraville in the Colony of Victoria – John Jones and Margaret Murtaugh (https://tinyurl.com/5be4kkme).

Marriages in the District of Wangaratta in the Colony of Victoria – Frank Heach and Matilda Moore (https://tinyurl.com/5e5ej3wu).

Marriages in the District of Wangaratta in the Colony of Victoria – George Moore and Mary Jane Armstrong (https://tinyurl.com/msu5wyrk).

Marriages in the District of Wangaratta in the Colony of Victoria – John Jones and Harriet Marum (https://tinyurl.com/2spu49jr).

Marriages in the District of Wangaratta in the Colony of Victoria – Thomas Marum and Harriet Moore (https://tinyurl.com/mr4y92hd).

Moore Considine Family Website – Alice Faithfull (https://tinyurl.com/j33nctz: access code –seemoore).

Moore Considine Family Website – Alice Rebecca Clark (https://tinyurl.com/j33nctz: access code – seemoore).

Moore Considine Family Website – Amy Ellen Porter (https://tinyurl.com/j33nctz: access code – seemoore).

Moore Considine Family Website – Charles Moore (https://tinyurl.com/j33nctz: access code – seemoore).

Moore Considine Family Website – Christopher Grear Cook (https://tinyurl.com/j33nctz: access code – seemoore).

Moore Considine Family Website – David James McEwan (https://tinyurl.com/j33nctz: access code – seemoore).

Moore Considine Family Website – Ellen Considine (https://tinyurl.com/j33nctz: access code – seemoore).

Moore Considine Family Website – Ellen Nelly Porter (https://tinyurl.com/j33nctz: access code – seemoore).

Moore Considine Family Website – Francis Heach (https://tinyurl.com/j33nctz: access code – seemoore).

Moore Considine Family Website – George Earl Moore (https://tinyurl.com/j33nctz: access code – seemoore).

Moore Considine Family Website – George Moore (https://tinyurl.com/j33nctz: access code – seemoore).

Moore Considine Family Website – Harriet Jane Moore (https://tinyurl.com/j33nctz: access code – seemoore).

Moore Considine Family Website – Henry Faithfull (https://tinyurl.com/j33nctz: access code – seemoore).

Moore Considine Family Website – Jane Molina Dawson (https://tinyurl.com/j33nctz: access code – seemoore).

Moore Considine Family Website – *John Jones* (https://tinyurl.com/j33nctz: access code – seemoore).

Moore Considine Family Website – John McEwan (https://tinyurl.com/j33nctz: access code – seemoore).

Moore Considine Family Website – John Moore (Jnr.) (https://tinyurl.com/j33nctz: access code – seemoore).

Moore Considine Family Website – Margaret Considine (https://tinyurl.com/j33nctz: access code – seemoore).

Moore Considine Family Website – Patrick Considine (https://tinyurl.com/j33nctz: access code – seemoore).

Moore Considine Family Website – Sarah Moore (https://tinyurl.com/j33nctz: access code – seemoore)

Moore Considine Family Website – Silas Porter (https://tinyurl.com/j33nctz: access code – seemoore).

Moore Considine Family Website – Thomas Moore (https://tinyurl.com/j33nctz: access code – seemoore).

Moore Considine Family Website – William Moore (https://tinyurl.com/j33nctz: access code – seemoore).

New South Wales, Australia, Assisted Passenger Lists, 1828 – 1896: Ellen Considine (https://tinyurl.com/y4y6z7x8).

New South Wales, Australia, Assisted Passenger Lists, 1828 – 1896: Patrick Considine (https://tinyurl.com/365wcyv3).

New South Wales, Australia, Convict Indents, 1788 – 1842: George Reynolds (https://tinyurl.com/vysxb54y).

New South Wales, Australia, Convict Registers of Conditional and Absolute Pardons, 1788 – 1870: George Reynolds (https://tinyurl.com/kvfkpmex).

New South Wales; Births, Deaths and Marriages – Marriages: Robert Humphries and Bridget Considine (https://tinyurl.com/4hfkj6xt).

New South Wales; Certificate of freedom (1835): Robert Humphries (https://tinyurl.com/3uu24t2n).

New South Wales Death Certificate, 1933 – Jane Harris (https://tinyurl.com/yyjclabu).

New South Wales Death Certificate – George Reynolds (https://tinyurl.com/2d7cpz6s).

New South Wales Death Certificate – Robert Humphries (https://tinyurl.com/akb4e8wk).

New York State Marriage Index. 1881 – 1967: LaVerne J LaBarr and Alice E Clinch (https://tinyurl.com/ck62ru5z).

North Carolina Board of Health: Certificate of Death – Alice Ellen Clinch LaBarr (1870 – 1950) (https://tinyurl.com/3f5n5erx).

North Carolina Board of Health: Certificate of Death – LaVerne Judson LaBarr (1870 – 1958) (https://tinyurl.com/7yku97dh).

Old Bailey Records – George Reynolds (https://tinyurl.com/kzsxjr8v).

Old Bailey Records – Robert Humphries (https://tinyurl.com/af8n358b).

The High Halden Register of Baptisms, 1558 – 1966 Joseph Moore (https://tinyurl.com/ycy8jp25).

UNSW Canberra, the AIF Project –Rupert James Cavanagh Moore
(https://tinyurl.com/bdftbha4).

Victoria, Australia, Assisted and Unassisted Passenger Lists, 1839 – 1923 for F. Heach
(https://tinyurl.com/mrcnbkhr).

Victoria, Australia, Wills and Probate Records, 1841 – 2009 for Francis Heach
(Supreme Court of Victoria, Probate and Administration No. 183211)
(https://tinyurl.com/z8cpsjyd).

Victoria, Australia, Wills and Probate Records, 1841 – 2009 for John Moore (Jnr.)
(Supreme Court of Victoria, Probate and Administration No. 72/380)
(https://tinyurl.com/29tx4wwv).

Victoria, Australia, Wills and Probate Records, 1841 – 2009 for Matilda Heach
(Supreme Court of Victoria, Probate and Administration No. 125502)
(https://tinyurl.com/ycy87jxm).

Virtual War Memorial – Moore, Rupert James Cavanagh
(https://tinyurl.com/3x4wss4f).

WikiTree – Eliza Buckman (abt. 1833) (https://tinyurl.com/y8bx7vw7).

WikiTree – George Buckman (abt. 1831) (https://tinyurl.com/y72hedud).

WikiTree – George Moore (1845 – 1875) (https://tinyurl.com/y7zherzr).

WikiTree – James Dunster (1794) (https://tinyurl.com/2zkcdj2r).

WikiTree – James Lonie Fulton (1856) (https://tinyurl.com/37d639h4).

WikiTree – John Moore (Snr.) (1816 – 1891) (https://tinyurl.com/p7m48bsu).

WikiTree – John Moore (Jnr.) (1843 – 1899) (https://tinyurl.com/359yhf4z).

WikiTree – Joseph Moore (1791 – 1819) (https://tinyurl.com/3yz2bjd9).

WikiTree – Mahala Buckman (1828) (https://tinyurl.com/y8gq4nns).

WikiTree – Margaret Considine (1818 – 1895) (https://tinyurl.com/4zu7wu66).

WikiTree – Matilda (Moore) Heach (1840 – 1912) (https://tinyurl.com/2c4t429a).

WikiTree – Michael Considine (bef. 1795 – aft. 1820) (https://tinyurl.com/43wp8n39).

WikiTree – Phoebe (Dunster) Buckman (1793 – 1866) (https://tinyurl.com/ycba75yz).

WikiTree – Sarah (Barman) Dunster (abt. 1750 – 1828)
(https://tinyurl.com/3etdx3cb).

WikiTree – Sophia Buckman (1835) (https://tinyurl.com/y9cwwlsq).

WikiTree – Thomas Buckman (1798 – 1865) (https://tinyurl.com/y8bv66p9).

WikiTree – Thomas Dunster (bef. 1754) (https://tinyurl.com/ybznj33j).

WikiTree – William Moore (1845 – 1908) (https://tinyurl.com/ybzx549h).

Woodchurch Local and Family History, Baptism Details (23 May 1844) – Elizabeth and

Margaret Willis (https://tinyurl.com/y4cc4dnc).

Woodchurch Local and Family History, Baptism Details (23 July 1780) – Elizabeth Dunster (https://tinyurl.com/yd4wn9ye).

Woodchurch Local and Family History, Baptism Details (29 October 1786) – Francis Dunster (https://tinyurl.com/y7zt7osf).

Woodchurch Local and Family History, Baptism Details (9 January 1791) – George Dunster (https://tinyurl.com/ycvkyzvf).

Woodchurch Local and Family History, Baptism Details (16 November 1777) – James Burt (https://tinyurl.com/hyt293u).

Woodchurch Local and Family History, Baptism Details (21 September 1775) – John Burt (https://tinyurl.com/y9q2dcr7).

Woodchurch Local and Family History, Baptism Details (28 April 1816) – John Moore (https://tinyurl.com/yapeul4o).

Woodchurch Local and Family History, Baptism Details (12 March 1784) – Mary Dunster (https://tinyurl.com/y848pwb8).

Woodchurch Local and Family History, Baptism Details (17 March 1793) – Phoebe Dunster (https://tinyurl.com/ybwpvctk).

Woodchurch Local and Family History, Baptism Details (14 February 1813) – Sarah Moore (https://tinyurl.com/y8n7448a).

Woodchurch Local and Family History, Baptism Details (5 October 1788) – William Dunster (https://tinyurl.com/y9dh4vly).

Woodchurch Local and Family History, Baptism Details (10 July 1825) – William Willis (https://tinyurl.com/y3tvkah2).

Woodchurch Local and Family History, Burial Details (8 April 1778) – John Burt (https://tinyurl.com/yxgyu2r4).

Woodchurch Local and Family History, Marriage Details (26 March 1780) – Francis Dunster and Sarah Burt (https://tinyurl.com/ya72ts4g).

Woodchurch Local and Family History, Marriage Details (19 April 1812) – Joseph Moore and Phoebe Dunster (https://tinyurl.com/ydycnspq).

Woodchurch Local and Family History, Woodchurch Parish Chest, 1633 – 1842: Joseph Moore (Record Details, P400/13/5).

Woodchurch Local and Family History, Woodchurch Parish Chest, 1633 – 1842: Joseph and Phoebe Moore (Record Details, P400/13/5).

Legislation

Poor Law Relief Act 1662 (UK) (14 Car. 2, c. 12).
Poor Relief Act 1691 (UK) (3 Will. & Mary, c. 11).
The Mining Companies Limited Liability Act 1864 (Vic) (27 Vict., No. 228).

Government Gazette

New South Wales Government Gazette (No. 760), Tuesday, 1 December 1891, p. 9448.

Other Government Records

Parliament of Victoria, *Sixth Report of the Commission of National Education for the Colony of Victoria for the Year 1858*, pp. 58 – 59 (https://tinyurl.com/36jpa43c).
Parliament of Victoria, *About Parliament, Re-Member (Former Members) – James Stewart* (https://tinyurl.com/ydb65wfe).
Public Records Office of Victoria, *VPRS*, 28/P0, Unit 580.
Public Records Office of Victoria, *VPRS*, 28/P2, Unit 316.
Public Records Office of Victoria, *VPRS*, 7591/P2, Unit 181.
Public Records Office of Victoria, *VPRS*, 28/P0, Unit 103.
Public Records Office of Victoria, *VPRS*, 7591/P0002, 225/736.
The 1841 England Census – Phebee Buckman (https://tinyurl.com/3tyxvzbw).
The 1841 England Census – Sarah Moore (https://tinyurl.com/374964a7).
The 1841 England Census – Thomas Willis (https://tinyurl.com/yxqe9ha4).
The 1851 England Census – Elizabeth Buckman (https://tinyurl.com/2pb5vcck).
The 1851 England Census – John Buckman (https://tinyurl.com/584dtme6).
The 1851 England Census – Thomas Buckman (https://tinyurl.com/yyg9xqbh).
The 1861 England Census – Elizabeth Buckman (https://tinyurl.com/4973svuj).
The 1861 England Census – George Buckman and Family (https://tinyurl.com/m6vbey34).
The 1861 England Census – Phoebe Buckman (https://tinyurl.com/5bas5xk4).
The 1861 England Census – Sarah Moore (https://tinyurl.com/3v8w4j3u).
The 1861 England Census – Thomas Buckman (https://tinyurl.com/39ffzbm5).
The 1861 England Census – Walter Heathfield (https://tinyurl.com/4pa85xxa).
The 1871 England Census – Elizabeth Buckman (https://tinyurl.com/yku2575u).

The 1871 England Census – Mahala Law (https://tinyurl.com/bdcubjfe).

The 1871 England Census – Walter Heathfield (https://tinyurl.com/4c6jxe7v).

The 1881 England Census – Walter Heathfield (https://tinyurl.com/4jbj5mpr).

The 1881 England Census – Alice Law (https://tinyurl.com/3bmky5tn).

The 1891 England Census – Eliza Heathfield (https://tinyurl.com/bddj88k5).

The 1901 England Census – Mahala and Harriet Law (https://tinyurl.com/y4zf67jb).

The 1875 New York State Census – George Buckman and Family (https://tinyurl.com/mpd7smhd).

The 1875 New York State Census – John Clinch and Family (https://tinyurl.com/2wsjshj4).

The 1905 New York State Census – George Buckman (https://tinyurl.com/4ud43sb4).

The 1905 New York State Census – John Clinch (https://tinyurl.com/3xxj9rds).

The 1915 New York State Census (https://tinyurl.com/y8xrqwu5).

The 1870 United States Federal Census – John Clinch (https://tinurl.com/2s42vks8).

The 1870 United States Federal Census – George Buckman (https://tinyurl.com/y75wdhsq).

The 1880 United States Federal Census – George Buckman (https://tinyurl.com/52t4ns7k).

The 1880 United States Federal Census – John Clinch and Family (https://tinyurl.com/2s3utnfu).

The 1890 United States Federal Census – John Clinch and Family (https://tinyurl.com/y4lfqoyl).

The 1900 United States Federal Census – John and Sophia Clinch (https://tinyurl.com/yeympdj7).

The 1910 United States Federal Census – John and Sophia Clinch (https://tinyurl.com/yj6zay8z).

The 1910 United States Federal Census – LaVerne LaBarr and Family (https://tinyurl.com/yhhvctah).

The 1930 United States Federal Census – LaVerne LaBarr and Family (https://tinyurl.com/3fjmzwb5).

The 1940 United States Federal Census – LaVerne LaBarr (https://tinyurl.com/46navp9s).

Newspapers

Albury Banner and Wodonga Express (Albury, New South Wales).
Border Morning Mail and Riverina Times (Albury, New South Wales).
Cork Evening Herald (Cork, Republic of Ireland).
Goulburn Herald and County of Argyle Advertiser (Goulburn, New South Wales).
Nagambie Times (Nagambie, Victoria).
North Eastern Despatch (Wangaratta, Victoria).
North Eastern Ensign (Wangaratta, Victoria).
Ovens and Murray Advertiser (Beechworth, Victoria).
Sydney Gazette and New South Wales Advertiser (Sydney, New South Wales).
Sydney Herald (Sydney, New South Wales).
Sydney Monitor (Sydney, New South Wales).
The Age (Melbourne, Victoria).
The Argus (Melbourne, Victoria).
The Australian (Sydney, New South Wales).
The Chronicle (Wangaratta, Victoria).
The Colonist (Sydney, New South Wales).
The Corryong Courier (Corryong, Victoria).
The Weekly Times (Melbourne, Victoria).
Wangaratta Chronicle (Wangaratta, Victoria).
Wangaratta Despatch (Wangaratta, Victoria).

Miscellaneous Unpublished Documents

Burke to the Secretary of State, 11 October 1836 (TNA, CO 714/114, p. 96).

Document authored by Charles Bertram ("Charles") Moore and dated 23 February 1987 (*"Charles Moore's 1987 document"*).

Document authored by Albert Edgar ("Bert") Moore in September 1991 and entitled *William Moore of Three Mile Wangaratta* (*"Albert Moore's 1991 document"*).

Document authored by Albert Edgar ("Bert") Moore, dated 1992 and entitled *RE William & Rebecca MOORE* (*"Albert Moore's 1992 document"*).

Marriage Entry No. 7 for John Moore and Margaret Considine in the records of Sts. Peter and Paul's Catholic Old Cathedral, Goulburn.

Trotter, Thomas: *Diary, 25 May 1836 – 6 August 1836* (State Library of New South Wales, ML, MSS 774).

Wren, Henry: *Private Journal, Ship Duchess of Northumberland, 5 May – 8 November 1836* (State Library of New South Wales, ML, MSS 763).

www.ingramcontent.com/pod-product-compliance
Lightning Source LLC
Chambersburg PA
CBHW041711290426
44109CB00028B/2838